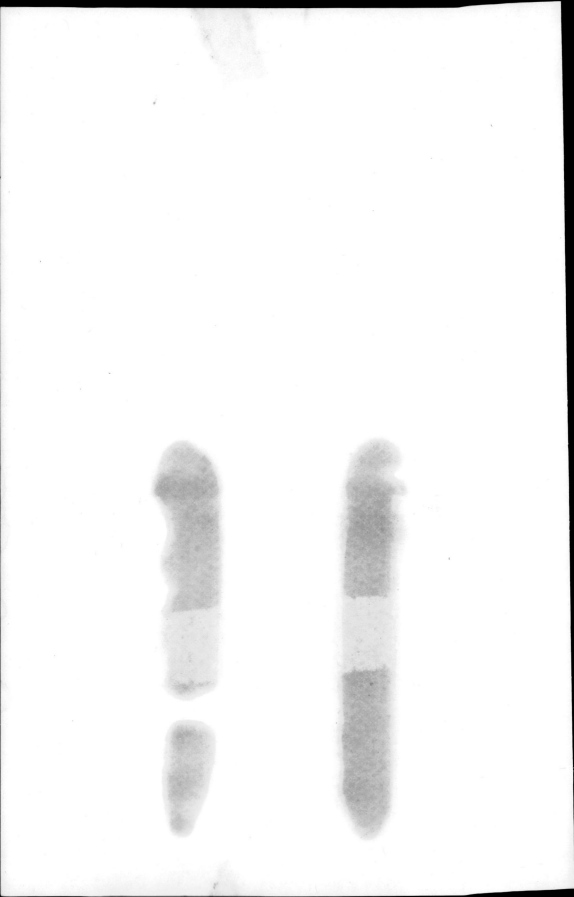

KNOWING THE SCORE

Notes on Film Music

Irwin Bazelon

 VAN NOSTRAND REINHOLD COMPANY
New York   Cincinnati   Toronto   London   Melbourne

Copyright (c) 1975 by Irwin A. Bazelon
Library of Congress Catalog Card Number 73-16701
ISBN 0-442-20594-5

Printed in the United States of America

Published in 1975 by Van Nostrand Reinhold Company
A Division of Litton Educational Publishing, Inc.
450 West 33rd Street, New York, NY 10001, U.S.A.

Van Nostrand Reinhold Limited
1410 Birchmount Road, Scarborough, Ontario M1P 2E7, Canada

Van Nostrand Reinhold Australia Pty. Limited
17 Queen Street, Mitcham, Victoria 3132, Australia

Van Nostrand Reinhold Company Limited
Molly Millars Lane, Wokingham, Berkshire, England

16 15 14 13 12 11 10 9 8 7 6 5 4 3 2 1

Library of Congress Cataloging in Publication Data
Bazelon, Irwin.
    Knowing the score.
    Includes index.
    1. Moving-picture music—History and criticism.
I. Title.
ML2075.B36   782.8'1   73-16701
ISBN 0-442-20594-5

Contents

TO THOSE OF US WHO SEE THE PICTURE

Acknowledgments

My thanks to Alfred Allan Lewis for urging me to write this book and helping to get it off the ground; and to Everett Aison for giving me the opportunity to put its theories to work in the classroom. I am indebted to Alan Seeger for the use of his extensive film research library and film music recording collection, without which the preparation of this manuscript would have been extremely difficult. In addition, I owe a personal debt of gratitude to Patricia Layman for her excellent photographs and invaluable assistance during the tapings of the interviews with the composers; Pat Gray of the London office of Van Nostrand Reinhold for her services rendered in my behalf; Brenda Currin for her time and effort in typing my material; and to composers Leonard Rosenman and Keith Robinson an appreciation for allowing me to bounce ideas off their heads all these years.

And finally, a special thanks to my wife, Cecile, for her infinite patience and her welcome suggestions.

Preface:
Opening Music Cue

In writing a book today on motion-picture music, I had the advantage of looking back over four decades of sound-film scores. As a composer and inveterate moviegoer, I have viewed a staggering amount of films, if you bear in mind that since the advent of sound more than 100,000 feature films have been produced, and it would indeed be a herculean feat to have seen every one. It has been my intent in compiling the material for this book to call attention to a sampling of film scores that merit serious consideration.

I have discussed particular films in detail and made repeated references to specific music for different sequences pertinent to my analysis. Some films are a cornucopia of musical gems. It is by design, not oversight, that I have chosen fewer rather than many scores. My selection of film music is a personal one; this book is not intended to be an encyclopedia of film scoring. I can only hope that the inclusions outweigh the omissions. Great films do not necessarily contain great music scores; and, conversely, sparkling, innovative music does not automatically indicate a superior film. There are only significant musical moments in single dramatic films, whether or not the films themselves are important. I have set myself the task to seek out and find these special, fleeting moments.

Another purpose I had in writing this book is related to a course I initiated a few years ago called "Music for Motion Pictures" for young film students at the School of Visual Arts in New York City. I had three objectives in giving the course:

First, I hoped to instill in these potential film-makers a pronounced awareness of music in films: to urge them to take music seriously and to comprehend its functions, emotional impact, capabilities and limitations, and not to go along with the myth propagated by past Hollywood film-makers that film music is only good and effective when nobody notices it. And I wanted them to consider the music sound track as an integral part of the objective planning of motion pictures; not to relegate the composer to the bottom rung of the creative ladder, but to give him status equal with the actor, writer, cameraman, and editor. (Throughout this book the use of the masculine pronoun for composer includes both male and female.)

Second, I wanted to advance the idea that when my students reached the

6

point of thinking seriously about a composer for their film projects—hopefully at an early stage—they would not visit the nearest discotheque or nightclub and hire the dance-band leader or pop singer-guitarist-songwriter-composer to write their music for them; that they would open their ears and minds to the entire musical horizon, listen, and assimilate all facets of the contemporary music world, inside and outside the pop-music milieu.

And third, I was determined to stress the importance of learning how to communicate with a composer so that they would understand the translation of drama into musical terms; to enable them, as film-makers, to converse with a composer in a mutual dramatic language about how they feel, what they want, what the possibilities are for innovative sounds and scoring, when and where to use music, what the composer can add to a scene that is *not* shown on the screen, and what kind of music will be written. For in all my years as a professional composer in the functional-music field, I have been amazed and distressed by the large number of film people I have encountered who are unable to engage a composer at the most elementary level of musical communication.

With more people involved in films today then ever before, I felt that a course of this type was both valid and timely. Millions of people view films and hear music. At an early age they are literally "earwashed" by musical kitsch. They become inured to bad taste and accept it as the norm—and this is the *reel* tragedy. Admittedly, much Hollywood film music of the thirties, forties, and fifties was banal in its own time. Today it is topically stale, and rehearing it via television, which regurgitates both the garbage of the past and the amplified refuse of the present, only reaffirms its commonplaceness.

I wanted these young, receptive students to see films with a new set of ears. And I hoped that my proselytizing would spur them to initiate change.

During my lecture sessions, I was pleasantly surprised to discover that a number of students had now and then attended a concert of music other than the pop-folk-rock variety. They did not know the works of avant-garde composers intimately, but the names rang a bell. I was optimistic that, with a little guidance, some students might explore the entire contemporary music scene and, ultimately, if and when they ever made a film, entrust the composing of music to a contemporary concert-hall composer—or at least give him equal consideration.

It is true that attendance at symphony concerts by young people has fallen off and that they prefer the movie theater and rock concert as their source of musical entertainment. It is also true that enrollment in film schools throughout the country has boomed. The camera has become the instrument of self-expression. For the most part, these young people want to create honest, thought-provoking, literate films. To do this, they must carry with them new musical concepts and take an innovative approach to the challenge of film-music composition.

It is to these young film students and the others to follow that this book is dedicated.

Irwin Bazelon
New York City, 1975

1. Film Music and the Composer

The film composer must invent forms and formal relations, not "ideas," if he is to write meaning-fully.

Hanns Eisler

It may come as a distinct surprise to many, including film directors and producers, but after years of listening to motion-picture scores, it is my firm conviction that you don't have to be a composer to write film music. (This is not to imply that being one is disadvantageous.) The basic structure of films and the nature of the music written for them are the reasons for this belief, which makes the question "What is a composer?" one of paramount relevance.

The fact is that music talent is not a rarity; many share the endowment. And a composer is not merely a person capable of expressing a musical thought. Nor is he someone who has discovered how to put a few sounds together, acquired a basic knowledge of chords as part of a limited harmonic arsenal, learned to fashion accents into rhythmic patterns, or demonstrated an ability to write pop songs, no matter how striking or tuneful the results. Just as a work of art excites the senses to a greater stimulation than surface agitation, the art of music composition is a little bit more involved than combining sounds or writing a tune. If writing a tune were the single criterion for recognition as a composer, we would be inundated by composers, for virtually thousands of people have this talent. The musician of unusual sensitivity is aware that musical art goes beyond the initial stimulus produced by a pleasant melody, a graceful poetic line, an unusual sound effect, a raucous rhythmic beat, or a frenzied kinetic release. More than titillation, the art of music engages the mind beyond the first impact into a deeper awakening. In this context, a composer, probing toward a heightened, more profound response, is an artist who can effectively incorporate his ideas into a musical mold and give form and structure to his imagination and fantasy. In essence, he is someone who knows how to put a *piece* together; whose technique, encompassing all the complex elements of musical composition, culminates in the creation of an extended, highly organized, totally developed work. This exercise in artistic fulfillment and self-discipline—the ability to put a piece together—distinguishes the genuine composer from all the bogus practitioners haphazardly writing notes on paper or playing directly into tape recorders who come under the general heading of music-makers.

The structure of films involves constant movement from episode to episode, camera long shots to close-ups, exteriors to interiors, dissolves, fast cuts, rapidly moving, alternating images, fade-ins and fade-outs, and other transitory cinematic devices. Because music is an art that exists in time, it can dramatically and psychologically underscore these visual sequences and by musical threads link the disparate scenes depicted. The ever-changing series of pictorial events allows a composer little time for extended development of musical ideas. The music tends to be as episodic as the scenic episodes. Fully realized musical elaboration, commensurate with shaping a concert work, is out of the question from both the standpoint of time and of sheer physical stamina; a composer may have to write forty minutes of film music in less than four weeks. Simple musical phrases, held notes, repeated figures, sharp accents, rhythmic punctuation, ostinati, drawn-out chords, and single, long, lyric lines become the rule of the day. The film composer is not required to act on his ideas, only to initiate them. The need for progression and a broad musical perspective is nil. He tends to fall back on repetition and restatement, cribbing from what he has previously invented, or borrowing liberally from others. Functioning as a composer in the sense of putting a piece together is never called upon: it is not necessary; indeed, it is not wanted. Film scores are not symphonies, concerti, or concert pieces.[1] In the main they consist of short forms, divertimenti, microcosmic time components, sketches and fragments of musical seeds—unfinished compositions with only the bare suggestion of character. In addition, the necessity of following cues in the film actively discourages large compositional canvases. The end results are abrupt, truncated phrases, mere snatches of music that are all beginning, no middle, and often a welcome end. "A little goes a long" way succinctly applies to film music. One small kernel of imagination—a chord, a few notes, an isolated germ of musical thought, a special sound or effect—can be stated and restated, fitting scene after scene, situation after situation, and fulfilling the dramatic requirements of the film more or less satisfactorily.

An example not unlike similar musical sequences in hundreds of films produced during and immediately after the Second World War illustrates the point that you don't have to be a composer to write film music:

SCENE:
World War Two, Pacific theater of operations (Burma). American troops sneaking up on Japanese supply depot in jungle to destroy oil tanks and ammunition stockpiles . . .

DRAMATIC REQUIREMENTS:
The scene calls for music that heightens the suspense and undercover excitement of the mission. There is little dialogue. The danger of possible detection by the enemy is always present and leads to increased tension.

From the example, one can say that the dramatic requirements have been fulfilled—superficially, at least. Without taxing the creative capacity of the music writer, the sequence works. There is suspense (trombone figure) and a military signpost (snare drum). But is this enough? Switching on a lamp also works, but is it the best possible diffusion of light? Simple, modest, and unsophisticated means can be effective, so the question here is not whether the solution is good or bad, right or wrong. What is germane is that one did not have to be a composer to have written it; anyone with the barest semblance of musical aptitude could have gone to the piano, selected three notes at random, assigned them to trombones, sketched in a comparable elementary rhythmic pattern, added a snare drum for patriotic color, and presto! a composer is born. If the repeated series were to continue for more than a minute or two, it would invite monotony—not entirely unwanted in this case—but with frequent pauses, starts, and stops, that problem could be surmounted, and the passage could cover the scene from beginning to end. Many people of varied musical skills can find solutions that work like this example.

In this same scene, a composer of superior imagination would not hesitate to expand the musical concept. He could augment and introduce additional musical lines, enlarge the compositional palette, add variety to the accompaniment figure, evoke a novel, exotic source of timbre, and investigate the unexpected—all to heighten the suspense and, in his special way, make it work better. A composer with extrasensitive insight can also add to the dramatic reality of the scene by altering the viewer's perception of the image. In this instance, by utilizing especially pungent music, he could accentuate the physical and emotional stress of the combatants over and above mere surface suspense.

In Orson Welles' film *The Trial*, the background track consists in the main of a low, unrelieved, deep drone. It accompanies the protagonist (Tony Perkins) from place to place and room to room, creating an aural vertigo complementary to the maelstrom on the screen. The combination of these two sensory invasions produces an eye-ear form of Op art. The dizzy feeling it evokes in the audience is strongly marked. The device works and creates a profound mood; but, again, one did not have to be a composer to have originated this idea or engineered its operation. Anyone with a visual-dramatic instinct might have invented this workable sound, and composing skill was not the foremost requisite in its construction.

Pictures like *Breakfast at Tiffany's* and *A Man and a Woman*, which employ a popular song specifically written for the film and functioning as its music track literally from ear to ear, are seemingly better suited to a songwriter's talents than a composer's. It is a debatable point whether these films and similar types have been "scored" in the strictest sense of the word. Any one of a thousand other songs could serve the identical purpose.

In the strictest musico-aesthetic sense, one can argue whether or not film music is music at all. The basic ingredients of composition exist: there is melodic line, harmonic texture, rhythmic agitation, orchestral color, and even a glimpse, now and then, of a musical germ. The composer's tools of trade are much in evidence. It sounds like music; it looks like music. But is it *really* music? About this point composer Leonard Rosenman writes: "While most of the elements of music as we know them appear to be present in the functional field, there is one element that is conspicuously absent. It is the propulsion of the score by means of 'musical' ideas."[2]

Without these ideas—the driving force of musical art—the finished product is vacuous and undeserving of serious consideration. It must be remembered that in films the literary ideas are dominant. Music serves the film as an accompanist to express these ideas, not the other way around. In this respect, the film composer's talent might be deemed more a mastery of the art of accompaniment than an ability to function as a composer of musical composition. Knowledge of his tools is taken for granted, but this is not the deciding factor in successful film scoring. What really counts is the composer's visual-dramatic awareness—his sense of the theatrical. Inherent in some film scores may lie the seeds for future compositions, but this is after the fact and clearly a by-product of film music's primary functional requirements. The rewrite job is not one of rearrangement. It is one of reconception and execution. Granted that aesthetic definitions of what is music and what is art are being drastically revised these days, the fact still remains that there is a difference between skilled, imaginative craftsmanship and the pure art of original composition.[3] Apropos of this, film music often calls for the talents of an expert, resourceful arranger or adapter of existing material to recompose or juxtapose, as it were, or the proficient services of professional orchestrators, whose creative instrumental imagery is underrated and generally misunderstood by the film public. Upon occasion, the line separating the individual skill of an orchestrator and the sometimes questionable powers of a composer blurs: the former's craft can approach extremely close to the latter's art. It is often a fine point of discernment.

Nonqualification as a composer is not a deterrent to one's being engaged to write film music and makes the list of available candidates infinite. In truth, today's competitive film-music scramble consists of both composers and noncomposers. Some of these musicians have as much in common with one another musically as an usher has to a film on the screen. Concert-hall composers, dance-band leaders, arrangers, bongo and guitar players, hummers and strummers, nightclub pianists, songwriters, assorted pop, rock, and jazz musicians, and pop personalities all compete in the musical melting pot and are seriously considered for film-scoring assignments. In this musical potpourri, contemporary concert-hall composer and all-purpose pop musician occasionally clash as competitors. Because of the prevailing pop-tune mentality of the feature-film business, the inevitable choice is the latter. In other words, in an arena where relatively few genuine composers are called, many others are enthusiastically chosen.

In the final analysis, film music is *almost* composing—but not quite.

---

1. This is true even if the occasion arises where the original music written for a specific film is adaptable to the concert hall, like Prokofiev's *Alexander Nevsky* or Copland's *Red Pony Suite* and *Music for a Big City* from *Something Wild.*

2. Leonard Rosenman, "Notes From a SubCulture," *Perspectives of New Music* (Fall–Winter, 1968), p. 131.

3. With the development of electronic music, an interesting question has arisen as to whether the science of sound is commensurate with the art of music. There are those who consider Stockhausen a physicist, Babbitt a mathematician, and Xenakis an architect, rather than composers. What is obvious is that music and composition in their latest evolution have now incorporated other branches of art and science, and the composer of the future may well be a combination physicist-mathematician-architect-electronic engineer-musician.

Film Music:
2. A Short History

*Old scores, if they're good, never die; they just
fade into subsequent films.*

Edward Connor

Film music was born illegitimately as a literal-practical child of necessity. It was
not the result of any artistic impulse or creative merger. In the early days, the
sound projector and the movie hall were in close proximity. Soundproofing
had not yet been perfected and the leakage of noise from the projector carried
over into the auditorium and interfered with the audience's visual enjoyment.
(This whirling sound is still noticeable in film classes or other screenings
where 16-mm films are shown with the projector in the open rather than
encased in a separate film booth.) The proprietors wanted not only to drown
out the projector but to alleviate a disagreeable (yet soporific) sound by
substituting a more appealing one—music. To accomplish this, they engaged a
pianist—tantamount to hiring a one-man orchestra—who incorporated
whatever sound effects—the clippity-clop of hoofbeats, the striking of chimes,
and other synchronized effects—he deemed necessary to accompany the screen
action. Psychologically, the silent film presented an interesting phenomenon:
sitting in a dark theater, immersed in a soundless world, created an aura of
unnatural stillness, broken only by a mechanical whirl and the sounds coming
from the audience itself. Coughing, sneezing, rattling candy wrappers,
popcorn munching, and a general restlessness filled the air, unrivaled by any
vocal resistance from the silent screen. Even today, this audience reaction is
noticeable. Viewers gradually quiet down during the main-title music and
reach the nadir level of noise as the picture begins to unfold. In addition, they
are much less fidgety during loud, violent action sequences than during soft,
intimate passages. Music was introduced to cover up the silence and
effectively combat audience disturbance. The early film-makers had no desire
to allow external annoyances to compete for attention with their visual
product: music was their panacea for encouraging audience empathy. In their
anxiety to bring about this rapport and lessen their fear of silence, they often
selected musical material bordering on the ridiculous: note, for example, the
countless silent films accompanied by marches, anthems, patriotic tunes,
operatic melodies, and whole segments of eighteenth- and nineteenth-century

13

symphonic repertoire, inserted without dramatic motivation to fill any and all situations. They were not meant to be listened to as music by the audience, but only to breathe musically across the screen as an aid and comfort to the muted picture, softly rocking the cradle in the darkness of the theater through quiet interludes, violent action, or intimate moments. This resulted in a fallacious premise: the audience should not be aware of the music in films. The screen represented drama, action, and dialogue; music was merely a subordinate detail—a window dressing. Anything that detracted from visual involvement was looked upon with suspicion. The actor was the financial investment to be protected at all times.

The early film-makers' dread of silence, coupled with their desire to induce audiences to focus attention on the screen, eventually led to a musical convention to open and proclaim the start of a motion picture. They bludgeoned the audience into a state of submission by adopting a musical ritual known as "main titles," which literally compelled the audience to concentrate its eyes and ears on the screen. This music signaled the beginning of an epic with fanfare, full orchestral rendition, and triumphal, whipped-up enthusiasm, which announced to the world that the film about to be shown had already achieved greatness even before it had been screened. Without subtlety, it musically directed the audience to pipe down and subdue its popcorn crunching and fidgeting, for "The film is about to commence." When the audience had been stimulated to the proper pitch of respect and excitement, this musical salute unfolded into blatant, overt advertising, transferring its artificially produced fervor by a twelve-gun musical salvo to the trailer for the following week's coming attraction: a picture positively guaranteed to surpass in action, drama, suspense, and greatness the now-playing masterpiece.

The main titles went even further than seducing a patron to come back again and again. They became the advertising slogan for the creators of the commodity as well. The composer was expected to accent the names of the people involved in the film—the producer, director, actors, and others—by cymbal crashes, forte chords, and other special effects, one louder than another, according to rank. Like hammer blows, the music punched home to the viewer those responsible for the epical masterwork they were about to see.

In *The Sand Pebbles* (1966), composer Jerry Goldsmith opened the film with an uncharacteristic main-title treatment: the music is soft, low, and soloistic, setting the Far East locale with restraint. The only dramatic emphasis is sounded over his own music credit. Inadvertent or not, it was one of the few times in film music that a composer called attention to his work. For all composers, it was a brief moment of putting the accent in the proper place.

The "moving picture" became part of show business at an early age. Originally a side-show attraction in the theaters of the county fairs around the turn of the century, its random growth was nurtured in the circus atmosphere of an amusement park, where director, owner, and distributor were one man. Motion-picture music, developing along similar haphazard lines, had the same pioneer spirit of the new entertainment medium. Playing in the dimly lit wings, the pianist was as much a gypsy and adventurer as his employer. Nobody had any technical expertise about the novelty they were introducing, and, feeling their way in the dark, they stumbled together in a camaraderie of ignorance. Because motion-picture music was regarded from its inception as a second-rate, auxiliary art, the first musicians who supplied illustrative music were often anybody who happened to be around and available; their basic qualifications were neither investigated in depth nor deemed worthy of concern. The artistic level of film and radio music was set by those itinerants flocking to the new medium by the attractive lure of monetary profit.

In the initial stages, the musical masters-in-charge had a virtual treasury of existing music at their disposal, including the cultural riches of the past and the inexhaustible supplies furnished on demand by countless music publishers eager to share in the rewards offered by the new ventures. One of these, the Sam Fox Company, flourished as the reigning silent-film-music storehouse. Stockpiles of illustrative pieces grew mountain-size; they were catalogued and pigeonholed for easy accessibility, with programmatically suggestive titles to cover practically any dramatic occasion, crisis, or mood that could arise in a film. It was the forerunner of the present-day canned-music library. Compositions with titles such as "Regatta Races," "Hearts and Flowers," and "Exhibition" became popular selections for background music. These pieces (many by J. S. Zamecnik), along with others of similar type, were piano compositions written in a late nineteenth-century style. They were often found in the homes of the general public as popular drawing-room favorites. Simple and naive, they were pale imitations of standard repertoire pieces.

In effect, the early silent-film pianists were the first practicing disk jockeys. They sifted through and arbitrarily extracted material to be used as they saw fit with the mood of each film sequence. They usually repeated the pieces for as long as necessary or until the end of a scene. In many cases, the actual titles of the compositions influenced their selection more than aesthetic considerations. (Needless to say, the pianistic performances left something to be desired.) From these humble beginnings developed an arsenal of stock compositions for mundane film situations. At the same time, certain empirical standards evolved that were rooted in misconceptions dictated by fashionable ideas of music and its function, prejudices that stemmed from the adoption of musical effects leading to banal clichés, and general bad habits that passed from one hack musician to another.

In their eagerness to ransack the symphonic literature for their own commercial purposes, the pianists, arrangers, editors, and conductors accomplished more than gentle rummage: they committed wholesale rape. No segment of traditional music was sacrosanct. They utilized "Asleep in the Deep" as the ship went down, the "Fate Theme" from *Carmen* for appropriate circumstances, the "Bridal Chorus" from *Lohengrin* to seal holy matrimony, Beethoven's *Moonlight* Sonata for moonlit nights and calm waters, the *William Tell* Overture for rainstorms and later for Western heroics, and countless other examples, including Wagner's "Ride of the Valkyries" for highly dramatic events or announcements, such as in D. W. Griffith's *The Birth of a Nation* (1915) to accompany certain horseback movements of the Ku Klux Klan. Film music of the silent era echoed the symphonic programs in American concert halls, which emanated from the creative output of the European composers of the late nineteenth and early twentieth centuries. The primary source ma-

HURRY MUSIC
(FOR MOB OR FIRE SCENES)

J. S. ZAMECNIK.

A typical example of silent film music. Copyright © 1913, Sam Fox Publishing, Inc., New York, N.Y.
By Special Permission.

terials were the composers' original scores, which were simply lifted from live performances and inserted into the new medium. The use of these musical signposts and other cue-book assortments became literal trademarks. As the industry boomed and reproduced its product with increased frequency and efficacy, the tried-and-tested musical solutions became the trusted allies of the powers that be. The formula "what worked before can work again" was their musical bylaw, traceable back to their initial thinking that an illiterate public could not be trusted. Positive that they alone understood the effect music would have on the audience, the entertainment entrepreneurs felt that any experimental or intellectual music was doomed to failure and poison to their product at the box office. This judgment, based in part on the belief that innovative music would call attention to itself, intrude into the film, and consciously upset people, set a precedent for composer-producer relationships that still holds today. Aaron Copland wrote about the producer's attitude toward film music in the forties: "The producers often claim, 'if I can't understand it, the public won't.' As a result of this the typical Hollywood composer is concerned not with the reaction of the public, as you might think, but with that of the producer. It isn't surprising, therefore, that all film music originating in Hollywood tends to be very much the same. . . . A pleased producer means more jobs. That alone is sufficient to explain the Hollywood stereotype of music."[1]

The result of this businessman philosophy on the part of insecure film heads was the deliberate standardization of motion-picture music. Creative imagination, whenever it dared to surface, was strangled by musical conventions and replaced by stock formulas; original poetic music became hackneyed, worn-out "pieces of eight." Inept, puerile musical trivia was given an official place in the order of things, and unobtrusive music that provided the background with a familiar and friendly sound was universally welcomed and applauded.

The transition of the motion-picture industry from small private enterprises to highly organized film companies took place in the early 1920s. These concerns had a clear-cut, no-nonsense design—to corner the commercial market. During this period, the first movie palaces were constructed; remnants of these prototypes are still visible in some places around the country. They were ornate, plush, superdeluxe edifices. Everything was devised to make these sumptuous castles and their superproductions a part of the American family's social scene. At this time, national advertising came into prominence and extensively covered the colorful events in the film medium—on and off the screen. The public was invited to share in this organized hoopla, to exchange its humdrum existence for the comfortable, easily accessible fantasyland inside the opulent movie palaces, and to escape for a few hours—amid a glamorous setting—the life-sized problems facing them in the actual world.

In the course of this feverish commercial activity, the piano player was gradually replaced by a live orchestra of varying size. Many theaters were equipped with organs capable of providing special sounds such as thunder, gunfire, and train sirens, plus a sound man in the orchestra pit who added to sound-effect possibilities. Often an organist played before, during, and after the feature presentation, a practice which continued even after the introduction of talkies. In the last years of the silent-film period, giant-size orchestras from fifty to a hundred musicians appeared in the more lavish cinema houses. Conductors of these ensembles selected the illustrative material from the ample supply already picked over like gnawed chicken bones by predecessors. They received enormous salaries for their cultural gravedigging and passed on their "musical wisdom" to an appreciative, essentially middle-class, uninformed audience. Many of these conductors came from dance bands, nightclubs, musical shows, and Tin Pan Alley. Later, after the birth of sound, they infiltrated radio and the film studios.

In the dying days of the silent film, huge, pretentious, "original music" scores were composed. They were of the same vintage as those previously utilized and not much different from the ones composed afterward for sound pictures. They had only to be recorded to complete the final step in the cycle: from piano to orchestra pit to silver screen—from silents to talkies—one score in one score.

The film industry promoted its product and Hollywood as the "eyes and ears of the entertainment world"—courtesy of Paramount Newsreel. But in winning the battle of size, sound, sex, sensationalism, and supersalesmanship, the industry pulverized the sensibilities of its audience into a state of stardust bewilderment. Values became clouded, causing people to mistake size for stature, violence for strength, showmanship for depth of content, earnestness for seriousness, and musical grandeur for cultural participation. In the meantime, as the dimensions of the theaters grew more extravagant and garish along with the exaggerated ads and the musical accompaniments received their fullest measure of added instrumental prestige, the music itself remained the same. This was so because as the film industry accelerated its development, it kept a firm hand on the throat of its musical machinery, effectively throttling any growth of style or innovation that departed from the rules of music convention. Now, instead of being pounded out by the pianist in the darkness, the identical pieces of trade—instrumentally arranged when necessary—were ebulliently performed by orchestras of elephantine proportions, complete with multicolored lights projected against the screen as virtual sounds of the spectrum—not unlike a contemporary discotheque flashing-light show. These monster-sized pit orchestras were counterparts of the powerful floodlights illuminating the cinema-palace exteriors and proclaiming to the public in high-voltage language the World Premiere Opening Night—a social event to be thought of in terms of a royal coronation.

To summarize, during the silent period there were four types of music:

Piano Improvization.   Pianists followed the screen with their eyes. They doodled, vamped, and attempted to reflect (by trial and error) the mood and tempo of the action. They improvised musical effects, mangled chords, arpeggioed up and down the keyboard, and filled in many sequences by playing popular music interludes.

Published Musical Extracts.   These were classified "cue books" distributed by music publishers and performed by pianists and pit orchestras.

The Score.   A score was prearranged by the director working with a musical assistant. It was derived principally from familiar musical sources—standard symphonic repertoire—e.g., D. W. Griffith in *The Birth of a Nation* (1915) and *Intolerance* (1916) worked with composer-conductor Joseph Breil.

Original Scores. These were created for specific films—on occasion by eminent composers. Some films that had original scores include:

Broken Blossoms (D. W. Griffith, 1919); largely original score by Louis Gottschalt.

L'Inhumaine (Marcel L'Herbier, 1923); music by Darius Milhaud.

La Roue (Karl Grüne, 1924); music by Arthur Honegger.

Battleship Potemkin (Sergei Eisenstein, 1925); music by Edmund Meisel.

The Big Parade (King Vidor, 1925); music by William Axt.

Berlin: The Symphony of a Great City (Walter Ruttmann, 1927); music by Edmond Meisel.

The New Babylon (Grigori Kozintzev and Leonid Trauberg, 1929); music by Dimitri Shostakovich.[2]

In any discussion of music and musicians, one cannot reject the past. In the early days, America imported its music from Europe. Art itself was never an organic part of our soil. We were too busy constructing an industrial-mercantile society, clearing the Indians off the land, and pushing westward to care about music and art. Music was not the bread-and-butter profession or life-style of vigorous pioneer progeny. The role of the musician in our social structure echoed the position he had occupied in the past; even Haydn took his meals in the servants' quarters. The musician was always an outcast, an outsider whose services were available to those who could pay for them. Music was a luxury to be enjoyed as relaxation, a diversion from the mind's primary concern with the war of business and the struggle for survival. Hanns Eisler's comments on the sociology of the musician are even more pertinent today in our entertainment culture than ever before, because, in a sense, the itinerant musician of yesteryear has returned, with his ever-present guitar strapped on his back and an amplifier at his side:

The practice of music is historically linked with the idea of selling one's talent . . . rather than selling one's labor in its congealed form, as a commodity; and through the ages the musician, like the actor, has been regarded as closely akin to the lackey, the jester, or the prostitute. Although musical performance presupposes the most exacting labor, the fact that the artist appears in person, and the coincidence between his existence and his achievement, together create the illusion that he does it for fun, that he earns his living without honest labor, and this very illusion is readily exploited.

Before the jazz age, most people used to look with contempt at a musician who led a dance orchestra. The deprecating glance is the rudiment of an attitude that has to some extent shaped the social character of musicians.[3]

Many musicians have always had an obsequious manner, from the dance-band leader who smilingly acquiesces to play your favorite selection to the strolling café violinist eager to ingratiate himself in hopes of a gratuity. This pandering to the paying audience is a rendered service of professional conformism. The ability of the musician to communicate with those who hire him assures him of continued return engagements.

The film composer is a temporary employee who can be discharged for any number of reasons, including the arbitrary judgment of his employers concerning the material he supplies. A cursory examination of a contract between composer and film company gives ample evidence of the composer's employee status. Upon signing to score a picture, the artist turns over all rights to his music to the company that engages him. Under the usual Hollywood contract, the composer functions as an indentured servant; he gets paid adequately for his creative labor but does not own any part of the music after he has completed the scoring assignment. The corporate powers reserve the right to use his work as they deem necessary: they can cut it to ribbons, arrange, rearrange, edit and readapt it for whatever purpose they desire. The disproportion between the corporation's power and the composer's impotence is plain. Only recently have the composers rebelled against this second-class treatment and fought back as a unit to regain lost rights and a measure of deserved respect. As of 1972, CBS (the first major corporation to do so) agreed to return all music rights to composers who have contributed music on their network shows; thus it allows composers to utilize their own work as they see fit and in whatever capacity they wish. Only a beginning in the long-overdue music-rights custody struggle, this action is indicative of a major breakthrough in attitude and relations between the musician and the film company.

From wandering minstrel to Hollywood composer is not as long a road as one might think. It is no more distant than that from roving troubadour in the Middle Ages to today's nomadic guitarist. The musician's heritage has contributed to the current image he maintains in the film industry. Only his power at the box office in terms of his track record—the films he has scored in conjunction with their financial success—gives him status in the film hierarchy. In the contemporary marketplace many composers, hit songwriters in particular, have earned a high personality rating—an added attraction that attests to their salability.[4] Their alliance with show business is not limited to a one-picture contract. A deeper involvement touches on social relationships and attitudes of mutual benefit. It is apparent that films ask more from composers than their music: the practice of the craft demands a certain flair, an up-to-dateness. The ratio of 90 percent showmanship to 10 percent artistry is not, in many instances, an unfair representation. Like the rise of court jester to king comedian, the ascent of many film composers to celebrityhood places them side by side with the actor, actress, and director. Together they make up the regal court of America's film royalty.

Hollywood began as an extension of Broadway. The initial music writers migrating to the West Coast in search of movie riches—California's early thirties gold rush—came from radio, pit orchestras, and the milieu of Tin Pan Alley. Arriving first, they planted their musical roots and entrenched themselves firmly in positions of management. Many acquired administrative posts and became heads of music departments in film studios. They hired the personnel, including, in many cases, the composers. These musician types had a perfect understanding of the aspirations of the film industry and an accurate knowledge of what kind of music was wanted and how it was to be utilized. Their musical tastes and goals reflected and coincided with those in executive authority. Rapport was their trump card, which allowed them to maintain their status in the industry, resist outside competition, and discourage newcomers or latecomers from making inroads into their inner circle. "Colleagues" in the strictest sense of the word, they functioned as cogs in the business wheel of studio operations, which were backed by corporate banking interests who took over economic control of the motion-picture industry shortly after its conversion to sound and inaugurated assembly-line mass production of feature films.

The counterparts of these Broadway-indoctrinated music administrators were the producers who came to Hollywood from the famed resort areas of the Catskills called "the borscht belt." Having served their apprenticeship in the entertainment-try-out theater—a perfect place to learn the rudiments of show business and the know-how of commercial enterprise—they were ready to graduate to the production of motion pictures. This included, when necessary, the hiring and firing of film composers, for which their "expertise" in matters of music and musical taste was supposed to qualify them.

In Lillian Ross' satirical dissection on the making of the film *The Red Badge of Courage* (1952), she quotes producer Dore Schary's opinion of what makes good film music: "Each time the music has the sense of warmth and nostalgia, it creates a mood that is helpful to the picture. As soon as the music gets highly inventive, it hurts the picture. . . . I think all music in pictures has to be cliché to be effective. Let's not debate it. I'll prove it to you. In Marine pictures, you play 'Halls of Montezuma.' In Navy pictures, you play 'Anchors Aweigh.' In this picture, the music that's effective is the sentimental-cliché music. It's a fact. Let's not debate it."[5] Thus in a few short phrases are summed up several generations of thinking on the subject.

The silent film was a one-dimensional sensory experience. Everything that could not be implied visually had to be communicated through printed titles. (This is strangely apropos in viewing foreign films, where direct language communication is absent although sound is present.) The emotion behind the various scenes had to be supplied and stressed by music. It was soon evident that the film needed something more than facial expressions and body movements. It needed sound and spoken words to give greater elasticity, eloquence, and a more immediate form of dialogue to achieve a semblance of equality with live theater. Roger Manvell writes:

The absence of the spoken word, of dialogue, forced the film to exploit the more elementary situations in drama and the more obvious kinds of characterization, because it was impossible except by indirect methods (the use of symbols, the elaborate construction of pictorial atmosphere, and the use of tricks in editing) to move nearer in to the complexities and subtleties of human thought and feeling. Many of the finest films of the silent period evolved a form of mime-acting which varied in subtlety with the artistry of the film-makers and actors, and this mime was directly related to the continuous stream of music which accompanied the film like the score of a ballet.[6]

With the advent of sound, following a transitional period between the birth of talkies and the final death of silents, music emerged from its tacit involvement into a more salient participancy. By trial and error it was discovered that, acting in a catalytic way, music could evoke emotional response; that it could alter a viewer's perception of the dramatic links between words and images; that it could stimulate feelings and reactions. With this unconscious revelation arose the theory that if the film-makers were unable to fulfill the dramatic requisites of their films—because of oversights, errors in cinematic judgment, or simple lack of talent—the composer could apply his witchcraft technique to soothe the sick film's ailments and, in some cases, completely cure it. In short, by doctoring the dramatic failures of the film, music could save the picture. From this conception of music as a placebo evolved the tradition of immense scores found in films during the period of the thirties through the fifties.

In many instances, pictures two hours long had almost every frame of film scored. In *Gone With The Wind,* for example, only thirty minutes out of 222 are without music. Warner Brothers led the way in adopting this notorious practice, and composer Max Steiner was its early devotee and principal practitioner. In the face of this supergrandiose musical assault, the very emotional responses film-makers were trying to kindle were literally choked to death. Music was used to cover and accompany everything: battles, hurricanes, earthquakes, catastrophes, and sheer noise were buried under an avalanche of musical sonority. Over, below, and through dialogue; nothing could stop it. Amidst the symphonic bombardment, the power of music to trigger emotions was rendered impotent. Its total saturation eliminated contrast, clouded ideas, reduced musical delineation to amorphous background sounds, and completely negated the placement of music in the proper dramaturgical context. But this backwash of sound and neutralization of musical components was exactly the kind of scoring that was expected. The audience heard the music without being distracted by its presence. Without diverting from the picture's action and dialogue, this type of background music kept the film going. It supplied a certain amount of melodic motion without making a point of its thematic content.

In fact, nothing changed musically in the transition from silent films to talking pictures. For while concert music veered off in another direction, seeking its own style of expression through innovative experiment—as with Schoenberg, Webern, and the twelve-tone school, in particular—movie music continued along the road of the silents. At first, it consisted of arrangements of existing music, but after a few years this practice was abandoned in favor of a new concept. Although the actual works of the old European concert composers were discarded as workable film scores, there arose in their place a new group of live film composers capable of writing—or, more accurately, rewriting—music in the exact late nineteenth- and early twentieth-century style of Rachmaninoff, Tchaikovsky, Mahler, Wagner, Strauss, Moussorgsky, and others. Later the impressionistic influences of Debussy and the rhythmic devices of Stravinsky crept into the musical picture. Now film music was flooded with imitations—minus, of course, the original name credits. Many of these qualified musicians emigrated from Europe, some as refugees from Nazi Germany at the onset of the Second World War. Their experience came from the opera houses and theater pits of European cities. They brought professional training, knowledge of the repertoire, and a heavy-handed emphasis on large-scale symphonic composition. Among others they included Dimitri Tiomkin, Herbert Stothart, Eric Korngold, Werner Janssen, Miklos Rozsa, and Ernst Toch. Along with Max Steiner, Alfred Newman, Victor Young, Franz Waxman, George Antheil, Bronislow Kaper, and Bernard Herrmann (whose musical style was actually closer to Aaron Copland's native idiom), they contributed many of the major scores for American films during the two to three decades following 1930. Their style reflected the lush, impassioned romanticism of mid-Europe in the late nineteenth century. For the most part it was pure schmaltz. While the violins throbbed and the woodwinds and brasses sighed and pulsated, the entire orchestra drenched itself in lachrymal sentimentality. The music was luxuriant, the embodiment of an emotional overflow. It didn't matter what the film was; even if the subject was a hard-boiled contemporary theme, the audience was still given its usual dosage of syrup and honey. This mellifluousness dulled the senses and acted as an opiate rather than a stimulant. And, it increased the viewer's susceptibility to the film's projected illusions by appealing to maudlin emotions.

During this period, there was a disproportionate setup of the orchestral components. The grandiose main titles and endings, indistinguishable middle voices, pronounced emphasis on violin tones, heavy brass chords, and undiscriminated woodwinds contributed to a standardization of sound reproduction. The small orchestra's reliance on strings for simple accompaniments behind intimate scenes and dialogue invoked a café-music sound. This usage compounded the overall effect and accentuated the uniformity of the music. In addition, inadequate recording techniques of the thirties and forties robbed film music of some of its potency and spontaneity. With rare exceptions—a woodwind solo, for example—the honeycombed sound of the orchestra had very little clarity or dynamic scope. The music underwent acoustical changes during its transfer to the sound track, gradually approaching a state of neutralization whereby its extroverted qualities were removed, its dynamic range narrowed, and its orchestral color destroyed. In this process the music was further reduced to an inconspicuous level by sound engineers' insensitivity to the subtle nuances of musical timbres. Today's eight-track stereo recording, offering separation and delineation of sound, was sorely missed.

The father of sound-film music was Max Steiner. Arriving in Hollywood around 1929, he was one of the first composers to score music for a large-scale, sound feature film—*King Kong*. His importance is not merely chronological. Steiner must be acknowledged for helping win recognition for the film composer and enabling him to receive his merited screen credit. He influenced many film people to accept the fact that music could serve a vital emotional function in their films, and he popularized music for motion pictures.

Steiner was one of the first practitioners of the device known in the trade as "Mickeymousing," a term derived from Walt Disney's early animations. These cartoons were the first efforts at precise timing-and-action relationships between picture and music through sound-track analysis or "reading." Steiner had a special weakness for this practice, which often vulgarized the scenes he was scoring. Using highly illustrative music to echo the action and mood of the film, he translated into musical terms the very movements depicted on the screen—sometimes in precise synchronization. This redundancy—the viewer already sees the action unfolding before him—acts as a distraction, amplifying its own musical shortcomings. By constantly calling attention to itself, the Mickeymoused score becomes offensive and tiresome. Whereas the typical background score made no dramatic contribution to the film at all, being practically irrelevant, the Mickeymoused score went to the other extreme, accentuating the obvious. Mickeymousing stressed the cleverness of the composer rather than the dramatic mood of the moment. The practice led to additional conventions as entire scenes were mimicked by music, with different instruments and orchestral devices showing the way. The bassoon became the village clown, usually inebriated; the tremolo on strings indicated suspense; mountain peaks evoked signallike horn figures. In effect, the music followed visual events and illustrated them either through direct imitation or by clichés associated with the mood and tempo of the scene. In the classic example, *Of Human Bondage*, both the protagonist and his musical accompaniment limp across the screen together in perfect rhythm; in *Gone With The Wind*, when the horses jump the fence, the music leaps in parallel motion. In *King Kong*, practically every movement on the screen has its musical counterpart; Steiner even gave the main characters and scenic locations their own *leitmotifs*. Slow or fast horizontal movement—people walking and running—is accompanied by music in a slow or fast tempo, which stops when the action halts and starts up again when the action recommences. Up-and-down vertical screen motion, as when Kong climbs the Empire State building, for example, is associated with music rising and falling in stepwise, melodic-scale fashion. In Mickeymousing, the anticipated action is often tipped off by the music. A heavy brass chord announces danger; a low, sustained tone echoes mystery; one ominous musical signal prepares the audience for the dramatic events to follow. Steiner was also fond of mixing realistic music with background music. A character whistling a tune during a scene is suddenly thrust into a different setting—out into a storm or shifted from an interior to an exterior. From out of nowhere comes an orchestra of eighty musicians giving forth with a full tutti rendition of the tune. This obvious device destroys all narrative illusion.

Many composers after Steiner adopted the follow-the-leader musical plan, and, in some films of the sixties (examples of which will be cited later), this idiosyncratic device can still be detected. Even today, highly illustrative Mickeymoused music regularly forms part of television-network series.[7]

An approach to film scoring other than Mickeymousing was that of Alfred Newman, who scored *How Green Was My Valley*, *Love Is a Many-Splendored Thing*, *The Grapes of Wrath*, and *Wuthering Heights*. In his scores, which were stylistically similar to Steiner's, he attempted to catch the emotional and dramatic flavor of a total scene rather than to imitate musically the small components and inner movements of each episode. This allowed the pictorial conception to remain intact and not get lost in the musical pyrotechnics of Mickeymousing. Newman's use of the string orchestra as background for intimate scenes had a depersonalized quality. The music could be sensed rather than actually felt.

As noted before, Hollywood producers rated the musical sophistication of their audience as decidedly low and, admittedly, with some justification. They were frightened to death by twentieth-century innovations coming to fruition in the concert hall. Contemporary music modeled on Schoenberg, Webern, Varèse, Ives, and others was declared out-of-bounds for movie music. The producers thought that the public ear was tone-deaf except for the most obvious, easily accessible, melodic music, typified by the late nineteenth-century mid-European concert style. What they failed to comprehend was the nature of films themselves in relation to this style. The bulky texture and large-scale structure is ill-suited to the sudden alterations in mood, time, and place, either for providing reticent, unobtrusive background accompaniments or for scoring the mercurial shifts in mood associated with Mickeymousing. The constant jumping around inherent in this latter technique weakens the music's sense of continuity.

It is easy today to take a pejorative attitude toward the technique of Mickeymousing, but one must think of the practice in terms of its time. In those days nobody really understood anything about film music, and the film-makers themselves were often as musically naive as their audience. Frank Capra writes about the music score for his film *Lost Horizon* (1936):

> Curiously enough, my biggest sweat was not the film. It was the musical scoring. I had given the job to a composer who had never before scored a film—Russian-born, ex-concert pianist Dimitri Tiomkin. To a man, studio executives had railed against such an unnecessary, perhaps stupid, gamble. But a little bird told me that Tiomkin would come up with new, fresh, novel music. The nervous Russian pleaded with me to hear and approve his themes for the picture. I refused. I wanted *his* music, not mine. But I copped a bet against possible disaster by hiring Max Steiner—Warner Brothers' great music composer—to conduct Tiomkin's score. I knew that if old Steiner thought the score inadequate, he himself would step in to rewrite it—fast.
>
> Curiosity had forced me to sneak unseen into the music-scoring stage to overhear Steiner's first orchestral rehearsal of the main-title music. I left with stars in my eyes. And after sitting for over three hours in that packed projection room, I still had stars in my eyes. Tiomkin's music not only captured the mood, but it darned near captured the film.[8]

What was this music that put stars in Capra's eyes? Incredibly schmaltzy to the point of dripping honey, Tiomkin's music was about as refreshing as stale ginger ale. The heavenly choir, serving as an allegorical narrative, only intensified an already overromanticized screen imagery. A puerile, laughable musical convention, the angel voices were dated years before *Lost Horizon*. The action takes place, for the most part, in Tibet, an exotic land filled with sounds strange to the Western ear, and yet not one single note of Tibetan musical language appears on the sound track. Last year, when I screened this film for my class in "Music for Motion Pictures," the students booed and hissed the music—and the film. This says something about the changes in musical styles and conceptions of sound since 1936.

The all-singing, all-dancing features of the thirties, such as the *Gold Diggers* series and various college musicals, were popular screen attractions. The human voice and rhythmic dance numbers dominated these films and relegated incidental music for dramatic background cues to a bit part. Sometimes the orchestra playing the scores was seen; other times it was implied. The musical film was different from the dramatic film with incidental music. The former was voice, singing, and dancing, and its drama was strictly subordinate to vocal projection and body movement.

During this period, music was used as a complement to the placement of a scene. Tunes were sung as background music in nightclub settings or as continuations of a scene that directly led to its rendition. The crooners of this era moved in and out and back and forth between their dramatic roles and the musical commentaries via lyrics set up by script formats. Action would stop while a singer rendered a torch number. Sometimes, in gangster films, the racketeers would be conspiring at a table in the foreground. Popular songs were featured or special numbers were composed for particular spottings. In fact, it was a short step from the instrumental pieces or musical-song excerpt from a dance film—as in the Astaire and Rogers and Bing Crosby musicals—to the more encompassing form of the theme melody.

It was soon discovered that Madison Avenue's techniques of supersalesmanship featuring the "see it, hear it, try it, buy it" message were psychologically more effective when musically packaged in the form of a tune, theme, jingle, or ballad, repeated ad nauseam. Thus, the theme tune during the lush, symphonic era arose as a built-in promotional advertisement heralding and selling the film in which it appeared. Coincidentally, the film brass discovered the value of box-office terms of a musical enticer—over and above background music, Mickeymoused or not—as a screen accompaniment. These broadly lyrical melodic gems contributed a financial dividend. Issued in sheet music and later availabale through recordings, they were an additional avenue of revenue. The theme tune itself was generally long and fatiguingly repetitious. Arranged differently upon occasion but present in one form or another, it intruded upon scenes regardless of dramatic motivation. Many had a poignant, exaggerated, romantic flavor especially effective in projecting sentiment and nostalgia. The theme tune could be played softly or assertively, depending on, or unmindful of, the constant mood changes on the screen. In some instances, it could function from start to finish as a replacement for the actual scoring of a film; and, indeed, it still does, as pointed out previously. Some of these early theme melodies, such as Steiner's for *Now Voyager* and Korngold's for *King's Row,* became extremely popular.

One of the earliest and perhaps the most famous theme song in film music is the haunting ballad composed by David Raksin for Otto Preminger's *Laura* (1944). An example of the felicitous use of a theme to convey nostalgia and brooding sentiment, it acts as a musical umbrella for the slightly above-average melodrama it covers. The song became a standard, and by giving the film an illusion of greatness and psychological intensity it did not actually possess, it helped the picture achieve the rank of a classic. Moreover, it literally sold the picture to the public. To a somewhat lesser degree this is also true of Miklos Rozsa's theme for Alfred Hitchcock's *Spellbound* (1946). Its eerie, darkly romantic flavor epitomizes the mood of the film and, in this respect, is highly effective.

Examples of another kind include the scores to *The Third Man* (1949) and the later success *Doctor Zhivago* (1965). Anton Karas's celebrated zither music in *The Third Man* is based on banal melodic lines amplified to center stage through the use of an indigenous solo instrument. Its main tune, repeated endlessly, is burned into the audience's psyche, but its effectiveness in selling the picture and setting the film's mood cannot be denied. Similarly, Maurice Jarre's "Lara's Theme" from *Doctor Zhivago* is an exercise in melodic futility, marked by musical imperfections such as wrong notes and badly chosen harmonies and progressions. And yet, pumped into the viewer's bloodstream by an oversized orchestra, it succeeded in promoting the film. (In this respect, the film producer is right in believing that he is getting his money's worth from the composer, for in his dollars-and-sense thinking, anything that creates an interest in his product or a commercial rapport between audience and film is the lucrative answer.)

Another famous theme song is the one written by Dimitri Tiomkin for *High Noon* (1952). Wrapped in Western trappings reminiscent of Aaron Copland's music, the theme explains and delineates the nature of the picture in naive musical argot. Although its sound track helps perpetuate the Western myth—a small town, lonely sheriff, "good" people—the added lyrics, sung throughout the film as a running commentary, paradoxically expose the mature message that the myth itself is phony. One of the first title songs in a dramatic setting to make sense, the commercial success of *High Noon* opened the dam and let in the tidal wave of title songs. It was the forerunner of today's hit-tune, main-title-song mania that preconditions both composer and producer to think "pop song" from the time of the film's conception. European films, especially the French cinema, suffered from the same predilection. The early scores of Maurice Jaubert and later ones of Francis Lai and Michel Legrand testify to this tendency.

Film music of the thirties through the fifties, in general, accurately mirrored its pop culture. Stylistically, the songs and tunes played for social dancing and on the radio were akin to those composed for films. Tin Pan Alley love ballads were as lush and sugarcoated as the movie schmaltz they emulated. Many of the film themes, including themes from the great masters' concert works, became popular song hits when lyrics were added. The

27

emotional sonorities of film music and American popular music were interchangeable—a fact of musical life even today. The public's willingness to accept the romantic facsimiles of nineteenth-century originals via the entertainment media was symptomatic of a chronic emotional attachment. In short, the melody became the malady.

By the fifties, the film-music scene saw distinct changes. Recording techniques advanced to a higher level of sophistication, improving the quality of the sound track. Given the luxury of additional time to compose his music plus the fidelity of the modern stereophonic speaker system, the composer's horizon of sound increased, widening his scope of imagination and dramatic effectiveness. The musical frontier began to push aside the lush romanticism of the late nineteenth century and move toward a more contemporary musical expression. Although not completely voided, the symphonic idiom's stranglehold on the movie industry's thinking weakened and commenced to wane. A backward step is occasionally taken, as with Miklos Rozsa's old-fashioned symphonic score for Wilder's *The Private Life of Sherlock Holmes* (1969) and Ron Goodwin's thick-textured orchestral background for Hitchcock's *Frenzy* (1972).

Even the concept of dissonance—that frightening, controversial, uncommercial sound—began to be reexamined, and this stronger musical language found its way into sound tracks with greater frequency. Gail Kubik's percussive use of the piano pounding out its rhythmic chords in *C Man* (1949) was a striking example of the new resources available to an enterprising composer. Once in a while the refreshing musical talents of Aaron Copland and Bernard Herrmann were allowed to shine through. Copland's earlier scores for *Of Mice and Men* and *The Red Pony* and Herrmann's scores for numerous Hitchcock films and especially his music—a classic in film-music circles—for William Dieterle's 1942 production of *All That Money Can Buy* (sometimes called *The Devil and Daniel Webster*) revealed a clean-cut, decidedly American musical profile in spirit and style, and even today these scores sound fresh and scintillating. Perhaps the most significant opportunities for progressive and experimental music were in the realm of mystery, horror, and science-fiction films. In the sixties, Jerry Goldsmith's superb scores for *Planet of the Apes, Mephisto Waltz,* and specific cues in *The Illustrated Man* became milestones in advanced music techniques and ingenious musical effects. Along with certain sequences from Leonard Rosenman's *Fantastic Voyage,* in which the composer experimented with *klangfarben* (the tone color of sound) and varied counterpoints of these kinds of sound, Paul Glass' pointillistic opening music for *Lady in a Cage,* Hans Henze's use of the voice in *Muriel,* Roberto Gerhard's sparse musical language in *This Sporting Life,* Toru Takemitsu's electronic score for *Woman of the Dunes,* Bernard Herrmann's chilling strings for *Psycho,* and Stanley Kubrick's use of Gyorgy Ligeti's "Atmospheres" for *2001* as part of the Star Gate sequences, they represent some of the possibilities inherent in motion pictures for utilizing contemporary music, especially certain uncompromising sounds. (Some of the examples in this chapter are discussed in greater detail in Chapter 5.)

During the sixties as the old-timers died off or faded into musical oblivion, a new group of composers appeared. Representative of this group are: Henry Mancini (*A Shot in the Dark, Wait until Dark*); Burt Bacharach (*Alfie, Casino Royale, What's New Pussycat?*); Quincy Jones (*In the Heat of the Night, They Call Me Mr. Tibbs*); John Barry (*Goldfinger, The Knack*); John Dankworth (*Accident*); and Paul McCartney (*The Family Way*). The road for this "new wave" was first traveled by Alex North in the fifties with his New Orleans-jazz-oriented score for *A Streetcar Named Desire* (1951). Later he used jazz in a primitive way for *Go Man Go*. These scores rang the bell for others to follow, notably Elmer Bernstein's New York jazz themes for *The Man With the Golden Arm*, John Lewis' chamber-music jazz for *Odds Against Tomorrow*, Johnny Mandel's jazz conceptions in *I Want to Live*, and Leith Stevens' jazz-influenced symphonic score for *The Wild One*.

With the Hollywood gates to employment swinging open, many composers, like Henry Mancini and Jerry Goldsmith, made the transition from television to feature films. The money for large orchestras was not available in television, and these men (Mancini in his jazz-driven *Peter Gunn* and Goldsmith's dramatic jazz elements for *The Man from UNCLE*) found that their use of small combos and instrumental groups was applicable to feature films and just as effective.

In recent years the influx of pop musicians and assorted rock composers has turned almost every major film into a kind of musical, with hit songs born overnight, exploited, and consumed like chocolate bars melting in the mouth. As a group this new breed has become the dominant force and the single most important source of music in contemporary films. Schooled in the idioms of cool jazz, rock, folk, and pop music, they have little affinity with the symphonically oriented music of the past. Their musical training, style, and thinking is diametrically opposed to the symphonic scores of Elmer Bernstein for *Hawaii*, Ernest Gold for *Exodus*, or Maurice Jarre for *Lawrence of Arabia*. Although their "finger-snapping" sound may not retain its freshness past tomorrow, it has the unmistakable commercial beat of "now." It is not merely up to date; it is up to the minute—the rhythmic dress of the mod generation.

Fashionable styles of film music should not necessarily be confused with progress. It is not always true that bigger, louder, or jazzier rhythmic tracks indicate superior scores. Even the fact that film music is seemingly better planned compared to an earlier period is no proof of dramatic excellence. Yesterday's incidental, often quiet background score—preferable in some instances—has been souped up and replaced by today's brassy foreground score. The result is often atrocious: a glossy, ostentatious front tacked on to a dull, prosaic rear. In many cases, we hear the ultimate in ordinariness performed by the ultimate in super-stereo-sound reproduction.

Concomitant with a changing scene and a more imaginative use of complex film technology, film-makers now more than ever encourage composers to write title songs and scores featuring theme tunes as a means of advertising their films and promoting the sales of the sound-track ablums. The figures behind this "money-rhythm" policy are difficult to refute: The Beatles' first album from *A Hard Day's Night* enriched United Artists by over two million dollars—triple what it cost to produce the movie. "Lara's Theme," part of the released sound-track recording from *Doctor Zhivago*, had sold over two million copies; Francis Lai's "Love Story" from the same-titled movie has sold over one million albums and 200,000 tapes and was recorded in 280 different versions.[9] Small wonder that Hollywood has beckoned with open arms and cash those musicians and young composer-songwriters who can write hit tunes and title songs, preferring them to all others. It does not seem to matter that the theme tunes have little relevance to the film's dramatic context. Usually placed at the beginning as a title song but occasionally at the end, as was Rod McKuen's song for *The Prime of Miss Jean Brodie*, the songs cash in on today's fast-changing youth market, ostensibly giving it pictures with a gilt-edged frame of catchiness. By influencing young people, the major consumers of pop-music recordings, to identify with their songs, their togetherness, their musical messages, film-makers have neatly packaged song and script.

The film industry's current hit-song mania is part of a deep-rooted pop-tune mentality. It is the result of a Broadway-show-biz heritage that has conditioned millions of people to accept each generation's pop culture as a valid barometer of musical excellence, creativity, and full value for the dollar. Through the mass-media loudspeaker system, the pop-music culture has rammed its product down the audience's throat and instilled in people, especially film personnel, a way of associating success and hit songs. By using instantaneously acceptable music, already packaged and presold in the pop culture, the film-makers display an adroit awareness of their audience's fashionable taste buds, and this audience, in turn, is a sitting duck for the industry's sales psychology. As we have noted, songs and theme tunes have been a source of revenue and promotion for studios for many years. What makes the present situation unique is the organized machinery behind the manufacture of hit songs in films today. Songwriting has become a success phenomenon laser-beamed into the hearts of Americans.

To comprehend what makes people susceptible to the musical message and massage of its pop culture, it must be understood that at heart America is a great songwriting-happy country. More prestigious attention is paid the pop songwriter in the mirror of public recognition than *all* the other representatives of the fine arts put together. Make no mistake: in the minds of most people, a composer *is* a writer of pop songs. The mass media have encouraged the public to accept this fallacy by elevating songwriting to the status of an institution. Respect and admiration are such that the pop-music song-and-dance ambassadors of show biz outnumber genuine artists 10,000 to 1 in receiving invitations from the President to the White House, where, along with professional athletes, actors, and actresses, they accept official accolades for giving a grateful nation its beloved music and entertainment.

This country began as a dream and was populated by an army of escapee-emigrants who "believed" the first love songs that extolled the limitless possibilities in the rich American earth. Through succeeding generations Americans expressed their hopes and aspirations in songs that often covered up a history of ingenuous exploitation. Myths based on legendary feats of bravery, personal heroism, and historic battles, including the vanquishing of the American Indian, abounded. The national pre-

version of melodic nostalgia instead of the eerie effects they now project, and everybody will rush to cash in.

Whether one is forced to absorb the latest rhythms blaring from music shops, hand-held transistors, or taxicab radios; whether one enters a bank, rides an elevator in an office building wired for Muzak, finds himself in a restaurant unable to escape the ubiquitous jukebox, sits in an airline terminal receiving piped-in reassurance, or attends the new movie house with its streamlined facade, extra comforts, and latest films with stereophonic sound equipment—the result is identical: assault to the ear and wall-to-wall musical enclosure guaranteed to make you a part of the pop-music scene whether you want to be or not. Nauseated or exhilarated, however you feel about it, the total effect is a loud, steady drone. The sameness of the music is like a movie loop going around and around, never stopping, never altering its beat except to play the tunes faster or slower.

If the public is accustomed to nonstop music in its everyday pursuits, it expects the same from its amusement outlets, and, unfortunately, film music is too often a part of today's ear pollution. With electronic equipment so sophisticated and elaborate as to dominate the musical stage completely and in some ways to overshadow the music it is forced to reproduce, it can truly be said that never before in history have so many had the opportunity to say so little so often with such overpowering amplification.

The fact is, the situation is not unique: the American money rhythm changes from generation to generation, but each age is positive that its own musical thumping is *the* beat. In rebellion against the romantic slush of thirties, forties, and fifties movie music and the Irving Berlin mentality in popular songs, today's pop-music-makers have replaced the schmaltz of yesteryear with a new kind of hopped-up fervor that is just as stupefying. To paraphrase a line from Noel Coward's *Private Lives:* It's astonishing and strange, the power of cheap music.

1. Aaron Copland, *Our New Music* (New York: McGraw-Hill Book Co., Whittlesey House, 1941), p. 262.

2. For a comprehensive list, see Dr. Roger Manvell, ed., *The International Encyclopedia of Film* (New York: Crown Publishers, Inc., 1972).

3. Hanns Eisler, *Composing for the Films* (New York: Oxford University Press, 1947), pp. 46–47.

4. Many film composers (including Quincy Jones, Michel Legrand, and Henry Mancini) play the summer music-festival circuit, leading an orchestra in selections from their film scores—mostly theme-tune arrangements.

5. Lillian Ross, *Pictures* (New York: Avon, Discus Books, 1969), pp. 145 and 148.

6. Roger Manvell, *The Film and the Public* (Harmonsworth, Middlesex, England: Penguin Books Ltd., 1955), p. 55.

7. One reason, perhaps, is that the television audience is not captive, and people watching in the comfort of their homes can easily leave the room or switch channels. Musical signposts tell them what is going on. Hearing the music away from the set keeps the viewer informed.

8. Frank Capra, *The Name above the Title* (New York: Bantam Books, 1971), pp. 217–218.

9. In *The New Yorker* profile on Joseph Levine, Sept. 16, 1967, the producer comments to director Vittorio De Sica about the music for *Woman Times Seven:* "You know, we have a chance to get Mancini for the picture." De Sica looked puzzled. "Henry Mancini," Levine explained. "The composer—the one who wins the Academy Award for music every year. I think we should get Mancini to do the score for the whole picture. All those goddam pictures and we've never yet had a hit song. It means a hell of a lot of money, you know."

10. One reason for the songwriting vogue may be historical: the voice came first; people sang at the beginning. Afterward they added movement, rhythm, and the dance. Then came instruments, initially as imitations of the human voice but gradually becoming more removed into electronic and mechanical expression. Possibly young people's desire to compose music reflects their need to use their voices and sing as a creative outlet.

11. Isaac Hayes is credited with composing the music; J. J. Johnson and Tom Macintosh, with the orchestration.

12. Unmercifully hammering out its rhythmic ostinato, today's beat beats the audience over its head. A pounding, ostinato figure, however, actually gives the feeling of movement and drive without being rhythmical. There is a distinction between ostinato, which is a rhythmic device, and rhythm itself. An ostinato is, in fact, a chain against movement, progression, and rhythmic variance. The music, reiterating a continuous pattern, literally stays put in one place. It is akin to rotating around a circle while being tied to a center stake.

3. The Contemporary Concert Composer in Films

There is too much interference doing films for serious composers to want to get into the medium.

Gail Kubik

Throughout the history of motion-picture music a significant creative force, seldom harnessed by the makers of commercial feature films in America, has operated outside the mainstream. It is the contemporary concert composer who has supplied this underground stream of film music. He continues to use his special dramatic insights and contemporary compositional techniques to compose imaginative music for those rare motion pictures he has been commissioned to score, but, relegated to a minority status by the film industry, he remains a victim of past and present prejudices.

Historical circumstances led to this state of affairs. Because of the early Broadway-Hollywood show-biz alliance, as indicated before, the concert composer was frozen out of a featured role in the industry at its very inception, and his position as an outsider was confirmed. It was and is an injustice that has become a fact of musical life in the functional media and is especially reprehensible when one realizes that it is the concert composer who, by virtue of his extensive training and artistic curiosity, possesses the articulate musical language and musico-dramaturgic syntax that comprises the culture. He is the keeper of the flame, and it is from his cultural arsenal that the pop culture has gleaned the materials to nourish its creative machinery.

It must be borne in mind that the motion picture, with its integration of all the technological elements such as picture, sound, dialogue, narrative, photography, and theatrics has emerged as contemporary culture's most representative medium. With all art, both serious and popular, becoming an amusement commodity for leisure-time activity, the film industry has absorbed the materials of traditional art in order to imbue its product with all the outer trappings of the genuine culture. In *2001* and *A Clockwork Orange*, for example, Stanley Kubrick uses the framework of classical music to give his films the veneer of art. In *2001*, he borrows liberally from Richard Strauss and others; in *A Clockwork Orange*, he avails himself of a recomposed electronic version of Beethoven, updating this composer from out of the pages of the

Anthony Burgess novel. This is reminiscent of the early days of film when the musical gems of the past were incorporated as background adornments.

With drama, mystery, psychological fiction, best seller, opera, soap opera, symphony, and musical soirée all being lumped together under one cultural roof today, the distinction between serious and popular art has become largely academic and no longer applicable. All art is sold in the marketplace and labeled "goods." The consumer can shop for packaged cultural bargains merchandised alongside the cut-rate treasures on display.

But while the pop culture has been extracting the best available from the culture and utilizing its outstanding literary, cinematic, and directorial talents, it has steadfastly refused to lay out the welcome mat for the contemporary concert composer. And although innovations in painting, sculpture, literature, and legitimate theater have been accepted, there has been a lag regarding contemporary concert music, with some small, esoteric exceptions. Film producers reason if the public is fearful of or adamantly resistant to avant-garde music in the concert hall, why should it welcome these painful sounds in motion-picture sound tracks?

Suspicious of an artist who is interested in spending only part of his time scoring an occasional film rather than becoming a full-time member of the film society, film producers distrust the concert composer for a number of other psychological and economic reasons:

They doubt his loyalty to the industry and do not believe he understands the aims and aspirations of the film business.

They are insecure about their ability to communicate with him on a common-language level—the old highbrow-lowbrow syndrome.

They fear the concert composer will not fit in on the film-making team; that his ego or difficult personality will disrupt the smooth-flowing music-to-film operation; that he will upstage everyone.

They doubt his ability or desire to follow explicit instructions, to get the job done quickly and efficiently, and to write good commercial music. (They also recognize that his track record as a songwriting attraction at the box office is zero.) And they fear that his inexperience in the film medium will cost delays and money and result in an unsuccessful recording session; that not knowing how to use basic mechanical equipment and techniques will cause a complete breakdown in the film-scoring process.[1]

They are afraid he will write ultradissonant music that will be inappropriate for the film, increase the music-expense budget (they will have to hire another composer to finish the assignment), and provoke audience hostility.

But there is the other side. For if the pop culture rejects the contemporary concert composer, the composer himself is unwilling or reluctant, as the case may be, to emerge from his academic shell, take advantage of the opportunities offered by the functional field, and attempt to change its attitude toward him. The hindrance is not the composer's presence in the contemporary-music field and his dedication to writing concert music but rather his obsessive preoccupation with maintaining his "serious-art" image that causes producers to back off and lessens his chances of entering the mainstream of film music.

Actually, "serious" is a misnomer, for I have rarely met any type of composer who wasn't seriously attempting to do the best possible job with his capabilities. Music means different things to different people, including composers.

In addition, the contemporary concert composer's life-style can be self-defeating, since it cuts him off to a great extent from the world of competitive action, of which the film subculture is an active part. Since many concert composers teach (either by choice or by coercion in order to earn a livelihood), Mother University watches over them and shields them from the business world, where making a living and competing for jobs demand personal sacrifices and artistic-survival compromises. The academic campus presents its own political intrigues, but it is still an insulated society that operates under rigid local administration. By staying in his own backyard, the concert composer perpetuates his ivory-tower image. For those who consciously prefer the emotional and financial security of the academic life, the rewards and personal achievements issuing from their work make their selection felicitous; there are many musicians who have a definite calling for the teaching profession and an abiding interest in student-instructor relationships. (Many concert composers, however, who are active in universities are not so much interested in attracting pupils as they are in indoctrinating disciples.)

But for those composers motivated toward other ends and not averse to competing in the outside world, the functional-music field offers an untapped potential. Whatever his final decision, the concert composer should consider the advantages of working in the profession for which he was trained, especially if he has a dramatic-visual awareness. Is it any more of a compromise to write less-than-adventuresome music for an inane film and be paid chunks of money for the privilege than to accept the drudgeries of teaching stilted, academic music courses?

Many contemporary concert composers in educational institutions look down their noses at anyone who receives money for writing music in areas outside the concert domain. It is all right to accept foundation grants and commissions for concert compositions, but earning money practicing one's craft in the functional-film field is sacrilegious. They see writing music for out-and-out theatrical features as denigrating, regardless of how imaginative the score might be. The few recognized serious composers who have been offered and have accepted the challenge have done so without any harmful consequences to their artistic integrity.

In today's films, especially those dealing with experimental images and literate ideas, it is now possible more than ever for a composer to write his own sounds—the same ones he uses in his concert music. The only stylistic musical restriction is the necessary dramatic adjustment to the cinematic context.

In Europe, since silent-film days, many distinguished composers have successfully worked on feature films. Among others, the list includes: Darius Milhaud, Arthur Honegger, Georges Auric, Hanns Eisler, Hans Henze, Roberto Gerhard, Vaughan Williams, Sir William Walton, Sir Arthur Bliss, Sir Arnold Bax, Malcolm Arnold, John Addison, Alan Rawsthorne, Humphrey Searle, William Alwyn, two extremely talented young British composers, Peter

Maxwell Davies and Richard Rodney Bennett, and, of course, Dimitri Shostakovitch and Sergei Prokofiev.[2]

In America, when a contemporary concert composer has scored a mainstream feature film (as have Copland, Kubik, Virgil Thomson, and Meyer Kupferman, for example), he has contributed dramatically effective music. Concert composers have scored many documentary and art films; indeed, in this field their talents have been eagerly sought. The reasons are not difficult to comprehend: small budgets and enlightened film-makers with imaginative ideas on the use of music make for a meeting of the minds between composer and film-maker. Because the tensions and financial liabilities attending big-budget commercial ventures are absent, the documentary field offers an ideal atmosphere for the concert composer's participation. Moreover, without love scenes, chase sequences, cops-and-robbers or cowboys-and-Indians settings, neurotic characterizations, fights, murder, and general mayhem—all the stock situations that mark commercial feature films—the composer can write his own music with less fear of interference.[3]

A few years ago I was commissioned by Skyline Films through Hewitt-Robins Corporation, a division of Litton Industries, to write a full-sized, twenty-minute orchestral work, which I entitled, "Overture to Tomorrow." I was given complete liberty to write my own music and use whatever contemporary compositional techniques and sounds I desired. The music served as the basic inspiration and format for an unusual industrial documentary. This was one of the rare occasions when a composer had been commissioned to write a score about the operations of a large corporation. Instead of composing music to fit a finished film, I worked with the creative team and spent hours studying unedited footage in order to understand the work done by this industry and its interpretation through the images of the camera. After the score had been recorded, the final version of the film was edited to the music. There are no sound effects in the film and, more significantly, no narration. Whatever sound effects I deemed necessary, I created myself out of musical materials. The composition itself served as the basis for a subsequent large-scale piece.

The hit of the 1964–1965 New York City World's Fair was a motion picture called *To Be Alive,* produced by Johnson's Wax Company and directed by Francis Thompson. In addition to the visual impact of a three-camera projection system, Gene Forrell's vibrant score was a major contributor to the film's success.* Similarly, concert composer Ezra Laderman's sensitive musical portrait for *The Eleanor Roosevelt Story* gives a special kind of poetry to this Academy Award-winning documentary. And mention should also be made of Canadian composer Louis Applebaum's imaginative scores for both documentary and feature films.

The fine-art film is a separate entity not primarily created for commercial exposure. As composer-film-maker Keith Robinson points out: "Many of these films are of a very abstract nature and have been inspired by existing music or created simultaneously with contemporary composers and musicians. In some

*Music excerpt on page 298.

cases, the music is so important and meaningful that producers have decided to eliminate dialogue."[4] These films present the composer with a more difficult problem than scoring for a dramatic narrative film, since there are no convenient dramatic signposts to hang his hat on. Some composers have responded to the challenge by using avant-garde techniques, electronic sound-producing instruments, and even aleatory devices. Films of this type have brought about a more complex amalgamation of the aural and visual art forms than ever before. John Cage and other composers have been active in these special projects.

In dramatic feature films, experimental, avant-garde techniques have rarely been given sufficient exposure to justify denying their worth. Although audience reaction has never been thoroughly tested, I seriously doubt that people would suffer extreme or even moderate discomfort, squirm, or flee the theaters damning the music. In some films where advanced writing has been used (especially for television), acceptance followed without any pro or con letters to mark the event. Yet if the same people heard the identical film sounds in a concert piece, they probably would stir restlessly and wonder what hit them. Obviously, dialogue and visual perception act as a filter screen, siphoning out whatever objectionable discords reach the audience's ears from the sound track.

The tolerance level for controversial sounds in conjunction with a film is surprisingly high. When a score is married to the screen, the screen image becomes a fusion of sight and sound, and the eye and ear practice a cheat. The musical background becomes a part of the whole—an aural accompaniment to the cinematic flow. This is true even when the score does not "fit like a glove"; it is still absorbed into the total perception. The most controversial contemporary sound, therefore, becomes tamer in films. And after going through the recording-session, mix, and editing stages on its way to final lockup with the film, a further neutralization occurs and markedly softens the aggressive nature of the score.

For example, if you play the score from Leonard Rosenman's *Fantastic Voyage* as it was recorded and then hear it with the film, the contrast is striking. On tape, the music has power, imagination, and a marvelous, contemporary sound texture. With the film, the composer's sound language is so watered down that it bears little resemblance to the recorded version. Other composers and films can be cited for similar transformations.

Composers, directors, and producers can hotly debate what will and won't work behind a given scene, but is it possible that almost any kind of music can serve the functional purpose, especially after it has been fused to the image and tuned down to a sufficiently low level in the recording studio? Considering the variety of film music I have been forced to listen to over the years, including reruns of silent-film absurdities, I am inclined to answer "yes," with only a few aesthetic reservations. One thing is certain: in all my experience viewing films, I have never been convinced that an unimaginative, cliché-ridden, infantile music track has killed a motion picture. Nor has an ultradissonant, contemporary score ever caused a film's demise. The music may not have helped. It may not have fit or fulfilled its dramatic potential; it may have caused a slight or intense choking sensation in particular scenes.

39

But never did it result in strangulation. The people who make motion pictures would have you believe differently, but a careful perusal of films and their history substantiates my contention.

The contemporary concert composer has certain advantages over native Hollywood types that could effectively be put to use. He has a historical background, a knowledge of the repertoire, and a style that can articulate dramatic comment and achieve mobility in relation to the film's imagery. Films that demand more than mere tunes, title songs, and jazz noodling, that call for a more sophisticated musical treatment, could be enhanced by the concert-hall composer.[5] Moreover, the nature of much contemporary music— its concise statement and inventive use of short forms—could be ideally suited to film scoring. Many concert composers' experience with chamber orchestras and small ensemble groups, their ability to make few musicians sound like many—both in size and in tonal reproduction—could be of distinct value in solving film-economy problems.

What advantages would lead the concert composer actively to consider lending his talents to the film culture?

He can stay close to music by pursuing his profession. Where else can he be paid so well for doing what he has been trained for?

He can practice his craft, conduct his own music, and function in all capacities as a full-time professional composer.

He can contribute his special dramatic insights and musical solutions to specific film projects.

He can hear his music played immediately by the best musicians in the world.

He can use the film medium as a laboratory to experiment with innovative sounds, ideas, and techniques and try out passages (sometimes from his own concert works) arranged for any group of instruments he desires.

He will remain constantly musically motivated. By having to write music quickly and with mature judgment, he can develop the discipline to organize his material with maximum efficiency—both in film and in the concert hall. This is superb conditioning and on-the-spot training, and the security it gives the composer about the sounds he hears is invaluable.

The composer who is unwilling to follow a teaching career to secure a livelihood now has the positive advantage of an alternate choice.

He can help create a genuinely cooperative art—an alliance embracing all the available arts, including multimedia—and work toward their democratic integration.

There are two schools of thought regarding the concert composer's entry into the functional-film field. The first, the "separation of church and state" theory, is that the composer should not confuse what he does in the film culture with what he writes in the concert hall; that it is better to keep the two areas distinct if at all possible. The composer should accept the cinematic-musical limits within which he must create. He should understand the separate goals and aspirations of his two fields so as not to suffer frustration and emotional desiccation from making a compromise in his own mind.

The second school avows no musical schizophrenia, contending that the composer should write his own music at all times and bend only in relation to the film's functional considerations. Since he makes no compromise in order to realize his own uncompromising sounds, his concert-music style and his film music are one entity.

It is easier for composers who only do an occasional score (usually under special circumstances) to maintain their concert style intact. For those who have jumped headfirst into the film world, it is harder to transfer their concert style—providing, of course, that they have one—into their film music. In the former case, the composer is called in as a specialist, while in the latter he works as a steady contributor and takes many varied assignments where the duplication of a style is not always possible or practicable. Many serious composers refuse to score films because they are unwilling to let directors take the irreverent liberties with their music that is often required. But which school of thought a composer accepts depends on such personal considerations as aesthetics, psychological motivations, and the extent of his commitment to his own principles of artistic conduct.

I often speculate on what might have been if, in the early days following the sound revolution, the contemporary concert composer just coming into his own in America had been invited to contribute to mainstream motion pictures on a regular basis. Cinema music as we know it, from past to present, might have taken an entirely divergent path. Assuredly, experimentation in new musical resources as a counterpart to the introduction of sound and experimental film-making techniques could have led to an increased awareness of music's potential as a dramatic force—at a time when the direction of films and film music was uncertain. What musical horizons might not have been explored had the vanguard of new masters of the twentieth century been engaged at the outset instead of the warmed-over old masters of the nineteenth century?

In my class, Music for Motion Pictures, I often conduct the following experiment: during the screening of *King Kong,* when the monster-hero hurls the elevated train to the street below, I substitute sections of Charles Ives' Fourth Symphony for Max Steiner's music. The students can then grasp firsthand the aural-visual effect of contemporary music. Ives' score is infinitely superior to Steiner's late nineteenth-century eclecticism, and the scene's violence and total hysteria come into sharper, more realistic focus with the insertion of a different musical vocabulary.

Today, the contemporary concert-hall composer has a second chance to enter the medium, at a time in films when his inventive talents are most needed to complete the picture. By making a concerted effort to be included, he can assist in breaking down the wall of resistance against him. The traditional gap between the artist-intellectual and the business establishment, based in part on mutual envy, can be spanned. The fears of one group toward the other can be overcome or at least immeasurably lessened. In this effort, the attitude of the artist is of primary importance. The door is ajar; it would not take a massive effort to push it wide open. An optimistic sign is that many young film-makers are more musically knowledgeable than their predecessors.

Playing contemporary-music tapes, including electronic compositions, for some of them, is not an act of irrational despair; they are aware of the contemporary concert composer's existence.

1. The fact is that the Movieola technique can be taught to anyone in fifteen minutes, and the art of the stopwatch in about five (see Chapter 4). As for the intricacies of the music run-through, where decisions are made as to which sequences of the film will be scored, these can be learned too.

2. Soviet movies are basically close to the people, and the sound track of a film is no exception. Individuality and avant-garde techniques are not usually encountered. A film has specific boundaries and rarely, if ever, allows the Soviet composer to be anything but illustrative, decorative, and occasionally inspiriting (see the discussion of *Alexander Nevsky* in Chapter 5).

3. The reader is directed to an excellent publication by composer Frank Lewin, "The Sound Track in Nontheatrical Motion Pictures," *Journal of the Society of Motion Picture and Television Engineers,* Volume 68 (March-June-July, 1959).

4. Keith Robinson, "The Right Music for the Right Film," *Making Films in New York* (December, 1970).

5. The tapping of this musical well holds further possibilities: the hiring of outstanding women composers, heretofore totally excluded, whose activities and participation in serious music are steadily increasing.

4. The Technique of Film Scoring

The film goes through the projector at ninety feet a minute, and it just doesn't go any faster or any slower, and the same scene takes exactly the same time every time, and your music simply has to fit.

Leonard Rosenman

In most cases, the composer's first contact with the picture takes place at the screening of a rough cut. This work print is pieced together in the form and order in which it will eventually be released for public viewing. It contains completed action, recorded dialogue, and, to a great extent, whatever natural sounds are required. Feature-film composers usually prefer to wait until this moment to begin their organized thinking about music, although presumably they have already read the script and have an overall comprehension of the film. This is understandable, for to begin composing from script inferences or directions, which are more often than not ridiculously inadequate, is foolhardy. A manuscript is a book; a script for a documentary film, approved by the institution sponsoring the project, is essentially the shooting instructions to be followed quite closely. But the script for a feature film is really a set of directions for the *making* of the picture, and what is on the page will change a thousand times during its long journey from paper promise to celluloid fulfillment. If the composer gets hung up on a musical conception of what he might eventually write for the film and then is forced to scrap everything because the picture is drastically altered, he will only be debilitating his creative energies.

In certain instances when a composer is hired long in advance of a film's shooting schedule, especially if he enjoys a relationship with the director that involves regular colloquies concerning the audio-visual problems, the composer can get a clearer understanding of the film's music potential. He may be able to play a larger part in shaping the film by influencing the director to leave a scene room to breathe and allow the music to contribute a more effective statement, even to the point of considering (however remote) the possibility of cutting the film *to* the score. In this way the composer becomes a real collaborator, and, instead of simply being tacked on, the music is part of the constructive scheme of the film. Special director-composer relationships have existed through the years: Sir Alexander Korda and Arthur Bliss on *Things to Come* (1936); Sergei Eisenstein and Sergei Prokofiev on *Alexander*

43

Nevsky (1938) and *Ivan the Terrible* (1944–1946); Jean Cocteau and Georges Auric on *The Blood of a Poet* (1930), *Beauty and the Beast* (1946), and *Orphée* (1949); John Ford and Alfred Newman on *The Grapes of Wrath* (1940) and *How Green Was My Valley* (1941); Pare Lorentz and Virgil Thomson on *The Plow That Broke the Plains* (1936) and *The River* (1937); Alfred Hitchcock and Bernard Herrman on *Vertigo* (1958) and *Psycho* (1960); Federico Fellini and Nina Rota on *La Dolce Vita* (1960) and *8½* (1963); Blake Edwards and Henry Mancini on *A Shot in the Dark* (1964) and *The Pink Panther* (1964); Bryan Forbes and John Barry on *The Whisperers* (1967); Peter Glenville and Laurence Rosenthal on *Becket* (1964); Franklin Schaffner and Jerry Goldsmith on *Planet of the Apes* (1968).

But generally during the period prior to film production, the composer's thinking is largely preliminary and inexplicit. He gets down to specifics after the film has been shot and edited in a form that enables him to perceive it from beginning to end—when it has been cut to length. Later there may be postproduction sound refinements, color corrections, montages, and optical effects such as dissolves, crosscuts, fade-ins, and fade-outs.

When the composer arrives on the scene, he is a latecomer playing catch-up, so to speak. Everyone else has been working on the film for some time. The producer and director are involved in getting their film shot, edited, and delivered to the theater for its hoped-for long run. They don't have much time to concentrate on any one aspect of production, such as the music. For the most part, they leave that to the expert in whom they have placed their confidence. Their immediate attention is drawn to problems of coordinated action, dialogue, actor's temperament, shooting schedule, and expenses accrued during the course of making the film. They may not even hear the entire music score until the recording session. (This is particularly true in television.) Their closeness to the project can even dull their perspective regarding the use of music, and the composer frequently has to spend time talking them out of music for scenes he feels do not require scoring. At the initial rough-cut screening the composer is either turned on or off by what is projected. If it is the former, he experiences all kinds of impulses and inner excitement as various wild possibilities filter through his mind, some of which he retains and utilizes and others that he discards during the composing.

Before discussing technical aspects and procedures of how a composer makes his decisions regarding the music—the process of scoring—it is important to note that a composer spends a great deal of his time in noncomposing activities: in dealing with agents and contracts, and with directors, producers, and contacts. (Composers are usually listed at price levels in competition with other composers, depending on their professional status in the industry.)[1]

It cannot be reiterated too often that the art of music means different things to different people. The feelings expressed about music and its function in films are not always clear-cut. Directors themselves have divergent opinions or none at all regarding the use of music in their films. Even today many still try to use music mainly as a cover-up or prop to support places in their films they consider to be weak. As far as musical expertise and knowledge are concerned, most film people are laymen. Their understanding of music in and out of film is limited to the ken of their experience, which, for the most part, is inadequate or, in some instances, totally nonexistent. (Of course there are exceptions: every composer who has worked on films has been impressed with a particular director who demonstrated an unusual musicality and an ability to engage in knowledgeable conversation.)

In our time film directors have become the great philosophers, projecting their comments and reflections on life onto a large screen, where their images speak for them with enormous impact, regardless of the content. And yet, it is not always true that the prestigious director knows more about the use of music than anyone else. He, like his audience, responds to music more or less enthusiastically, depending on his interest, curiosity, and exposure. Generally, he is more likely to be influenced by current popular-music sounds than by serious music. I have found that everyone, in and out of music, thinks he knows a good tune or theme song from a bad one. Everyone is an expert, from movie directors to account executives making television commercials, from the man in the street to the wives of producers. For the composer, this rock-bottom, pop-song level of communication is extremely frustrating, as he must listen to every self-styled expert who considers himself qualified to offer his opinion. And, in the end, if the tune is not acceptable for whatever arbitrary reason, out it goes.

The question of abstract music outside the limited area of writing tunes is another matter. Here the composer's position goes relatively unchallenged, because he is standing on his home ground. Frequently the director relays to the composer the sounds he wants in direct relation to something else he has heard and values, which in a sense is more confusing than having heard nothing—and is usually irrelevant to his film. The sound track for the picture *Easy Rider*, for example, is made up of a bunch of records that appealed to the people who put the film together. As a pop-music mélange, it demonstrates the theory that anything goes as long as it works.

Most directors and producers want to hear what they are buying *before* it has been written. This is one basic reason why the same people are engaged to do film after film and why a composer who has scored a Western, cops-and-robbers thriller, war epic, love story, or psychological drama will invariably be hired to write another one. His track record is well known, and there is little guesswork about the outcome. "Having done one," especially a successful one, palliates fear and promotes film-company security. In this respect, the directors who have engaged a composer with limited or no film experience to score their pictures deserve a great deal of credit: Elia Kazan for using Alex North for *A Streetcar Named Desire* and Leonard Rosenman for *East of Eden*—Rosenman's first film and a blockbuster—and Sidney Lumet for hiring Quincy Jones to do *The Pawnbroker*.

In response to what the director may want, the composer in turn can't explain what he is trying to do or pinpoint what he hears or hopes to do, because he is still attempting to put it together in his own mind; he is unable to relate it to anything else the director knows. If the director's head is full of music he is absorbed in (from whatever source), he may vigorously oppose the composer's ideas simply because he is incapable of tuning in to the latter's wavelength. But if, for example, the director and composer are in conflict about where a music cue is to start and end, the question should be related to dramatic intent, not to the director's thinking about one kind of music and the composer's about another. Since the director has only the foggiest notion of what the composer is talking about until it is in concrete form and laid out as a fully realized music cue, in effect the composer literally has to compose the score in order to get across his thoughts and musical intentions.

Film-makers who are just getting their feet wet in the medium have serious doubts about everything, let alone the music. They tend to hire experience to help *them* and not just the film. Many, however, go to the other extreme, constantly annoying the composer with free advice on how and what he should compose and with endless conversations relating to the psycho-dramaturgical content of the film (many times a figment of the producer's imagination).

The problem for the composer in communicating with a nonmusical person is to be able to present his work and ideas in terms the film-maker can understand and relate to, even if this presentation must be made on a primitive level. This is a difficult task, since the composer spends his entire life *in* music, working out specific musical relationships, while the director spends his time *out* of music, involved full-time with films—a visual medium—and only part-time with music, as it affects his film.

How then does a director who is unfamiliar with the language of music communicate with the composer? For one thing, he does not have to be a musician to have an idea of what he wants and how he feels, and he can express these things in general dramatic terms relative to musical elements— slow, fast, loud, soft, high, low, assertive, inconspicuous, pastoral, lyric or rhythmic, light or heavy, tense or relaxed, and the like. And if he is unable to talk intelligently or express himself on this subject of vital concern to his film, he should be willing to learn how to do so. Unfortunately, this communication gap between composer and director remains one of the biggest problems.

Composers differ in the way they try to solve these difficulties. Some have achieved such stature that the director will defer to their judgment and leave them alone to work out the musical solutions. Others develop a technique for giving dramatic readings of the score at the piano, accompanied by their voice. They imitate instruments, sing lines, delineate rhythms, and play themes—anything to give the director some insight into what they are doing and thinking—in order to keep the recording session from being a director's surprise party. Taking a director unaware with sounds he is not anticipating invites trouble. If, however, the composer's position is insecure, he is unwise to play his music on the piano if he can avoid it. Earlier, I pointed out that a score divorced from its associative word-and-screen context changes the aural perception. People respond differently to the same music—especially highly dissonant, controversial sounds—in the concert hall. This phenomenon has always been understood by composers. In their dealings with film producers and directors they quickly learn to be cautious about playing their scores on the piano. Chances are it will make an unfavorable or at least a confusing impression, especially if the composer is not proficient at the keyboard. After all, the score is written for instruments, and the piano cannot convey the sound or color of a tuba, xylophone, or violin. One thing is certain: in composer-director-producer relations, a bad impression is worse than no impression. This applies equally to an audition or contracted musical assignment. It is always better to screen a film, if possible; otherwise, a composer must exert discretion in selecting and playing his musical tapes as demo tracks for film-scoring opportunities, lest he run the risk of being fired before he is hired. Ideally, the music should be recorded and married to the screen action before the director, out of an adverse reaction to an unsatisfactory piano performance, can discourage the composer's inventiveness. I can attest from my personal experience with documentaries, animated films, and television tracks (including TV commercials) that had clients (analogous to film producers) heard the music I was composing for their productions before it was recorded and fused with the image, more likely than not I would have been dismissed; and many film composers have had similar experiences. Non-musicians simply cannot comprehend the total effect of music until they hear and see it locked into the cinematic context. Still, questions of style, texture, thematic material, form, sound, and intent must be discussed in advance. To wait until the recording session to iron out conflicting points of view is to court disaster.

In his album notes on John Barry's music for *The Whisperers*, director Bryan Forbes comments on working with the composer:

> I have always felt that film composers work under very adverse conditions. They alone, of all the creative elements involved in the making of a film, are seldom, if ever, given a second chance. Take the fact that the screenwriter can and very often does submit half a dozen drafts before the final screenplay is accepted. Take the fact that the director can, of course, shoot each and every scene over and over again before pronouncing himself satisfied with the result. Take the fact that once the editing stage has been reached, those same scenes can be rearranged, clipped, flipped, optically revised, or distorted in a thousand different ways: there is literally no limit to the number of variations.
>
> But the poor composer never enjoys these luxuries . . . This has always seemed to me grossly unfair. So when I first started discussions of *The Whisperers*, I resolved to try another approach. It was decided that John would write his music at the same time that I was shooting the actual film. This meant that by the time I came off the floor John had finished a complete score. He had the script the same time as the actors, he saw assembled sequences of the film at frequent intervals and spent a lot of time actually on the studio floor observing work in progress. In this way he became part of the production from the very beginning.
>
> We recorded his complete score, not in snatches or short lengths to fit pieces of film, but as a musical whole. . . . Then—and only then—did we discuss the needs of the film. And, of course, we then both enjoyed the luxury of choice. I could indicate to John those themes I liked most—he didn't have to hum them or pick them out, chopstick-style, on the piano: they were on tape with a full orchestra. He was then able to go away and develop those themes at something approaching leisure. We

thus came to the final recording sessions fully aware of each other's needs.[2]

Needless to say, this kind of working relationship between director and composer is not the general rule, but it represents an attempt at collaboration, a way of including the composer in the total picture.

In the screening room, the composer sees the rough cut as many times as he deems necessary, or, as one composer remarked, "as long as he can stand." He can run the film or sections of it over and over again. Before he gets to work on timings, synchronization points, and musical layouts, he must break down the film into those sequences he intends to score: where the music is to come in and go out and—of greatest importance—those places to be left silent. Where *not* to have music may be more significant than where to insert it. Music can enter and depart in various ways: for example, on a dramatic accent synchronized with cinematic action or sneaking in under dialogue; fading out the same way; cutting off abruptly; or, perhaps, dissolving into a natural sound (e.g., telephone ringing or door slamming). Bringing music in is more complicated than taking it out: an entrance is twice as conspicuous as an exit. Moreover, narration and music cannot enter simultaneously: the music drowns out the words. Apropos of this, a high-pitched speaking voice (or voices) tends to become fuzzy when accompanied by instruments of similar range; this is also true of low-pitched timbres. However, the combination of voice and orchestra in the same register can create a special effect—a matching blend wherein one absorbs the other into an indistinguishable tone color. The scoring of a low-pitched instrument against a high voice (or vice versa) sets up a contrapuntal flow that has all the ingredients for dramatic dialogue.

Becoming intimately familiar with the film, discovering its musical potential, and making decisions as to when, where, and how to use music all come under the heading of "spotting" a picture. In deciding which sequences will have music, the composer asks himself: Is music needed? What is it supposed to do for the scene? How is it to be utilized? Is there an opportunity to say something *not* on the screen that will enhance the spectator's involvement in the picture? If so, in what direction is the motivation to be? And, finally, what kind of music should be written? After these questions have been resolved and decisions about the music's entrance and exit reached with the director's approval and sometimes the producer's, the composer is ready to commence his work.

The composer's right-hand assistant is the music editor. From the initial run-through to the final breakdown sheet prepared by the editor, their close collaboration is an absolute must. The music editor can assist the composer with any technical problems or details which may arise prior to, at the beginning, or during the writing of the music. Following the preliminary first screening, the composer and editor meet again and run the film together. They screen the picture on a stop-go projector, which can be halted at any point, reversed to a specific spot, and run forward again. During this viewing the composer indicates the sequences he is interested in scoring, and the editor marks them accordingly— by reel, scene, and action. The next step is to transfer the film to a Movieola, a small sound-and-image viewer equipped with a film-footage counter and a foot pedal for stop-go and forward-backward motion: it is actually a portable movie projector with a built-in magnifier that enlarges the film and eliminates the need for a separate screen. The music editor makes a detailed breakdown from his initial run-through notes of each sequence being scored. This preparation sheet is the composer's guide in writing music for the entire film.

Film travels through the projector at ninety feet per minute (35-mm film) and there are sixteen frames in a foot. Three feet equal two seconds. The Movieola registers footage, which is changed into time segments, and every single frame of film footage is converted into minutes and seconds. These timings are the measurements around which the composer designs and fits his musical elements. It is important to understand that the timing breakdown completely recreates for the composer everything that is happening on the screen for each specific scene occupying his attention. This includes second-by-second details, dramatic action, camera movements, panoramic backgrounds, positions of the actors and their dialogue, entrances and exits—the total "picture" on paper. By studying his breakdown guide, the composer knows where he is at every step of the way and at every second in each relative scene. It is complete precision; there is no guesswork. It is laid out exactly as reproduced on the screen.

Actually, the only mechanical gadget a composer needs is a stopwatch. Generally he writes to timings of the nearest second (one-third of a second is close enough, although some composers cut it even finer), depending on an elasticity of performance during the recording session to achieve a closer image synchronization. The sequences to be scored are broken up into numerous music cues and so designated. These cues are relatively short—upon occasion, only a few seconds. Rarely is a cue longer than a few minutes, and, if necessary, it too can be subdivided. It amounts to a few seconds here and a minute or so there, adding up in some instances to a twenty- to forty-minute film score, all measured with a stopwatch or time clock against script and screen action.

There are no set rules about how to match sound and image; indeed, the motion picture requires no special compositional techniques vis-à-vis a musical technique relevant to this art form. Nonetheless, film music relies on a unique blend of musical-dramaturgical considerations, which hinges on the composer's dramatic talent—his ability to see and hear and act upon the possibilities available to him when he combines music with visual action. In the process, he borrows and adapts certain compositional methods used in autonomous music—that is, music written for purposes of performance outside the literary-image medium.

While some composers use a Movieola in their homes to enable them to look at the film as often as they want and even to try something out on the piano and see how it goes with the scene, most work exclusively with the editor's breakdown notes. Composers all have their individual working methods and, like good cooks, are reluctant to divulge their recipes; but, generally, they make a blueprint, a planned framework, for each music cue. This paper outline is constructed before the creative work begins and may include some first-impression sketches. Basically, it is the filling in of the music at each particular spot in the total planned framework that is the essence of composing for films. The composer's problem is to keep this process from becoming so dull and contrived that it deteriorates into mere padding. Only his creative spontaneity and freshness of material guarantee that this will not happen.

The composer knows the length of the music cue. If, for example, it is a one-minute segment, he knows that this is the equivalent of fifteen four-second bars or thirty two-second bars in 4/4 time, depending on whatever basic tempo he establishes. On the metronome the former is circa quarter note = 60; the latter, circa quarter note = 120. Naturally, this implies a constant rate of movement from beginning to end, which in fact may be interrupted by fermatas or changes in tempo—faster or slower—that disrupt the regular metric pulse in order to accommodate changing images and dramatic action that may require synchronization between selected musical elements and part of the sequence. In any case, the overall timing of the cue remains unchanged, even though the steady, rhythmic beat associated with a uniform tempo may be broken.

Some of the younger film composers use a computerized timing guide that eliminates technical errors in timing synchronization. This is especially useful in scenes where dissolves and crosscuts occur at irregular speeds. The guide furnishes the precise tempo the composer needs to synchronize his points of attention, enabling him to smooth out his musical transitions.

The number of places in a cue that may demand fixed synchronization between music and image varies from scene to scene and will depend on the composer's film-scoring approach. More often than not, synchronous points are dramatic highlights that motivate the composer to stress their importance over other moments in the sequence. By marking them accordingly, the composer assigns these places in his score a position of special prominence. Of course, with too many synchronous points he runs the risk of creating distracting illustrative music—a problem he has to consider. He pays particular attention to these conspicuous spots, but the intermediate timings between synchronous points also serve the conductor as smaller reference markings in the overall rhythmic flow of the music.

Example 1 (page 55) and Example 3 (page 61) are breakdowns from timing sheets. Example 2 (page 56) and Example 4 (page 62) represent musical solutions to the two breakdowns, with the synchronous points, if any, indicated by large circle markings around the appropriate timings.

In sequences where close synchronization is required, as with rapid action on the screen or fast-changing or moving images, a "click track" is sometimes employed. The composer decides on a basic tempo, and the music editor converts the metronomic markings into frames of film, which in turn correspond to electronic impulses. These impulses or clicks are synchronized with the film sequence and fed into earphones that the conductor and the orchestra wear. The conductor hears the clicks clearly and without interruption; they become in effect his "headbeat." The composer can cut up the musical cue—barring the music as he sees fit so that the strong accents "hit" the proper spots—in any manner he desires to produce simultaneous correlation between music punctuation and the cinematic action. In this way, he can musically underline any image without fear of missing a synchronous point in fast tempo. The click track can consist of any choice of basic note values and include varying rhythms and changes in tempo. For the sake of simplicity, the basic meter in Example 5 is written in quarter notes at a constant tempo. Example 6 illustrates one solution to the click sheet (see p. 73).

Compositional techniques for television are essentially the same as for dramatic feature films, so the basic problems are similar. But there are some psychological and technical differences relating to the question of sound reproduction. The TV set is equipped with an undersized speaker, inferior in tonal reproduction to that in the motion-picture theater. This affects a composer's thinking and writing. Also, films have larger budgets covering musicians' expenses. Television limits, in most instances, the number of performers available, but this is not a drawback. The composer's skillful instrumentation can make a few musicians, properly miked, sound like many. Because television dramas are compressed into tighter time units, action is usually executed in shorter time spans, and the music must keep even closer pace than in feature films. Endings cannot wait. They have to be summed up quickly in time for the commercial message, which follows the last chord so closely as to be considered the next music cue.[3]

Film music is impatient. It has a function to perform and must make its presence felt without procrastination. It has to be extremely flexible and capable of immediate alteration, for music and picture must coincide and fit each other perfectly; to attain this synchronization, changes are frequently necessary—they may even be desired. For this reason, a film score contains within its musical elements both organized notation and a place reserved for unwritten material—a kind of preplanned improvisational design that is there in the composer's mind, ready if needed. Every film composer has experienced both planned and unplanned happy accidents. Things that are not always anticipated occur during the composing stage and on the recording stage. The composer should be attuned to these possibilities so that he can take advantage of them when they occur. Some unusual, innovative effects can be the result; moreover, it is the composer's added personal touch that produces a new excitement that may give a scene a different characterization, perhaps more effective in its dramatic impact than what was originally intended. It is, in a sense, a kind of "spontaneous creative combustion."

In some ways, the recording session is more fascinating than composing. Whereas writing music is a personal thing, recording the score is a collective enterprise that requires coordination between composer, conductor, orchestra, and recording engineers. The recording session may also involve the director in several ways: he may not appear at all, leaving the session to the composer's judgment; he may be present, giving support and counsel or interfering with the session's smooth operation by arguing questions of style, interpretation, and dramatic suitability—issues that should have been settled earlier. Sometimes an astute director is instinctively right, and it is to the composer's credit if he can recognize this and make the relevant adjustments in his score.

Everything is organized toward one objective: complete synchronization of music and picture. Apropos of this is the complex arrangement and placement of microphones, headphones when needed, musical instruments, and film-projection equipment. In essence, the recording session is a kind of private concert conducted for eventual public hearing, and while no one expects in the rehearsal time available (which can be considerable in big-budget films) to attain a perfectly executed concert rendition, one does expect and receive from the excellent musicians on call a highly respectable, lively performance-reading. This is especially worth noting since the musicians do not see the music they are performing before the recording session.

Prior to the recording session, the composer must carefully review his music and decide what kind of musicians will best perform his score. There are some musicians who lean toward a more classical interpretation, others who favor jazz, and a great many who are at home in both styles. Any musician employed for film recordings must be able to sight-read with considerable skill; this art goes with the profession. Musicians are incredibly instinctive. They can express the composer's directions and contribute their own special nuance and creativity. The conductor (who may or may not be the composer himself) first rehearses the orchestra. He records initial takes—sometimes the first one hits the target—to get a feeling for the cue and to check balances. After a few run-throughs, some composers who conduct their own music prefer to go into the engineer's booth and listen to the music while someone else conducts. This allows them to hear more objectively and have a closer, critical, "earsight" view of the score. The conductor chooses the cues to record in whatever order he desires. Part of his job is to check instrumental balances frequently and keep things moving smoothly and in sequence. Synchronous cues outlined by the composer to catch specific points of action are given to the conductor by the editor, who marks a red-pencil line across the film for several seconds prior to the contact intersection that culminates in a white dot at the synchronous point. To the nonmusician, the problems of conducting the score, staying in tempo, eyeing the timeclock located adjacent to the conductor's stand, cueing the musicians, and at the same time following the screen action probably seem impossibly complicated. Technically, a good film conductor's task and approach to the score is commensurate with that of a good concert conductor: flexible in spite of the music's seemingly formidable obstacles standing in his way. In the past, some conductors were dubbed "human metronomes" because of their ability to accomplish this meticulous timing operation; in some cases, their musicianship stopped right there.

The recording session is the composer's last chance to polish his score by augmenting, embellishing, or deleting. He must be tuned in every second of the way, focusing his attention on all the countless little details—such as phrasing, dynamics, and instrumental effects—he may have held in abeyance and on which positive decisions must now be made.

Laurence Rosenthal's observation, "The recording stage is the composer's golden moment; after that everything is downhill," refers to the fact that following the rehearsal period, the takes and retakes, the stopping and going, and the exhilaration culminating in the final recording, the composer no longer maintains control of how the music is used. It may be cut to pieces, edited and reedited, with different segments spliced together, cues used out of context from their original conception, volumes lowered indiscriminately, balances destroyed or severely altered, entrances and exits changed—everything, in truth, to make a composer hearing the music in conjunction with the film for the first time wonder what happened to the notes he wrote. More than discouraging, the experience is frustrating, often to the point of making the composer hate his own score. A number of film-music expressions have come into existence to describe what is done to the music: "Bring the music up here," "Take it down there," "Hold it under this scene," "Fade it in slowly," "Fade it out gradually," "Lower it under the dialogue," "Bring in the sound effects," and others. The nonprofessional must remember that the final sound level he hears in the movie theater results from mixing and adjusting the track to the film. The score itself probably was recorded at a much higher volume—or at what composers commonly refer to as the "all-purpose, studio mezzo forte."

Composers love to relate among themselves some of the incidents that take place on the recording sound stage, usually between composer and director. In the old days if a director had a dissolve or wanted to create a foggy fade-in or fade-out effect—one of those countless situations where blurred imagery was desired, notably in flashback sequences—he would solicit the composer's help; the latter solved the problem by calling over to the percussionist: "Hey, Mac, give me a vibe mist." This vibraphone-scale glissando, with all tones sustained by the pedal, served as a simple panacea and created the "haze" needed to blend one scene into another. I recall working on a documentary film for which the director had engaged one instrumentalist who was capable of performing on several woodwinds. While conducting a flute passage in one sequence, I heard the director's voice booming over the intercom: "Build it up, build it up." The incongruity of the situation struck my funny bone: one musician playing his heart out and the director screaming at the top of his lungs for power and dramatic force—from a single flute, no less. Then, there's the story about the composer conducting his music for a film dealing with lesbianism. After hearing the main-title theme, the director complained to the composer that the music wasn't right. He explained that he wanted "a good lesbian theme." I asked the composer what he did. He replied, "I kept the heterosexual idea, just added a few wrong notes." The director was pleased as Punch.

The sound the composer hears in the recording studio is deceptive. Hearing it in all its glory at the proper level with amplification and full-presence, eight-track-stereo playback is a mind-blowing experience. But listening to it reproduced on a monaural, optical track through one or two small theater speakers after the track has been arbitrarily doctored by the nonmedical team of director, sound engineer, and editor, with noises, dialogue, and sound effects added, is a tremendous emotional letdown. The neutralization of the score is one of the tragedies connected with the mechanics of recording and sound reproduction, as good as they are. Acoustical changes are a fact of life that every composer is aware of and forced to submit to in one way or another. Some of the composer's best moments end up on the cutting-room floor, swallowed up by other elements that the director deems to be of greater value—dialogue, theatrics, natural effects, or just plain capriciousness.

There isn't a film composer alive who doesn't want his music to be heard. If the actor protests that musical paint is brushed over his dialogue or squeezed out of the tube over his finest lines, the composer complains that his precious sounds are being buried under garbage passing for narration. In the final analysis, the composer loses, because it is not his film. Maybe this is why so few composers really care about the score (or the film) they have sweated over after it has been recorded and mixed with the action.

The composer dreams of the day when all theaters will be equipped with multitrack stereo systems capable of playing more than one magnetic track. The different layers of sound will then accommodate everyone and everything: the actor and his dialogue, sound effects or noises, and music—all working together without one wiping out the others, and reproducing outside in the theater what the composer creates and hears inside the recording studio.

1. The life cycle of the composer in the film hierarchy is a moving platform. On this treadmill are three kinds of composers: 1. the older, battle-scarred veteran (fifty and over); 2. the middle-aged expert (thirty-five to fifty); 3. the young, up-coming talent (twenty to thirty-five). Not unlike the business world, where the old-timer is put out to pasture when he reaches retirement age, the film-composer veteran is gradually phased out; the expert becomes the veteran, the young talent moves up to expert status, and a new group of bright, enthusiastic, young eager beavers step on the conveyer belt. In the concert field, the veteran composer would be hitting his prime (after all, Brahms wrote his symphonies in his sixties), increasing his creative output, and becoming more venerated. But not so in films. The turnover is an endless current of circulating manpower—from induction to promotion to unofficial yet tacitly approved, forced semiretirement.

2. Bryan Forbes, original motion-picture sound track of *The Whisperers*. Music composed and conducted by John Barry. United Artists Records (1967).

3. A word about the musical commercial. It started with the radio jingle and was superseded by the television singing commercial of varying length—usually thirty or sixty seconds, but occasionally only five, ten, or fifteen seconds. The commercial created a specific demand for all types of original music talent. During the period 1955–1965, the television commercial was a highly experimental field for the use of advanced musical resources, notably animation. I myself created many of these innovative music tracks (no jingles), consisting of short compositions scored for unusual combinations of instruments—tuba, xylophone, trumpet, piccolo, piano—and fused to the screen as an integral part of the image. The young art directors creating these storyboards were enterprising and eager to explore heretofore unopened avenues of musical sound. It was in many ways the golden age of TV commercials. The advent of rock had a standardizing effect on the musical backgrounds, and before long, all commercials began to exhibit the same pulse behind the image. Jingles, rhythmically dressed in pseudorock attire, sing the praises of soaps, cereals, refrigerators, and automobiles. With contrast eliminated, individual style has been discarded in favor of an all-persuasive pop language.

Example 1

Reel 12 Ml	SECRET CEREMONY Richard Bennett		
		fts.	time
Music starts on C. S. Cenci crying "No" as she gets up from chair		0	0
Cut to M.L.S. (medium long shot) gallery		1½	1
Cut to Medium Long Shot Cenci sitting in armchair		8	5⅓
Cut to C. S. piano top (pills gone)		14	9⅓
Cut to high angle hallway, Leonora picking up Cenci's coat		20	13⅓
She lays coat on packing case		43	28⅔
Cut to ext. empty passage		44	29⅓
Cut to low angle Cenci on gallery above, door in foreground		49	32⅔
Door starts to swing at:		52½	35
Sound of door slamming at:		60½	40⅓
Cut to ext. Leonora walking down passage		65	43⅓
Cut to int. passage, Cenci's shadow visible on wall		71	47⅓
Cut to Leonora walking down ext. passage		78	52
Cut to medium close shot Cenci staggering down passage		84½	56⅓
She stumbles		88	58⅔
Supports herself on edge of balustrade, also on this footage cut to medium low angle shot of gallery, Cenci crouched behind it *mouthing*.		95	1–3⅓
Cut to Leonora walking down exterior passage, shot through foreground gate		107	1–11⅓
Cut back to low angle shot gallery, Cenci *mouthing*		110	1–13⅓
Cut to close shot Cenci looking over balustrade		119	1–19⅓
Cut to high angle Cenci starts to fall dead, camera zooming in towards her		122 131	last chime 1–27⅓
Her head hits floor		135½	1–30⅓

SECRET CEREMONY. Composer: Richard Rodney Bennett.

Example 2

SECRET CEREMONY (Film score). By Richard Rodney Bennett. Copyright © 1969 by Leeds Music Ltd. Used by permission. All rights reserved.

SECRET CEREMONY. Composer: Richard Rodney Bennett.

SECRET CEREMONY. Composer: Richard Rodney Bennett.

SECRET CEREMONY. Composer: Richard Rodney Bennett.

SECRET CEREMONY. Composer: Richard Rodney Bennett.

Example 3

Reel 2. Cue #5   War Action SURVIVAL-1967 Irwin Bazelon

0:00   1. Music starts immediately. Zoom in on airborne jet fighter plane.

0.02   2. Close-up shot of jet plane

0:04   3. Plane banks sharply to left.

0:08   4. Plane begins steep dive.

0:12½   5. Plane strafing, joined by other jet planes.

0:17   6. Cut to jets destroying enemy planes on ground at airfield.

0:20   7. Plane on ground being hit by gunfire.

0:22⅔   8. Plane explodes.

0.26   9. Cut to tanks.

0:27½   10. Camera pans over field as tanks move in.

0:29   11. Close-up camera shots of tanks firing.

0:32   12. Cut to med. shot . . . waves of soldiers attacking across desert.

0:43   13. Battlefield shots . . . camera moves closer to action.

0:46   14. Artillery fire . . . assorted shots . . . different camera angles.

0:53   15. Cut back to planes in "dog fight".

0:58   16. Explosions . . . bomb hits.

1:07   17. Sudden cut to close-up of burning tanks and equipment.

1:13–15 18. Music fades out as camera approaches and goes through smoke of burning debris.

WAR ACTION. Composer: Irwin Bazelon

Example 4

WAR ACTION. Composer: Irwin Bazelon

WAR ACTION. Composer: Irwin Bazelon

WAR ACTION. Composer: Irwin Bazelon

WAR ACTION. Composer: Irwin Bazelon

WAR ACTION. Composer: Irwin Bazelon

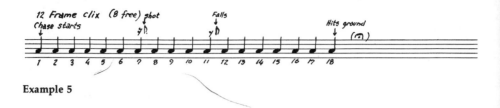

Example 5

Example 6

Film Moments:
5. What Does Music Actually Do?

*To the delights of music he was equally insensible;
neither voice nor instruments, nor the harmony of
concordant sounds, had power over his affections,
or even to engage his attention. Of music in
general, he has been heard to say, "It excites in
my mind no ideas, and hinders me from con-
templating my own."*

Boswell's *Life of Johnson*

*Even program music like Respighi's "Pines" or
"Fountains" does not evoke pines or fountains,
but only images in the minds of people who would
rather daydream than listen.*

Pauline Kael

Play the note A on the piano or any instrument. What you hear is the pitch A.
Strike other notes at random or in disciplined order. The resulting combinations make phrases, chords, and lines—segments of purely musical associations expressing intervalic relationships of tone and pitch. The sounds do not
expound philosophical ideas or denote heroic deeds. Speaking through its
written notes, the language of music expresses only musical aesthetics: it does
not convey an image or verbal impression. Despite contradictory theories
attempting to explain the affective power of music and copious program notes
by past and present composers and musicologists ascribing profound literary
meanings and pictorial connotations to music compositions, the fact remains
that music in its pure and absolute state does not *describe* anything. By acting
directly on the central nervous system, it can, however, arouse an intensely
emotional response. Music is a potent stimulant. But the images it seems to
conjure up in the listener's mind's eye are not implicit in its pure sound
environment. These responses are daydreams, programmatically triggered by
an individual's own range of personal experience, by undirected or lazy
listening habits, and perhaps by associations deep-rooted in childhood. The
more sophisticated his musical horizon, the less apt he will be to evoke
images in conjunction with the musical sounds he hears. It is like the layman
who feels compelled to find the proverbial, recognizable frame of reference in
an abstract painting in order to appreciate it.

If pure music cannot describe a picture, it often suggests an image. This subtle response is not easily explained. Nor is it consistent in its reactive effect, for usually no two persons imagine exactly the same mental images. It is this persistent habit of visual association with music that invariably makes us think of the sea when listening to Debussy's *La Mer*, or evokes the imagery surrounding the play of water when we hear Ravel's piano piece *Jeux d'Eau*. Debussy's lyric poem is not the sea in musical form; it is a poetic expression by the artist, using musical notation to convey impressions and emotions—his *feelings* about the sea. Given a different title, *La Mer*, through its atmospheric color splash, could easily express mirrored reflections and thus induce diverse sensations and pictorial associations. In this work, the composer's rich, impressionistic canvas makes *La Mer* a sea of musical imagery. This piece actually depends more on its sense of line, phrasing, imaginative orchestration, and rise-and-fall impulse than on the sea, its inspirational motivation. Similarly, *Jeux d'Eau* need not have implied rippling water or a bubbling fountain. It could just as easily have been identified with forest rustlings or some other equally picturesque impression. In both examples, the music is evocative rather than descriptive. Richard Strauss' *Sinfonia Domestica* does not literally describe a family at the dinner table. It would continue to function as music even if the composer had called it, more or less graphically but certainly not inappropriately, *Dance for Two Chickens and Twelve Eggs* or perhaps *The Adventures of an Airborne Perambulator*.

Some of my own music originally composed for children's games and activities and in my mind expertly married to the visual imagery was reproduced some years later as a television background track for two early Fritz Lang films, *Lady in the Moon* and *Metropolis*. The music seemed just as at home in Lang's futuristic world as in its original context. Other music has played an equally ubiquitous role. For a long time Elmer Bernstein's *The Magnificent Seven* theme was used in television commercials to sell Marlboro cigarettes and thus became inextricably linked with the Marlboro he-man image. And at this writing Lalo Schifrin's *Cool Hand Luke* music is being utilized by ABC-TV's daily local-news show in New York City as an opening and closing theme, thereby associating this score with news events.

Music is supposed to bring out the essential human element in listener and spectator alike. It has been thought to work directly on the emotions, either to relax or to intensify. But these emotions are difficult to pinpoint. They would seem to comprise a kind of nonrational response, an opposition to drab reality. The greater the poverty of this reality, the more excessive the melodic overflow. The undercurrent revealed in this apparent discrepancy points up a truism visible not only during the depression and postdepression years of the thirties but still a fact of life in our present-day technological society. Many people lead uncreative, humdrum existences brought about by social conditions that breed frustration and rejection. Attending movies and listening to favorite radio programs began in the twenties as social events deliberately planned by the ambitious originators but quickly developed into escape outlets that enabled people to forget, at least for a short time, the very conditions that fomented their discontent. Laughing instead of crying—a well-known emotional contradiction—is expressed in Preston Sturges' *Sulli-*

van's Travels (1941), which stars Joel McCrea as a film director of musical comedies who wants to make films of social consciousness. Through a series of events, he finds himself imprisoned and forced to serve on a chain gang. After watching prisoners laugh heartily at a Mickey Mouse cartoon, he realizes that these hapless human beings, rejected by society and relegated to its backwash, have nothing in their lives to look forward to but an occasional opportunity to laugh. At this precise moment McCrea decides he can better achieve his social aims through comedy rather than pretentious social dramas.

The entire amusement industry is founded on this idea of making people laugh in spite of how they really feel inside. Because of its strange power to weave a spell and to create an aura of sound, music is ideally cast in the role of a soothing agent to help forget the realities of everyday existence. Even contemporary rock music, which sings, screams, and shouts its defiance, creates its own world of fantasy, a special brand (X, I presume) of self-induced musical hypnosis. Its initial impact excited by its freshness and honesty, but now commercial exploitation has reduced freshness to frenzy and adulterated honesty into something less than genuine. What once stimulated through abrasion now merely irritates.

To see, the eye must be open. The ear, on the other hand, is physically open at all times, but how much it grasps depends on its degree of receptivity. Seeing before hearing, however, is not always what happens in today's film world. It is true, that, unless he attends a special film glorifying rock- or folk-music heroes, the viewer buys a ticket to *see* a film, with or without musical accompaniment. And yet, considering the importance and promotion of sound-track albums these days, many film patrons entering a theater may prick up their ears before putting on their glasses.

The serious musician has trained his ear by systematic effort to a high level of receptivity. He literally thinks with his ears. Aesthetically, music attempts to transform the listener's passive ear into an active organ of serious concentration. The listener's unwillingness to exert himself in any innovative aural direction that might cause an "earache" is the basic operational theory, both commercially and scientifically, of Muzak. Canned music is beamed at the layman's innate tendency to daydream or be titillated via his ear, dulling and soothing an organ already partially quiescent.

As an art form and because of its affective power to stimulate response, music makes an ideal partner in the successful merger with the screen image. Whereas in pure music the listener dreams up his mental pictures, in film music he has the visual supplied to him and no longer has to imagine anything. The suggestive quality of music is intensified when a cinematic perspective is added to the musical form. As previously mentioned, the marriage of screen and music results in a sight-sound fusion; the musical background is assimilated into the total visual entity. While film music frequently supplies another dimension to the screen, its mere presence makes the spectator aware that it is a *movie* he is viewing. In this way, film and film music are inextricably entwined in the common purpose of creating an illusion of reality.

The basis and origin of music in films actually stems from its theatrical application and not, as is generally thought, from the piano-music backgrounds for silent films. The staccato roll of the snare drum signifying the entrance on stage of an impressive personage, the dramatic flare and trumpet fanfare signaling the arrival into the circus arena of the lion tamer and his daring act, or the extralong drum accompaniment building to a feverish climax before the high diver leaves the platform for his incredible death-defying leap into a small tub of water are all aimed at shocking and exciting the audience. This is live, on-the-spot drama. As a theatrical adjunct, film music is before-between-and-after-the-acts music. It is essentially dramatic, not descriptive, adding an extra emotional dimension to the cinematic assault already being waged on the visual senses. At the same time, music can freshen the pictorial image and restore to the total portrait some of the lifeblood that photography tends to drain away.[1]

Audiences have been preconditioned by the nineteenth-century Romantic tradition and repertoire to accept description of imagery (program music) at face value, reflecting accurately what the composer has indicated it is supposed to describe. In this light certain primitive and naive programmatic responses are inevitable: rippling arpeggios suggest waterfalls, shimmering rays of light, or wind rustling through trees; low, agitated tremolos portend danger or hint suspense; massive block chords imply religious connotations or invite comparisons with great epical events. Out of this preconditioned suggestivity evolved the adoption of puerile, musico-visual associations leading to stock clichés and standardized effects.

The Physiological Impact of Music

The preceding material is a lead-in to a broader, more analytical approach to the aesthetics of film and music. Although numerous articles exist on the techniques of film music (including historical surveys and elaborate illustrative materials), there is much less data on the affective power of music in films. What does music actually contribute to a film? What is its relationship to the visual perspective in functional and emotional terms? When and how does music become an integral part of the drama or the film's thematic idea? How does it enhance or detract from the viewer's involvement in the film? And what about musical sounds or effects and the use of other sounds (mechanical, electronic, and naturalistic) as "music"?

In an excellent article, "Face the Music," William Johnson casts light on these aesthetic questions:

> In the last four decades—the era of the sound film—the dramatic use of music has been brought to a fine pitch of precision. Music can be tailored to fit the film's action—or, in some cases, vice versa—to the nearest twenty-fourth of a second. The dynamic balance between the music and the film's other sounds can be controlled with any desired rigor. And the blending of music and film, once made definitive, can be repeated unvaryingly time and time again.
>
> Music accompanying a film does not usually work on the spectator in the same way as "pure" music works on the listener . . . The affective elements which do apply with equal force to "pure" and film music are few and relatively clear-cut. They operate on the physiological plane.[2]

The "physiological plane" Mr. Johnson refers to is the impact music has on the human body. This musical impact makes itself felt in various ways and to different degrees; primarily through rhythm (rate of movement, accents or stress, and articulation—legato or staccato), pitch-range register (high or low), and dynamics (loud or soft); secondarily, and with less definite measurement, through its harmonic texture (thick, heavy, light, or thin), style (baroque, classical, romantic, or contemporary), lyric contour (melodic patterns), form and meter (marches, dances, songs, chants), spectrum of sound (broad or narrow, delineated or amorphous), and orchestral tone color (choice of musical instrument for dramatic communication from very dark shadings to extreme brightness).

Inside both the concert hall and the film theater, people respond more readily to fast, rhythmic music than to music of a slower, more deliberate nature. Music with a definite pulse—a beat—is both potent and provocative. Even the musical unsophisticate responds to this physiological identification; witness the effect on today's rock generation. Play a simple, rhythmic drum pattern for a child and watch his reaction: it may vary in degree, but it will not be negative. Perhaps the stepped-up, strident tempo of contemporary urban life is partly responsible for a predilection to rhythmic response, but the primitive African tribes also exhibited this affinity before advanced technology or complex stereo amplification.

In the pure music environment, Stravinsky's pounding, rhythmic devices in *Rites of Spring* and Bartok's driving frenzy in his String Quartets stimulate through their fast, energetic vigor. Slower music works on the emotions in different ways, but sometimes the responses they induce are the same as those experienced by listening to fast music. Wagner's *Tristan and Isolde* and Ravel's *Daphnis and Chloe,* with their progressively rising melodic sweep, pushing forward with every phase, succeed in pulling the listener along to an impassioned climax.

Mr. Johnson is presumably correct when elsewhere in his article he correlates one's physiological action response to a musical beat with "certain natural tempi of the body, such as the heartbeat or breathing rate." Increasing the speed of the music tends to accelerate the body stimulation. Excitement is built up by a rapid, forward thrust of the musical stimuli, usually accompanied by a dynamic crescendo. As an illustration of this phenomenon, Mr. Johnson cites an especially felicitous musical and cinematic example: William Walton's music for the charge of the French knights in Olivier's *Henry V.* Others can be mentioned, but one in particular stands out in my memory—the incredible moment in *All That Money Can Buy* (1941), when Walter Huston as Satan performs "Pop Goes the Weasel" on the violin during the country-dance scene. Accelerating faster and faster until it is almost impossible for any human to execute at that speed, the music, laughing and impudent, is exhilarating in its devilish insouciance.

The blending of rhythmic excitement and ceremonial drama creates a ritualistic dance of white heat in Hiroshi Teshigahara's *Woman of the Dunes.* Wearing masks and carrying torches, the villagers on top of the sand dunes shout, laugh, mock, and hurl insults down at the man and woman below, urging them to perform sex in the glare of the fire. The relentless, hammering beat of an amplified drum and other percussive sounds accompanies this bizarre imagery. Accelerating in tempo, growing louder and louder, the music compels the man to chase the woman around the sand house. The frenetic drive of the drum's rhythmic explosions is a musical sexual assault that accents the film's mood of terror and allegorical symbolism.

For the main titles of his score for *Psycho* (1960), Bernard Herrmann uses jagged, high-driven rhythms that set the film's pace and put the nerves on edge. Nothing is shown but the credits. Indeed, an image is not needed. By his nervous energy the composer points up the mood, tempo, and emotional fervor of the ensuing narrative. For the overture to *North by Northwest* (1959), Herrmann used, in his own words, "a rapid kaleidoscopic virtuoso orchestral fandango, designed to kick off the exciting rout that follows." As a stimulant to increase the heartbeat, it is high-blood-pressure music, full of verve and buoyancy.

The amazing virtuosity of the Harlem Globetrotters in *Go Man Go* as they execute a sports ballet, dribbling and passing a basketball back and forth, is a spectacular display of professional wizardry, made even more bedazzling by the finger-snapping, whistling rendition of their theme song, "Sweet Georgia Brown." The staccato impact of the opening percussion crescendo leading into "Rock Around the Clock" (Bill Haley and his Comets) in *Blackboard Jungle* (1955) is exhilarating; and so is the rebirth orgy scene from John Frankenheimer's *Seconds,* with naked participants thrashing around in a sea of grape juice shouting "Stomp the grapes" in a spontaneous display of rhythmic intoxication. Contrasts in rhythm, style, and instrumental-vocal color create an exciting scene in *Zulu* (1964). The rhythmic chant and splintered percussion sounds of the native warriors preparing to attack the besieged British brigade is answered by the soldiers singing a Welsh folk song. While the clashing vocal tones point up the confrontation of two distinct cultures, the frenzied beat of the Zulus acts both as rhythmic counterpoint and accompaniment to the song's lyric flow. Jerry Goldsmith's frenetic tempo and pounding beat for the ape chase in *Planet of the Apes* (1968) features piano and percussion soloistic elements. As the apes on horseback attempt to round up the humans on foot, the music engenders cinematic superexcitement. This scene has one of the longest sustained music cues without dialogue that I have ever heard in a film. Of similar force is Leonard Rosenman's fast-driven motor propulsion for the wrestling scene in *The Savage Eye.* The music soars over the crowd noises and emphasizes the bestiality of sport and spectator. It electrifies the audience. The same composer's machine-gun attack for the hook fight in *Edge of the City* (1957), through its relentless rhythmic bombardment, succeeds in practically blowing the viewer out of his seat. Indeed, critic Pauline Kael wrote about this music: "When he completed the score, he must have cut another notch on his gun—as a composer, he's out to slaughter the audience."[3] Lalo Schifrin's pulsating jazz for the first part of the two-car chase scene in *Bullitt* (1968) intensifies the exciting maneuvers of the cars as they twist and turn through city streets. The tension is built up further by a cinematic device: when the bad guys shift into high gear in a desperate attempt to elude hero Steve McQueen, the music cuts off abruptly and is replaced by the realistic sounds of screeching car tires, grinding gears, screaming brakes, and traffic noises. As the race accelerates, the excitement mounts, and the spectator is forcibly drawn into the action by the sound effects operating as a second-stage, quasi-music sound track.

As part of the music track in an exciting discotheque sequence in *Point Blank* (1967), spectators grunt, make noises, and shout key words in rock argot while blinking and flashing strobe lights illuminate the go-go dancing girls. What makes this psychedelic scene even more nerve-shattering is that the music prominently in the foreground functions as background for a violent fight going on backstage between Lee Marvin and several hoods. The ostinato, rhythmic pounding of the go-go beat hammers at the mind with the brutal force of fists on the body. As the music continues, the bodies Marvin has racked up are discovered. There is a scream, but nobody reacts. Easily incorporated into the hysterical rock beat as a vocal solo, the patrons think it is part of the electronic frenzy. If this scene had had a forties or fifties nightclub backdrop, the scream would have stopped the music cold and created a furor.

A high degree of spectator excitement is generated by Alex North's music in two diverse films. The revolt of the slaves in *Spartacus* (1960) is accompanied by fast-moving music that heralds a rousing call to action, creating a striking panorama of sight and sound. In the scene depicting the gladiators in training—jumping, attacking, thrusting, counterthrusting—the music is discordantly aggressive, full of violence and abrasiveness. Its stress and counterstress help convey how men are turned into robotlike killing machines. Later, the music expands into a full-fledged dance piece as the gladiators prepare their army recruits to meet the Roman legions. In his fast music, North often employs techniques reminiscent of Aaron Copland. This is especially noticeable in his use of short rhythmic figures that start, proceed, back up, and proceed again, gradually growing larger and longer as the pattern repeats itself, piling the phrases one upon another.

For the mustang roundup in *The Misfits* (1961), North creates a veritable four-part ballet. In the opening music (Part 1) an airplane piloted by Eli Wallach takes off to spot and chase horses through the mountain pass onto Nevada flats where they can be captured. In the following scenes Clark Gable and Montgomery Clift attempt to rope the horses from a cartop (Part 2) and to lasso them on foot so they can be tied down (Part 3). The climax (Part 4) comes when Gable single-handedly fights a stallion to subdue him, ending as both collapse in exhaustion. The music builds from one episodic part to another with extraordinary vitality. At the same time, the ballet is not continuous: there are pauses between the sections, and the musical parts are sharply contrasted. At times the music is dissonant, percussive, and abstract, with wild horn passages alternating against woodwind figures and percussion interjections. At other moments, it is almost heroic, with sweeping horn lines against strings in contrapuntal dialogue. The combination of rapid tempo, energetic music, and fast-moving action is highly stimulating. But North's music catches something more: it conveys a feeling of the romanticism and high adventure of yesteryear and touches upon the loneliness of aging cowboys whose way of life has passed.

Excitement assumes a more violent, sinister nature in *To Kill A Mockingbird* (1963). When a stranger grabs the children as they walk alone through woods filled with shadowy figures, Elmer Bernstein's music takes on a nightmarish quality not previously heard in his tender, evocative score. The incisive chordal attacks in uneven rhythmic patterns rise to a screaming pitch as the children battle for their lives. Its sound fairly leaps out of the screen, intensifying the viewer's feeling of fright. A colder anguish is felt in Ingmar Bergman's *Hour of the Wolf* (1968) when Max von Sydow imagines himself killing a boy who stares at him. Lars Werle's electronic score sets up a rapid, steady oscillation of beats that heightens the sense of hallucination. During the powerful scene near the end of Alain Resnais' *Muriel* (1963) when Helen's (Delphine Seyrig) former lover (Jean Pierre Kerien) meets his brother-in-law, who has come from Algeria to induce him to return to his legal wife, Hans Henze's obtrusive, dissonant music pulsates and pounds, lashing the brother-in-law's rage across the screen.

In the jazz-nightclub scene in *Odds Against Tomorrow* (1959), I still recall Harry Belafonte crashing down hard mallets on the metal bars of the vibraphone in a rhythmic paroxysm of frustration, frayed nerves, and emotional anxieties that directly motivates his cinematic characterization. His temper tantrum epitomizes the film's tempo of threat and criminal intrigue. And in *The Sweet Smell of Success* (1957), Elmer Bernstein's twisted rhythms of modern jazz—the "Broadway Beat"—are a perfect frame for the movie's theme of the jostling, corruptive world of Broadway press agentry.

My score for Jules Dassin's documentary on Israel, *Survival-1967*, contains another example of how progressively faster speed tends to stimulate physiological response. The film's climax is the opening of the gates to Jerusalem to pray at the Wailing Wall. The scene begins at daybreak over the Old City. A slow, two-part horn passage sets the stage for the great day. It is plaintive, not heroic, music. A man appears on the road. He is joined first by one, then another and another, some on crutches, others hobbling. With their appearance, the music tempo increases. A contrapuntal, running cello figure is introduced, followed by a folklike theme in flute and clarinet. Soon there are dozens of men, women, and children on the road, singly and in groups. As more and more join the parade to the Wall, the music's pace steps up, becoming sharply agitated and swelling in orchestral sound. When the crowd size has increased to thousands, the breaking point occurs. Unable to be contained any longer in disciplined ranks, the people commence to run in wild disorder. The screen is pandemonium, a blur of running, shouting, crying, jubilant humanity. By rapidly accelerating in speed and sound, the music intoxicates the surging crowd to a feverish pitch and explosively propels their joyous dash to its climax. In addition, through its excitement and fervor, the music engulfs the audience and projects it into the screen action. When the Wailing Wall is reached, the score echoes the entrance into the Promised Land and ends on a high, sustained trumpet note simulating the shofar, an ancient Jewish instrument used in religious services. Then, fade-out.

In this music there is an ecstatic, lyric sweep, which expresses as much as music can the indomitable spirit and faith of the Israeli people. It was important that the music not be heroic in a military sense; otherwise, it would have focused attention on the Six-Day War victory and caused the emotional

81

outburst during the impassioned rush to the Wall to be misconstrued as exultation over a military success rather than what it is—a call to rejoice in prayer and thankfulness.

Musical tempi slower than the body's natural pulse can be either stimulating or relaxing, depending on musical considerations and the dramatic context of the scene, including the actual rhythmic pace of the screen image. As a means of heightening the excitement and tension of the car chase in *Bullitt,* for example, it would have been inventive to write against the flow of the picture, utilizing music slower then the visual rate of movement. Tightly spaced, longer-held notes with sharp, intermittent punctuations could be effective by creating a contrast between the slower music and the faster picture. The sporadic spraying of musical interjections, pushed forward by impulse accents (not perpetual movement in sixteenth notes), evolves a slow but fast-sounding piece. Working against the speed of the screen image and holding back the thrust of the music spikes the score with a special brand of dramatic seasoning, over and above the typical, fast, percussion jazz usually found in these prosaic screen situations.

During the surrealistic ballroom sequence in *All That Money Can Buy* (a veritable gold mine for musical examination), Bernard Herrmann's music sounds assume a slow-motion, almost frozen dance tempo. The effect is eerie and chilling; it provokes rather than soothes the senses. In *Psycho,* the same composer's slow, underplayed phrases behind much of the footage actually relax rather than tighten the dramatic suspense, thus setting up the audience for the knife murders that occur without warning. The music never gives away the impending horror of Hitchcock's script. Herrmann's score is a paragon of how a composer, by staying out of the picture beforehand, can increase shock value through subtle undercurrents of nonviolent music. The use of strings without any orchestral colors complements the black-and-white photography with a black-and-white sound. It is one of the rare occasions in films where a string orchestra has been used from beginning to end.

Whereas fast or faster, animated musical tempi increase body stimulation and build excitement, the effects of slow or slower music are often conflicting and diverse. They may be neither relaxing nor taut. In *The Whisperers,* John Barry's slow, muted, main-title music, using the old-fashioned sound of the harpsichord interlaced with warm, lyrical string phrases, effectively characterizes the plight of an old woman clinging to life by escaping its realities. The music's plaintive, leisurely pace expresses her dreamworld. The identification is suggestive, not descriptive. It is the harpsichord that serves as the instrument of direct communication between screen image and spectator. Later on, her carefree husband is mirrored in the more vigorous sound of the piano, thereby musically contrasting the temperaments of the couple.

The slow-paced tunes of Henry Mancini for *Breakfast at Tiffany's,* of Francis Lai for *A Man and A Woman,* and Simon and Garfunkel for *The Graduate* are essentially relaxing and easy to listen to, even if the first two, in particular, call attention to themselves by constant repetition. The tunes are nostalgic. Leonard Cohen's opening song for *McCabe and Mrs. Miller,* although ostensibly relaxing, does not work on the spectator in the same way. It is a narrative prologue in vocal form to announce the coming of the errant stranger, the familiar antihero of dozens of Western epics. The song is simple, for the film is a fable of the Old West possessing a once-upon-a-time quality. By comparison, the sustained tones and slow-moving musical flow, often overlaid by a special impact sound, in Fred Karlin's score for *The Stalking Moon* tauten the nerves and heighten the suspense of this above-average Western tale.

A languorous musical tempo accompanies Charles Chaplin's ballet scene in *The Great Dictator* (1940) as he balances an inflated balloon of the world, gently hitting it with his fingers, knees, posterior, head, and foot, arching the rubber bag to the ceiling in an expression of poetry in motion. Again, the music neither relaxes nor tightens but acts symbolically to establish Chaplin's smug state of mind. Through the imagery of the dance, the spectator is made aware that, as Hitler, Chaplin thinks he is master of the world, with mankind at his mercy and the universe at his fingertips dancing to his tune. Suddenly, the balloon bursts. The bubble and the dream are shattered. Echoing the altered tone of the film, the music segues into a military marching step to convey without subtlety that it is the armed might of his enemies that has destroyed his dream of conquest. In *City Lights* (1939), Chaplin's hilarious fight sequence is cut and edited to an upbeat musical rhythm he created himself and to which he dances around the ring with style and grace. The integration of music and motion are in perfect balance, yet with an independence of movement that allows the musical structure and cinematic elements to maintain separate paths, even as they circle or parallel each other in synchronization with the boxer's gestures. The musical impulse, by its shape and fluidity of line, emphasizes the character and spirit of the sequence, giving it a sense of light-hearted continuity.

In *The Chalk Garden* (1964), during the scene where Deborah Kerr and the old judge who sentenced her for murder years ago and who is now unaware of her identity meet over the luncheon table, Malcolm Arnold's music combines a nervous, fluttering anxiety with essentially slow, pulsating drumbeats. Working up to a dramatic climax, the alternating currents of tempo and contrasting musical figures are unsettling, heightening the suspense and elucidating the emotional agitation of Miss Kerr over her fear of discovery. The alternating current of fast and slow music can sometimes do more than merely raise or lower the excitement level of the viewer. To an indeterminate degree it can brighten or darken the visual image—and induce a corresponding response in the spectator through the sudden intrusion of one tempo upon another. In Aaron Copland's score for *The Heiress* (1949), the composer mixes mood sequences and orchestral colors as a direct result of the screen action. Switching from music of lightness and sparkle in the running-up-the-stairs scenes to somber texture behind the father, Sir Ralph Richardson, underlines the dramatic value of the cinematic crosscut. The spirited and gay music of the stairs sequence, punctuated by short pizzicato passages in strings, brightens the view and, indirectly, the mood of the viewer. On the other hand, the essentially low woodwind phrases of the slower music are devoid of warmth and darken the view, throwing into sharp relief the father's unsympathetic character and indirectly acting as a depressant on the viewer.

Pitch and dynamics also influence body reactions: they can disturb or calm and, in so doing, stimulate disagreeable or pleasant feelings. As compared to rhythm, these stimuli arouse responses neither more nor less intense. But the musical beat, with its primordial motor drive, would seem to have a more immediate gut effect on listener and viewer alike. Musical register and shadings are restricted as to the body responses they can induce by certain acoustical principles—elements dealing with the science of sound and aural perception. How people hear music and their tolerance level for and adjustment to extreme ranges of pitch are important factors in measuring physiological reactions. Whereas soft music gradually fades out when the sound level is reduced beyond the ear's capacity to distinguish an aural sensation, loud music has a saturation level above which it is almost humanly impossible to tolerate, at least not without ear protection. (In seeming contradiction to this is the amazing ability of pop-rock fanatics to listen to their music at an amplification level that is unendurable for most people.) High notes played forte (loudly) sound shrill and piercing. Although I doubt that they cause actual pain, they can produce considerable discomfort and, on occasion, intense fright. The same notes played piano (softly) are mysterious and ethereal, hanging suspended in midair. Low notes played forte, especially on brass or strings, sound rough and coarse and tend to growl when sharply attacked; performed piano, they have an ominous, deep-dark coloration. High or low tones played staccato (short and clipped) have a different physiological effect than identical tones played legato (smoothly). Soft music can be restful and easy to listen to, or, by the use of special musical devices involving accents or changes in embouchure (attack by the performer), it can become dramatic and cause apprehension. One example is the old radio cliché called a "sting," usually performed forte-piano and fading into soft agitation; another is the string tremolo for suspense, frequently played softly. Nonmusicians must realize that notes at the extreme ends of the pitch-range register are by no means easy to perform—and even less easy to listen to, especially for any length of time. At these outer limits sounds are perceived physically rather than aurally.

Loud background music may be irritating, but its precise functional impact can only be measured in relation to the cinematic context. In *Hangmen Also Die* (1943), as a portrait of Hitler appears in a banquet hall, Hanns Eisler's music stops on a multi-toned, widely spaced, piercing chord. Its loud resonance is not merely jolting but a powerful means of conveying a sense of evil. As a pure sound, it describes nothing. But as a cinematic adjunct, its contemporary sonority fairly shrieks hostility. Given an audience predisposed toward repugnance at the image, the music becomes a vocal expression of their feelings, literally shaking a fist in Hitler's face. Jerry Goldsmith's satanic score for *Mephisto Waltz* also goes beyond physiological disturbance. In the scene where the devil comes to kill the young child over the mother's pleading, the loud, quasi-electronic music actually scares the hell out of you—as it did even the composer on initial hearing. The eerie, thundering sound vibrations raise the hair on one's body. Also frightening to the spectator is Lalo Schifrin's music for the Wolper Productions film on insects, *The Hellstrom Chronicle*. During the horror montage where the insects become cannibalistic and start eating each other, Schifrin's loud electronic sounds, synchronized piano effects, and percussion explosions, together with the picture, create an atmosphere of physiological turbulence.* Music loud enough to cause severe physical and mental uneasiness was deliberately composed by Richard Rodney Bennett for the agonizing suicide scene at the end of *Secret Ceremony* (1969). Swelling to an excessively high pitch of sustained sound, Bennett's score rings in the ear, reinforcing the hallucinatory tone of the film and contributing a stunning aural climax to a picture suffering as much from heavy-handed direction, pretentious script, and self-indulgent histrionics as the psychotic infantilism it depicts.

In countless outdoor adventure, Western, and spectacle films of the thirties, forties, and fifties, loud, unrelieved music, sweeping melodic phrases, and brassy fanfares whipped up excitement and enthusiasm much like main-title music. This excessive loudness was usually not meant to produce physiological anguish. And, in many romantic dramas of this period, routine emotional churnings in the form of musical crescendos posed as impassioned dramatic outbursts. Often the swelling of music plus cinematic images—a stallion rearing, blazing logs in the fireplace, exploding fireworks in the sky, breaking waves on the seashore—testified to the presence of sexual passion. (Today we see in full-screen close-up what the music and visuals previously suggested.)

Loud music also served the purpose of shouting the headlines at the audience during montages in films of this period, such as *Meet John Doe* (1941). This was a favorite cinematic device where newspaper streamers or rapidly changing datelines flipped by quickly, obviating the need for detailed exposition. The music jarred the viewer and stressed the dramatic importance of the front-page black type.

In addition to assaulting one's eardrums beyond the point of endurance, constant loudness is also debilitating. This can be seen in many films of the last decade that use rock and jazz background tracks. With the amplification turned up to the highest sound decibel, the audience is pounded into a mesmerized state of submission that eventually leads to apathy. On the other hand, soft music can be listened to indefinitely, especially in strings, which have the capacity to depersonalize themselves. This type of unobtrusive background scoring has been the bread-and-butter music for countless sequences involving pastoral images and scenes that do not require musical comment but only an atmosphere of tranquil inconspicuousness.

In the concert hall, extremely soft music can be anything but relaxing and, indeed, can cause body unrest, for the ear must strain to hear anything at all—and without benefit of a visual image. Many avant-garde composers have capitalized on this aural phenomenon. Their pieces, some lasting fifteen to twenty minutes, are performed at an exceptionally low sound level, defying the listener to pick up the vibrations. Music that can barely be detected by the ear cannot be criticized, at least not in a conventional sense, and is often a form of direct hostility. The composers' response is that music played consistently at a very low threshold of sound and for extended lengths of time

*Music excerpt on page 301.

demands intense concentration and unwavering preoccupation with the music itself. Tantalizingly present, it can be more unsettling than loud, aggressive sounds. Compounding the issue, certain contemporary composers repeat the same notes (sometimes one note) and chords over and over again, with little variance and no discernible fluid motion. Loud or soft, the hypnotic effect is monotonous and physiologically disquieting.

The effect of soft music in films is not definitive. It depends on its usage in the cinematic frame of reference. Behind the image it tends to evanesce and go unnoticed unless some special stress focuses on its presence. Soft music is not an automatic sedative. It can be suspenseful, unnerving, gently lyric, or dramatic. And, as in the famous slapping incident in *Patton* (1970), it can also be disturbing without being obtrusive. In this episode, Jerry Goldsmith's music is forcibly eloquent, yet restrained. There are overtones of an earlier trumpet triplet figure with vibes, brass, and strings. The music has a lyrical flow on top, with dramatic accent punctuations on the bottom. It reflects Patton's conflicting emotions in his impulsive behavior toward the battle-fatigued G.I. he physically rebukes. The composer often uses soft trumpets (an amplified, reverbed, quasi-subliminal sound) to set up distant military signposts without resorting to blatant emphasis. Although the score incorporates large-scale orchestral waves of attack and counterattack, it echoes contrasting plaintive elements of loneliness and despair. In places Goldsmith's nonheroic approach actually softens George C. Scott's superbly played portrait of the bellicose, egotistical general.

In the aforementioned *The Stalking Moon* (1968), Fred Karlin consistently utilizes a soft background level of sound. His low brass chords, on a separate track, are hardly audible, but they create suspense, anxiety, and dramatic continuity. This is a good example of how subliminal sounds can be interesting and inventive. Many jazz-oriented composers introduce indigenous jazz ornamentation, often played unobtrusively behind screen action. These special effects instill an unsettling, nervous reaction in the spectator, no matter how softly they are performed, because they involve some distortion of the normally produced sound vibration. Altering the pitch causes a rise in tension. This unique musical language is evident in Quincy Jones' score for *In the Heat of the Night*. Jones uses soft-spoken vocal tones amplified through a flute to reflect alienation and resentment, and Don Elliot's voice, closely "miked," creates novel percussion effects and a strange rhythmic vitality that enhances the mood and theme of the film. Again, in *The Getaway*, Elliot's unusual talent for turning vocal inflections into instrumental timbres, along with the insolent, growling sound of the harmonica, adds an extra dimension of excitement to Jones' music. In contrast, Johnny Mandel uses a human voice imitating a musical instrument as part of the ensemble to accompany Sandy Dennis in *That Cold Day in the Park* while she walks around the kitchen busily cooking. Although not readily identifiable, the soft, intimate sound is beautifully expressive and evokes a mood rich in melodic fragments.

In *Psycho*, the knife murders are matched by high-pitched, piercing upper strings. The shrillness of the violins and violas in this register is more excruciating than any human cry could possibly be. Near the beginning of *Planet of the Apes*, after the three astronauts sight the unearthly scarecrows mounted on scaffolds atop cliffs, Goldsmith introduces high, exotic percussion sounds—metal twangs produced by stainless-steel mixing bowls.* The effect on the audience of this shrieking, wounded-bird cry is spine-tingling. At the end of *This Sporting Life,* after Rachel Roberts has died of a brain hemorrhage, Richard Harris hollers her name with a sense of futility and loss. Roberto Gerhard intensifies Harris' personal grief by a loud, high-register musical scream that is the very essence of agony and torment. A striking effect of physiological disturbance is achieved by Lalo Schifrin in *Hell in the Pacific* when Toshiro Mifune, a Japanese soldier marooned on a Pacific island beach, hears the peculiar, shrill sounds of cicadas. Schifrin starts his music with two extremely high-pitched, screeching piccolos. Coming out of the insect sounds and duplicating their voice, the effect evolves into a music cue.

Leith Stevens evokes an uneasy response of a different nature in *Destination Moon,* one of the early space-journey films. Consisting of soft, high, long-held, sustained tones, his music hangs like icicles over the bleak moon landscape and gives an ethereal feeling to the panorama. Even though his overall interpretation is basically romantic—almost Tristanlike in thematic content—the unfamiliarity and coldness of the terrain lend a strange aura of suspense.

At the other end of the scale, the ominous, low notes on the string bass in Quincy Jones' score for *In Cold Blood* capture the musical essence of the two killers. The bass instruments function as musical counterparts, sliding and gnawing their way through the film with a neurotic attachment for the psychopathic personalitites they mirror. In *Citizen Kane,* Bernard Herrmann uses the grave, low notes of the double bassoon to underscore and dramatize the opening scene when Kane is dying. And, in *All That Money Can Buy,* he introduces a low, distorted, gonglike sound that adds to the mystery of the chilling moment when Simone Simone as Satan's daughter makes her entrance. In *The Heiress,* during the intimate scene between father and daughter when he tells her she is not attractive, Copland employs the somber bottom range of the bass clarinet. Goldsmith's portentous low notes on the bass guitar that open the film *Hour of the Gun* give this rerun-of-the-mill Wyatt Earp legend just the necessary nervous throb it needs to heighten the tension leading up to the O.K. Corral gunfight. In Robert Flaherty's *Louisiana Story* (1948), Virgil Thomson's coarse, barking trombone motif in the low register dramatically launches the young boy's fight with the alligator. For *Night Slaves,* a feature film made for television, Bernardo Segáll uses the bass accordion. An unusual instrument that extends the lower range of the normal accordian down an octave, its deep-throated, suspenseful sound causes a sickening feeling of fright in the pit of the stomach and makes the spectator wonder what is going to happen in the scene where the aliens come to claim their slaves for the night. Since Segáll treats this science-fiction film as fantasy rather than horror, his music is mysterious without the usual unearthly sound effects.

Because cinematic context is the dramatic key, it must be considered in

*Music excerpt on page 302.

gauging physiological response, making the exact effects of rhythm, pitch, and dynamics anything but explicit. Harmonic texture, lyric contour, form, style, tone color, and other musical components act upon the audience in even more intangible ways. The scope of musical experience a listener brings to the film theater can exert a strong influence on his reactions as a spectator to the sound track. I have had the occasion to view a film more than once with various people and have found the effects of identical film music on different individuals to vary greatly as to the emotional impact or uneasiness aroused by levels of musical discord. It is true that persons familiar with the musical language of Babbitt, Berio, Stockhausen, and Xenakis are not going to be upset by far-out film scores. Their concept of cacophony differs from those musical unsophisticates who still regard Brahms as modern, but even the less adventuresome are not apt to be too disturbed by the obliquely jagged sounds they occasionally encounter in a film house. After sixty years, Stravinsky's *Rites of Spring* has lost much of its shock value in the concert hall, and the version in Disney's *Fantasia* further waters down the dissonant impact by being absorbed into the total eye-ear concept.[4]

For Robert Altman's *Images,* John Williams' percussion effects, performed by soloist Stomu Yamashta on Baschet sculptures, fuse with abstract cinematography to create a collage of sound, a nightmare world of reality and illusion. The blend of sight and sound softens the avant-garde musical techniques of Williams' amplified percussive textures. And the strange, intriguing sounds of Gyorgy Ligeti's *Atmospheres* hardly seem disconcerting or unduly exotic when wedded to the phantasmagoria of the Star Gate sequence in *2001: A Space Odyssey*. In all cases, the stitching is complete; no one part of the seam shows through.

In their innate response to all kinds of contemporary music, the discerning concert-hall listener and the discriminating movie spectator often part company when they enter a theater. Whereas the former might notice the music—its degree of complexity or its stylistic idiom—the latter becomes caught up in the story to the extent that he is less apt to notice disagreeable music, unless the director has focused attention on strident interjections, as in *This Sporting Life* and *Muriel*. Lindsay Anderson's sudden, jarring flashback cuts set against hypnotic backgrounds that include the brutality of the rugby field combine with Roberto Gerhard's darkly poetic, fragmented music to convey the violent inner tensions of the two leading performers. In *Muriel,* Alain Resnais' abrupt editing fits hand in glove with Hans Henze's jolting, discordant musical phrases. With the music and deliberate cutting, enhancing each other by support and opposition, Resnais stresses the ragged-edged life patterns of his assorted characters.

Historically, dissonance—harsh, controversial, disconcerting sounds—has been treated in films as a negative factor implying neurosis, evil, agony, and pain, the opposite of good and right, sweetness and light. Even television commercials emphasize the negative qualities (before swallowing) by discord and reinforce the product's benefits (after swallowing) with music of radiant purity. It is as though a halo of consonance were placed over the head of the hero and a Satan's tail of dissonance tacked onto the villain.

By examining two films of an earlier period wherein the protagonists play the role of composers, one can grasp how Hollywood fostered artistic deceit about the use of discordant sounds. As a boy, I remember viewing *The Constant Nymph* and watching Eric Korngold struggle with the task of writing a cantata for his screen alter ego. After the initial performance of the piece, our hero is told by friends, with typical movieland logic, that the music fails to communicate because its heart has been smothered under a blanket of dissonance. Here, good and effective are judged synonymous with uncomplicated and euphonious, while bad and passionless are associated with complex and athematic. Because the melody is submerged beneath muddy textures, it is unable to shine through and express the essence of all good music of that era: the harmonic-rhythmic symmetry that is the synthesis of Hollywood romanticism circa 1940. Korngold, who with Steiner and Newman greatly contributed to the lush, symphonic style of the golden age, was often criticized for getting overcomplex in his film scores. Having had a serious musical background, he conceived his music in the large-scale classical mold. He considered films as music dramas and dramatically interlaced his themes to form a unified orchestral work. In this movie the hero's musical problems not so subtly mirrored his own.

Moral implications are sharply drawn by the use of discordant sounds in *Hangover Square* (1945). The composer-protagonist is a reasonably normal, gentle neurotic who is subject to inexplicable blackouts when he hears noise. The clanging of steel pipes, the knocking over of musical instruments that results in the gut snapping of violin strings, or any nerve-rattling discord shatters his mental stability. The impact of these screeching sounds is mind-blowing, and turns Laird Cregar into Jack the Ripper. Bernard Herrmann's high, piercing sounds, augmented by screaming piccolos, are ear-splitting. They serve as distorted musical extensions, reverberating sound waves, emanating from the initial shock. The inference is clear: dissonance destroys sanity and gives rise to violence, which is symbolic with evil, even murder.

Herrmann's concert music is exactly the kind one would expect from a young composer at the turn of the century, and the performance of the concerto at the end of the film cinematically and musically sets the house on fire. Cregar dies in the blaze, pounding out his chords at the piano on a deserted stage. The screen lesson is that, like a child playing with matches, contact with dissonance can only lead to disaster.

Looking back, traditional music allowed little dissonance. Through overkill, whatever dramatic punch its harmonies once possessed has long since been reduced to a soft nudge. Because the cinematic art aims essentially at creating tension, contemporary harmonic sonority, with its high-voltage friction, can be extraordinarily effective for scenes of fear, chaos, shock, and anxiety. But the converse is also valid: advanced music, including electronic sound manipulation, is also applicable to tenderness, tranquillity, longing, irony, and wonderment. It stimulates in two ways: by engaging the ear in sensations that startle and excite by their unfamiliarity and by communicating a fresh insight or different point of view about the visual perspective.

In the past, dramatic film music fell into well-established categories such as love music, beware-the-danger music, mystery-background sounds, sighing melodies of passion, throbbing crescendos of excitement, ghostly violins, flute figures, and other established formulas. Although faced with essentially the same prosaic visual situations, disguised by contemporary film techniques but still variations on an old, familiar theme, composers today are utilizing new musical resources to change musical associations. Innovative sounds can serve as a blood transfusion to help cure the musical anemia caused by depletive practices of an industry that manufactures and consumes its creative product as fast as it is produced, sometimes turning fresh techniques into clichés within a short time. This is conspicuous in the music of many jazz-oriented composers. The novelty and imagination of their inventive devices, including sounds that can be dramatic without being especially musical or creative, have been worn thin by the simple process of overexposure and supersaturation.[5]

One of the last vestiges of motion pictures' melodramatic heritage is the presentation of sensational material, exaggerated full-screen. The film superseded the pulp novel, incorporating the latter's literary trash into cinematic cash; and today, by virtue of progressive shocks and discoveries, we are seeing the ultimate sensationalism in sexploitation films.

Yet it is elements of sensationalism that give motion pictures dramatic surprise. Dynamic sound tension—the heartbeat of contemporary music—is ideally suited to sharpen surprise and heighten the cinematic perspectives of the human dilemma.

Naturally, avant-garde techniques for the sake of being up-to-date are not the objective. Inordinate complexity or excessive fussiness only confuse, making the screen action less meaningful and thereby weakening the total effect of the film. Complicated harmonic intricacies can be commonplace; indeed, they are often unimaginative and mechanical, while simple functional elements handled in an inventive manner can be just right. The requirements of the film's dramatic structure are the keys to the compositional techniques employed. Success depends on how the material is constructed and utilized to meet the exigencies of the film and whether the composer can break away from routine practices.

Associations to Musical Elements

The film composer's use of contemporary musical resources cannot be examined in isolation. It is part of a larger, more complex relationship of action to sound that includes the importance of *associations*. Perhaps the most powerful factor in determining the filmic impact of musical elements, notably harmonic texture, tone color, form, and style, lies in the spectator's ability to attach associations to diverse musical patterns and their often commonplace dramatic meanings, even though he may be only vaguely aware of these elements and the role they play in shaping his responses.

In the early Westerns, for example, the clichés of the silent era reigned over the sound tracks. The viewer's associations to simple, rhythmic figures and harmonic stylization had already been established through constant repetition. Certain "noodlings"—sequential patterns in specific cadences—were repeated in film after film.

Fast

The above pattern, or its equivalent, came with every Western chase. It was intended, I suppose, to set up a sense of movement and dramatic urgency. The harmonic progressions posed no problems of discord or disturbance—the excitement kicked up by horse and rider were no more significant than a short-lived dust cloud. But why should they be? The chord sequences had been used for over two centuries, and they fitted in with the hackneyed plots in a perfect merger of little with nothing. But as greater narrative sophistication and camera techniques made innovative inroads into the Western mystique, directors began to underscore the psychological tensions of its traditional heroes and antiheroes, figures raised by the media to myth status. The composer also began to utilize a different musical vocabulary. In the forties and fifties, for example, Aaron Copland's Western style lyrically and rhythmically influenced an entire generation of film and concert composers, many of whom wrote Coplandesque music without bothering to sign his name to their scores.

An unpretentious little Western, *A Gunfight* (1970), illustrates how style and harmonic texture trigger spectator associations. Two legendary retired gunmen (Kirk Douglas and Johnny Cash) meet in a small southwestern town. They are forced into a confrontation by the bloodthirsty local citizenry, eager to wager on which one can outdraw the other. Spurred on by financial needs and desire for self-reaffirmation, they agree to a staged shoot-out in a bullring across the border, the ticket-sale proceeds to go to the winner. In this movie Laurence Rosenthal mixes two musical styles. At the beginning and periodically throughout the film, he supplies simple background music as window dressing, underlining in a conventional harmonic style imagery already apparent. These musical stereotypes include typical Western-tune accompaniments behind commonplace town settings, scratchy-violin country-dance music for café scenes, and characteristic rhythmic guitar figures for a south-of-the-border flavor. By changing idiom and introducing an astringent harmonic texture based on the natural tension in unresolved major-minor second intervals, the composer initiates contrast and involves the spectator in the subtle tug-of-war between the two old-time gunslingers. Clashing tones and sharp, pinched-nerve twangs intermingle with Western tinkling—guitar plucking and banjo picking. The mildly discordant intrusions heighten the tension between the two men. By alternating simple incidental music with taut, abrasive sounds, the dual tonality of the musical styles is persistently unresolved and in continuous opposition. This creates mounting suspense up to the finale, which takes place in a circus atmosphere. As the two men meet in the center of the arena, the spectacle becomes a theatrical production introduced by trumpet fanfares. The use of stereotyped bullfight music is effective and surrounds the combatants with the excitement of a real bullring contest. But the most interesting musical sequences occur after the gunfight. In the first-version ending, Cash shoots Douglas. Immediately there is a chilling, altered sound. As the stunned crowd disperses, sound clusters pulsating over suspended tunes (amplified instruments plus Echoplex for maximum reverberation) give the spectator a sense of alienation, almost anticipating the bizarre twist of director Lamont Johnson's double ending. In slow-motion flashback, as the camera hits Cash saddling his horse, altered church-bell sounds introduce the second-version ending. In this cinematic replay, Cash is killed by Douglas. The sound clusters, distorted by reverb and Echoplex, create an aura of unreality that draws the viewer into the enigma of which version was genuine.

For Jan Kadar's *The Shop on Main Street* (1965), Zdenek Lisko utilizes two different musical styles simultaneously. The shopkeeper (Josef Kroner) is afraid he will be arrested for shielding an old Jewish lady (Ida Kaminska) from the Hlinka Guards. Though the latter have instructions to deport all Jews from the small village in German-occupied Slovakia, her name has mistakenly been omitted from the list. He tries to get her outside the store into the town square, but the old woman is deaf and does not understand what is happening. She lives in a world of fantasy, and the foreground music, dreamlike and gossamer, reflects her world of unreality. At the same time, in the background, martial music and strident orders from the commandant blare forth through loudspeakers outside the store. The clash of subtle tensions between the two people inside with the powerful, realistic aggressions of the military order outside is vividly dramatized through the juxtaposition of musical styles. And it is the associations elicited by these diverse musical patterns that arouse in the spectator feelings of pity and empathy not only for the old woman's plight but for all people caught in similar tragic events.

Music for this film is sparse. A whimsical, violin-solo passage, repeated several times, connects scenes depicting episodes of the shopkeeper's domestic life. A great believer in nonillustrative music for his films, Kadar uses few sequences of follow-the-action scoring. A local open-air band plays a charming waltz at the beginning of the film and during the surrealistic slow-motion scene of Kroner and Kaminska dancing through the town square at the end. The waltz is not a title song or theme tune. Its special impact depends entirely on associations. It is through the music's nostalgia that the audience is made aware of how things once were; in effect, the waltz becomes a lyric portrait of peaceful life in a small provincial town before the Nazi invasion.

In *Five Easy Pieces* (1970), not only do the stylistic differences in the music command attention, but also the contrasting life-styles of diametrically opposed music cultures in the film itself. Again, spectator response depends on associative connections. Antihero Jack Nicholson vacillates between two conflicting worlds: the cultural surroundings of his musical family, representing the life he deserted, are in sharp contrast to the world he now inhabits, dominated by the pop-music scene. The clash in values between the commercial rhythms of the one and the so-called classical purity of the other are sharply etched. Nicholson always feels he is better than the people with whom he associates because of his serious musical background, although "five easy pieces" are all he remembers. In addition, the cultural rift is further split by shifts in time and place. The pop scene is essentially identified with urban life, while the classical settings take place in a quiet, Waldenesque ambience.

For Joseph Mankiewicz's *Sleuth* (1973), John Addison's main-title music is an old-fashioned, turn-of-the-century overture accompanying backgrounds of miniature stage sets from Sir Laurence Olivier's mystery novels. The composer's selection of this particular musical form and style is a deliberate attempt to delineate Olivier's character and suggest his involvement with the past. This association is immediately apparent by the disparity between the music style and the opening camera shots of the contemporary landscape surrounding his stately country manor. Inside the house, with its quality antique furnishings, is a room devoted to costumes, toys, music boxes, games, and gadgetry.

A two-character tour de force (Olivier and Michael Caine), *Sleuth* has all the ingredients for dual musical interplay built into its mystery plot. Unlike *Hell in the Pacific,* another two-character movie for which Lalo Schifrin's music anticipates every moment of suspense with ominous drumbeats and exaggerated phrases, Addison's score is restrained and often understated. In the outdoors sequence, for example, as Caine in clown's costume scales a ladder to an upper-floor window while playing the thief game (a rehearsal for the fake robbery cooked up by Olivier), the music is comical without the usual stereotyped illustrations of buffoonery. Here the clown music is decidedly more contemporary than the old-fashioned sound of the harpsichord with which it is contrasted. By imaginatively playing off one kind of music against the other, the audience is made aware of the nature of the two men. The piquancy of the harpsichord suggests Olivier's eccentricity as he fancies himself the detective-hero of his own books. Addison's music catches the droll spirit that marks the battle of wits between Olivier and Caine. At the same time, it leaves the tense dramatic elements to the individual artistry of the actors. Their deadly game of intellectual thrust and counterthrust creates its own rhythm and suspense.

In the scene where Olivier dances around the room to Cole Porter's popular standard "Just One of Those Things," the music is accompanied by a collage of sounds coming from music boxes, chimes, bells, and mechanical devices. The surrealistic color sounds plunge the spectator into, and whirl him around, Olivier's private world. And, at the end as he stands amid his toys and music boxes, enveloped in their bizarre sounds, the music tells us that Olivier has become one of his own wooden figures.

Contradictory associations result from the use of two harmonic styles in the previously cited film, *Images* (1972). The film would seem to have two composers working at the same time but on different musical planes, since there is a discrepancy in styles that both enhances and detracts from the picture's dramatic intensity. The credits, shared by John Williams (music) and Stomu Yamashta (sounds), are a misnomer, however, for the entire score is

Williams', including the organized, composed sounds performed and interpreted by percussionist Yamashta.

Williams' opening music, featuring a piano solo and colorful orchestral textures, is basically romantic. As Susannah York recites her own self-indulgent children's story, "In Search of Unicorns" the music paints a wind-on-a-misty-hill tone poem.* By contrast, the sounds played by Yamashta on Baschet sculptures (glass tubes and prisms of stainless steel), both with mallets and by rubbing the fingers on the tubes, are strikingly contemporary. In addition to the Baschet pieces, Williams' score utilizes Inca flute, Kabuki wooden percussion instruments, bells, wood chimes, and other exotic timbres. Combined with avant-garde devices (slides, glissandos, blowing air through the flute) and magnified double-life-size through amplification, echo chamber, and reverberation, the sounds are strange, exciting, and unusual.

The composer's musical design was twofold. First, he supplied a lyric thread to stitch together the episodic ramblings of Miss York. The effect of this music is a moot point. By giving her imagery a warm and atmospheric musical landscape, is the composer or director suggesting that her children's book is profound and artistically significant? Viewers will differ in their aesthetic response. Second, Williams' musical sounds are inextricably entangled in Miss York's day-and-nightmares that mix up her husband, dead lover, live lover, and a little girl who resembles her so that nothing is what it seems. Shadow and light, voice and sound continuously weave in and out of focus to make the viewer uncertain when reality is fantasy and illusion is fact. In a dazzling, kaleidoscopic display of rotating prisms, lenses, and other light optics, the camera illumines a shattered mind.

In some places, however, the sounds get overly melodramatic, too much "in the picture." They force the contrasting music to be their accompaniment: that is, the music plays in the shadow of the sounds. Perhaps the undue prominence of the sound track tells us something about the script; its deficiencies need musical camouflage. As a composer, however, I am elated to hear this kind of score, put together with skill and inventiveness, in mainstream film music.

The sound effect of hanging glass bells from the car's rear-view mirror frequently sets off Miss York's hallucinations in the same way that the jangling of harnesses or the ringing of doorbells in Buñuel's Belle de Jour cue Catherine Deneuve's daydreams. The use of musical sound to create an impression of credibility is never better demonstrated than in the scene where Miss York supposedly stabs and kills her lover. The knife attack is accompanied by a blood-curdling sound that explodes in the eardrum, then falls into soft, bell-like tones as blood drips across the rug.** It is the dynamic power of this sound chord that makes us feel that what we are seeing has actually happened. The musical impact is so strong in associating force with murder that it is not until later that the viewer discovers the event never occurred.

The split personality of the two distinct styles of music in Images is accentuated not only by harmonic texture and style but also by tone color. The

*Music excerpt on page 303.
**Music excerpt on page 305.

impressionistic, lyrical music is scored predominantly for strings, woodwinds, and piano. The contemporary quasi-electronic sounds are almost exclusively percussion. Near the end of the film when she drives her car through a sea of multicolored lights, Miss York is enveloped by a broad spectrum of sound.* The slightly off-center resonances of the Baschet sculptures, along with other percussive, avant-garde effects, lend themselves perfectly to the hallucinatory atmosphere and, through their alienation from familiar timbres and musical patterns, impress on the viewer her final derangement.

The use of percussion instruments does not always evoke the associations just described, no matter how unconventional or weird the sounds produced. Sometimes they are exotic or terrifying, as in the cave and scarecrow episodes in *Planet of the Apes*. At other times the effect is primarily dramatic, as in any of 1001 popular action-suspense films. As mentioned before, many jazz-oriented composers single out individual instruments in various color combinations and use percussion effects as atmospheric coloration, neutral background-filler, tension heighteners, or, more familiarly, as a source of rhythmic drive and excitement.

Alex North's percussion music elicits a sociological association in the gathering-of-the-forces scene in *Viva Zapata* (1952). Lan Adomian describes the sequence:

Zapata is captured by the reenforced "rurales." He, like the old peasant whose lasso was cut by Zapata, is now walking the dusty road, his neck in a lasso. Here occurs one of the outstanding moments in the film. The camera picks up peasants in the plaza, in the fields, on the streets. Their faces are impassive, but their hands are making clicking sounds by knocking little stones against each other. This is a sort of primitive telegraph—apparently spreading the news of Zapata's capture. As the clicking rises in volume you hear a measured beat of bongos and tuned timbales. The orchestra has started a kind of Mexican bolero. We hear next flutes, guitars, plucked strings. All this is without dialogue. The camera picks up figures of peasants seemingly emerging from nowhere, but all gravitating toward the bound Zapata and his captors. The music rises in volume, expressing the unspoken demand of the peasants for the liberation of THEIR Zapata. The "rurales" thus surrounded are compelled to free Zapata, who joins his people.[6]

North's percussion takes off with the exact rhythmic pulse that the peasants have established with their clicking stones. The music acts as a rallying cry, an instrument of rebellious defiance.**

Even today an audience viewing *The Lost Weekend* (1945) rarely laughs when the camera zooms in on a whiskey bottle hanging by a string out of an apartment window. This scene is made meaningful by the music. Produced by the rich, pulsating tones of the vibraphone, it sets up a strange, shivering soberness. Had Miklos Rozsa used the xylophone in place of the vibraphone,

*Music excerpt on page 306.
**Music excerpt on page 308.

for example, he would have risked changing the serious mood to one of comic irrelevance. The xylophone's contrary tone color could twist the viewer's associative response from sympathy to out-and-out snickering. This is so because the xylophone's sound, produced by wooden resonators, is essentially brittle, sardonic, and frequently suggestive of the *danse macabre*. Its cartoon characteristics, coupled with the sight of the whiskey bottle dangling out the window, could precipitate laughter and destroy the film's serious theme.

A particularly happy example of the xylophone's capabilities is in Charles Eames' documentary, *Toccata for Toy Trains*. When the old toy train races the old toy car, Elmer Bernstein's music sets a fast, frolicsome rhythm. Along with the piano, the clickety-clack of the xylophone adds immeasurably to the merry spirit and makes the people in the audience feel that they are passengers on a delightful excursion through yesterday's countryside. Maurice Jarre employs the instrument extensively in *Night of the Generals* (1967) in a contrasting way. First, he uses it as percussion color over the opening music's military march; later, its biting crackle becomes the main ingredient for his segue motif. And finally, when the French prostitute is being driven to her apartment in the General's (Peter O'Toole) car prior to her murder, the instrument's hard staccato snaps home the jangled nerves of the General, exposing his degenerate psychotic personality. The xylophone's special timbre turns the imperious German martinet into a dehumanized cartoon.

I rather doubt that Walt Disney movies could have existed without the xylophone, since it provided an amusing if tiring musical accompaniment for many of the simple-minded dog-cat-and-mouse chases prominently featured in these and other animated films. The marimba, another mallet instrument, deeper in pitch, mellower, and with greater resonance than the xylophone, has in its lower range a striking tone quality not unlike that of a pipe organ. Composers have used the marimba not only for musical stereotypes in films set in Central American or Mexican locales where the instrument is popular, but also for other instances where a ritualistic or symbolic association with the church is desired.

Returning to the vibraphone, the instrument's ability to create overtones through its power to vibrate is exploited by John Lewis in *Odds Against Tomorrow*. Carrying over suspended notes from one episode to another, the music literally melts into ensuing sequences. While the vibe tones act as a continuous lyric line and reflect Harry Belafonte's anguish and emotional instability, they also bind together the constant shifts of disparate scenes.

What associations are evoked by the now-familiar background of percussion noodlings that composers use to keep things moving (or the audience awake) remain a mystery. On a simplistic level an audience might react to brushes on cymbals and cool-jazz drum-rhythm patterns by eating their popcorn a little faster, while marking time in anticipation of dramatic action. This formula for achieving continuity is an easy way out for the composer, who can write or improvise it at the recording session, a simple solution for the director to effect a knitting together of loosely constructed scenes, and an easy-to-listen-to rhythmic flow for the spectator. No sweat; no tears. But occasionally, the use of percussion borders on the ridiculous. Such is the case in *Is Paris Burning?* During a scene inside the office of the high command, Maurice Jarre, for no apparent reason except an absence of musical taste and dramatic insight, punctuates the dialogue with cymbal clashes. These ringing interpolations coming between narrative exchanges are absolutely meaningless.

A positive use of percussion occurs in *Alexander Nevsky* during the final scenes of the battle on ice depicting the total rout of the German knights. When the invaders break through the ice and are drowned as they retreat in wild flight, Prokofiev uses drums, timpani, and cymbals to pound home a lesson to all invaders: the folly of those who would attempt to conquer the Russian people.

The associations summoned by an ensemble group's or a solo instrument's tone color are well documented. Tone color (instrumental timbre) is especially significant at the beginning of a film, since opening music has the special associative impact of being there *first*. It is commensurate with a composer's opening bars for a concert piece, which usually contain the notes and intervalic relationships of greatest importance. By placing them first, the composer shows that he considers them superior aesthetically and prefers them over any other tonal combinations.

Tone color is seasoning—salt and pepper to a film. Initially it adds to the flavor by perking things up, but if overindulged, it palls and makes scenes flat and bland. Nina Rota's score for Fellini's *Satyricon* (1970), based on the satirical novel by Petronius, avoids his predilection for exaggerated romanticism. Instead, he projects arresting orchestral textures at the beginning of the film that surround the air of antiquity with a flamboyant color design. However, due to the inordinate length of the film and a lack of sufficiently contrasting musical elements, interest is not always sustained. This is also the risk with exotic and unusual timbres. A good illustration is the Ondes Martenot in *Secret Ceremony*. After the initial exposure to this monophonic electronic instrument, which at first is eerie and evocative, the sound becomes less stimulating with each repetition.[7] The same is true of the theremin in *Spellbound* (1945), which creates an atmospheric mood that permeates this psychological thriller with a peculiar, somber romanticism, only to become, with protracted use, too obvious. It has seldom been employed since *Spellbound*, so closely is its sound associated with this film. Even percussion staples can be tiring if overplayed. Composers know, for example, that it is the first entrance of the snare drum that creates the strongest, most successful impact, and that continued use diminishes the instrument's special pungency.

The listener's response to opening music is not only one of the more intriguing aspects in the film mystique, it is the most emphatic. Early associations leave a strong imprint, a memory bank, that retains impressions, no matter how varied. This remains true even as the film's subsequent moods are developed or altered by ensuing cinematic episodes. Many films, both past and present, are introduced by brief overtures over the titles that create an overall, sometimes artificial mood. The overture, considered the quintessence of main-title music, frequently sets up the dramatic character for the opening scene or establishes the proper mood during the opening sequence itself. It can even introduce and accompany screen action that commences behind or prior to the title credits. Occasionally there is a tease—expository material that precedes both the initial music cue and the credits. Through the years, opening music was often misused, marked by loud, brassy fanfares and whipped-up enthusiasm. Because these devices still appear—dressed in modern musical attire—much opening music remains a jazzy, jet-propelled stream of meaningless froth.

The value of opening musical statements to create an atmosphere or convey a feeling is especially beneficial in comedies and fantasies, for both these forms seem to require assistance to elicit audience response. When Jerry Goldsmith opens *Lilies of the Field* (1963) with a lyrical, solo-harmonica phrase (which is later used as the main motif for the "Amen" chant sequence), then joins walking bass, banjo, accordion, and strings in an arrangement punctuated by country-music markings and Western-style rhythmic patterns and melodic contours, the music style immediately reflects Americana. But more important than environmental associations, the music introduces the warm-hearted spirit of the film. The score for this lively little comedy is not meant to overwhelm but to arouse empathy for its characters, which grows with the visual development.

To this day the opening to *Citizen Kane* (1941) remains a brilliant example of the total fusion of music, sound, and symbolistic imagery. Bernard Herrmann's low, ominous array of sounds intones dramatic doom. Accompanying the camera as it moves slowly up the gates of Xanadu, the music evokes portentous associations and feelings of awe at the vacuous grandeur of God-Kane's castle. Extraneous voices and echoing sounds act as counterpoint, enriching the tonal ambience and enhancing the images. Prokofiev's opening music over titles for *Alexander Nevsky*, the epic film about thirteenth-century Russia, also speaks in dark, portentous overtones. The music is dirgelike, heavy, and brooding—and yet heroic. The opening scene depicts a desolate landscape, with skeletons pierced by spears telling us of other wars and deaths. Through its solemn, intensely nationalistic feeling, the music conveys the incandescent spirit of the people, and hints at the rise of a new patriotism, crystallized later by the entrance of the Chorus, which sings of Russian strength and valor in Nevsky's earlier victory over the Swedes. Prokofiev uses a solo oboe, whose tone color elicits a plaintive response as the viewer reflects on the scene's barren isolation.

The overture to *Nicholas and Alexandra* (1972) by Richard Rodney Bennett is also a setting for a segment of Russian history, this time the last months of the Romanov dynasty. The opening motif in horns is taken up by the strings in a large, full-scale symphonic rendition that includes a chorus. The music's emotional, lyric sweep is eloquently expressive and heavily influenced by Russian music of the late nineteenth century. Associations are clear-cut. As the film progresses the music texture gets more complicated and parallels the tragic downfall of the czarist family at a time of changing social values and rising Bolshevism.

In contrast, Bernard Herrmann's overture to *All That Money Can Buy* is full of playful touches that set the place, the time, and the spirit of this Faustian tale in unmistakable musical language. Similarly, John Addison's opening for *Tom Jones* is a fast-paced, mischievous romp that launches his romantic adventures and sets the impudent tempo to depict those halcyon English days of Henry Fielding's mid-eighteenth-century novel. The overture features the piquant flavor of the harpsichord in the foreground against the robust tone of the piano in the background. The listener's response is influenced not only by style and rondo-variation form, but also by the composer's choice of instrumental timbre to expose the contradictions in Jones' personality. Full of ribald trombone slides and other belly-laugh musical effects, the score blends perfectly with the action, embellishing rather than illustrating.

The main titles of Truffaut's *Jules and Jim* use a kind of circus-carnival overture. Georges Delerue's rollicking music reflects the spirited friendship between the two young men. And John Barry's opening music for the James Bond films he has scored, in particular *Goldfinger*, positively announces his nonsubtle approach to Bond's adventures—at sea, in Fort Knox, and in bed. The spoofing, Mickeymoused assortment of musical babble is loud, brassy, and irritating, but decidedly apropos.

The taut, rhythmic vitality of Elmer Bernstein's overture to *The Man with the Golden Arm* is excitement of another type. It sets the story's dramatic mood. The piercing orchestral sound, featuring piccolos, clarinets, and brass marked "screaming, nasty," gives a percussive drive to Gail Kubik's opening (over the credits) for *The Desperate Hours* that anticipates the suspenseful sequences that follow. In *The Cobweb* (1955), Leonard Rosenman broke ground with his use of the twelve-tone-series technique. The main theme contains the following row:

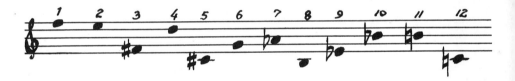

Performed in a high register for maximum shrillness, the opening music serves as exposition for the film. Its strident sound and oblique contour is just off enough to jangle the nerves and suggest that emotional disorder is the principal affliction (not counting the plot) of the film's cast of neurotic characters. What is germane is not the style or idiom of this music—for the Schoenbergian system is only one way of organizing material—but that the composer makes this technique effective within the framework of the dramatic context. His expositional recipe, therefore, is not an exercise in musico-mathematical virtuosity. Sometimes nervous and uneasy and at other moments forceful or restrained, the score always reinforces the action, not by mere backdrops of sound but rather by supportive back-up. (Besides the music, the only thing I recall in this Grand Hotel nuthouse is the sight of pianist Oscar Levant as a patient, popping pills and singing "Mother.")

Contrasting orchestral styles and forms to introduce cinematic action and evoke diverse associations can be seen by comparing certain films: André Previn's curtain-raiser for *Bad Day at Black Rock* (1954)—a scalding film about a war vet (Spencer Tracy) who uncovers a town's secret—accompanies the image of a streamliner rolling across the western plains and pulling into a flag stop. The train is propelled by Previn's aggressive rhythms, which include a motif with sharp echoes of World War II. The title is brought on in rhythmic synchronization—*Bad-Day-at-Black-Rock*. As Previn's music literally blows the train into a small western town, it symbolizes the fast tempo of the outside world invading a place steeped in the past and mistrustful of strangers. The music sets a rapid pace for the film, but it by no means anticipates the subsequent screen action: its primary function is to get things started. However, in Miklos Rozsa's opening for *Brute Force* (1947), his heavy, brooding, symphonic sound hangs like a pall over the prison gates and sets the mood for this hard-nosed drama about convicts and penitentiary life. Alex North's opening music is even more pointed in *Spartacus*. His sharply chiseled bass line, weighted down by the tuba, gives a contrapuntal sweep and majesty to the title credits. The emotional force of the music suggests the momentous consequences of Spartacus' slave revolt. Ending with divergent lines that come together on one distorted chord, it focuses musically on a symbolic Roman sculpture breaking into fragments.

Behind newsreel footage of the middle thirties, David Raksin's main titles for the horror-suspense film *What's the Matter with Helen?* (1970) is musically complex.* Regarding his thinking for this sequence and its anticipated effect on the audience, the composer writes:

This score must not begin like any old horror film score, but ought to add to the element of mystery. The idea was also, to some extent, to remain a pace behind the revelation of Helen's real nature; it is *not* the job of the music to give away the story. The rhythmic ostinato takes care of the basic dramatic requirement of the title music . . . . and the dramatic objective must be accomplished without lapsing into melodrama. Starting the rhythmic pattern off with percussion was a quick afterthought. The pattern, which could—with different notes and chords—show the brighter aspect of its jazz origins, is indeed relentless, partly because of its pace (a quarter note equals twelve frames), but much more because of the notes chosen, their relation to the shifting harmony and to the open beats and percussive beats that make the pattern a duple-rhythm.

Then, over this pattern, with its tragic and propulsive drive, there appears a theme—an alto-sax "poignant" solo. Again, it is a matter of the notes chosen, in relation to everything else that is happening. To fall into the sin of anachronism by introducing ideas and feelings that belong later in the drama at too early a stage is a risky business; it is quite legitimate to introduce thematic or other material that will later develop and metamorphose with the story. Not only is this dramatically and musically sound practice, but I believe that properly handled it can help to unify the film through the strong integrative power of musical forms, as well as the ability of music to evoke memory. As to the interpolation of the pop tune "Goody, Goody!" into the middle of this already complex process, it is meant to be kind of a shocker, a seeming irrelevancy, and therefore a challenge.[8]

---

*Music excerpt on page 312.

For *Lady in a Cage* (1964), Paul Glass' opening music is off the beaten path for mainstream features. The story concerns a crippled lady (Olivia De Havilland) who is trapped in a stalled home elevator and attracts big-city human animals. Glass' uncompromising sound is conceived as a chamber concerto played by a small ensemble. The assorted city scenes—couple in car embracing, man lying on pavement, dead dog in gutter, debris thrown from rooftops, garbage can exploding in air, screeching traffic noises—play behind Glass' terrifying, sometimes violent sounds. His staccato phrases, sharp accents, pizzicato figures, percussive explosions, abrupt rhythmic interjections (loud, big sounds followed by soft, small ones), and moments of silence are encased in a twelve-tone-series framework. It is restless music with more than a touch of hysteria. Partway through the opening sequence the composer introduces a haunting lyric line in conjunction with fast camera shots of the house where the drama will unfold, which contrasts with his overall music design and lends a quiet, personal touch to that particular setting, isolated from the city's rumblings and violence. The jarring musical intrusions, blended with the fragmented imagery of a hostile environment made vivid by abrupt editing techniques, induce in the viewer an acrid sense of disgust. This is a good example of where drawing on contemporary music pays off. In addition to establishing a mood of chilling suspense, Glass' personal language helps create a feeling of estrangement—a modern-day fact of life. The music's personality is so distinctive that when the elevator's emergency bell rings, the clang seems to emanate from the score as a percussion interpolation rather than a cinematic sound effect.

Gerhard's opening music for *This Sporting Life* is sparse and pointillistic. Similar to Paul Glass' sound framework, its atonal language is interpreted for the most part by single instruments—flute, drum, xylophone, short string lines, and harmonics (high, flutelike, partial tones faintly produced by a string, pipe organ, or human voice through the vibration of fractional parts of a string or air column). These elements, plus sharply accented chord impacts, suggest the strain and violence of English football as a spectator sport.

Opening music of a completely different style and tone color dominates Johnny Mandel's atmospheric score for *The Sandpiper* (a dreadful movie but a good musical example for purposes of contrast). About this film, the composer writes in his notes from the album jacket: "Usually, a cinema composer tries to dazzle the listener with the wildest possible variety of sounds and tempi. For *The Sandpiper*, I have, instead, tried to sustain a constant mood throughout. It's a haunting mood matching the poignancy of the story, underscored by the beauty and loneliness of the magnificent Big Sur location. I have attempted with this music to capture the sounds of the surf, the grandeur of the mountains, the beauty of the land."[9] What evolves is a lush, full-brass harmonic flow—an impressionistic, jazz-influenced tone poem that arouses nostalgic associations connected with the romantic ocean landscape.

Incompatibility marks Maruice Jarre's main titles for the brilliant Visconti film, *The Damned* (1969). The initial music over factory backgrounds has a mechanized, contemporary, rhythmic thrust. Suddenly and with no preparation, Jarre switches idioms and introduces a romantic theme with movie-music flavoring. This clumsy change of style is incomprehensible, unless the composer or director naively believed that it would influence the audience to respond with new associations analogous in some way to the decadence of Visconti's characters. The mixture of prosaic, unctuous music with Visconti's baroque expressionism—including his imaginative use of weird colors and unorthodox makeup—seems to be entirely incongruous. And even if it was meant to create a musical flow contrary to the visuals for dramatic purposes, the cinematic effect of the stylistic change is dubious. One gets the distinct impression that there was indecision between film-maker and composer about the opening musical statement's style and content.

Going from the ridiculous to the sublime, the lyrical warmth of Aaron Copland's opening music sets the mood for *The Heiress.* The stamp of the composer is clearly recognizable as soon as his name appears on the screen; prior to this, at the beginning of the main titles, there is one minute of music footage that is not part of his score. Flowing into the opening scene, the initial music gives Copland an opportunity to establish the ambience of the period and the special charm of New York City's Washington Square at the turn of the century. The music is tranquil and pastoral. In this film, as in *Our Town* and *The Red Pony,* Copland stresses a softness of texture and sparse instrumentation. The simple directness of his lyric style is deceptive, for in spite of easy-to-understand musical language, its power to arouse profound feelings and stimulate associations is considerable.

Lyricism of another sort, a singing yet sadly sympathetic quality, marks Laurence Rosenthal's opening music for *The Miracle Worker* (1962). As Helen Keller (Patty Duke) gropes her way through a maze of wash hanging from a clothesline, she becomes entangled and falls to the ground. Her mother rushes out of the house, extricates her from the sheets, and holds her close. Rosenthal's lyrical line suggests both the loneliness of a little girl trying to find her way through the maze of exterior and interior darkness and the pain of the helpless mother. Although the screen image itself is evocative, it is the intensely emotional music that enhances the spectator's involvement in this moving episode. This time it is not just an individual tone color or definitive musical form or style that creates a distinctive atmosphere but the poetic sensitivity and expressive warmth of the total musical statement.*

The tone color of instruments, individually or collectively, so varies in its impact and consequent association with the visuals that it is a potent weapon in the composer's arsenal of musical resources. One of my favorite examples is Jerry Goldsmith's first musical statement for *Planet of the Apes.* Coming after expository cinematic action—Charlton Heston, leader of a space-exploring team, has entered notes in his flight log, given himself a sleep-inducing shot, and settled down to await the moment of his future awakening—the shock of Goldsmith's opening phrase is extraordinary. He employs one repeated, "stopped" note in the low register of the piano (the instrument's most dramatic range) and gradually increases dynamic volume as the pattern is telescoped by a bass slide whistle, which emits a glissando sigh of unearthly sound. With the simplest economy of means and a brilliant stroke of

*Music excerpt on page 315.

imagination in his choice of timbre, the composer manages to put the spectator in another time and a different place within the short space of only a few bars of music. The effect is immediate and stunning.

PLANET OF THE APES (Main title). Composer: J. Goldsmith.

The piano is also used against different visuals in *To Kill A Mockingbird* to convey other associations.* Elmer Bernstein opens the film with a piano solo playing little phrases, accompanied by a child's humming and talking. After the titles, the music becomes a simple children's song—intimate, restrained, and sparsely orchestrated. The evocative and nostalgic music is distinguished not only by tone color and an easy, flowing tempo, but by its style and form—a three-part A-B-A pattern commencing with a children's song, continuing into a middle section where the music swells to a fuller sound, and finally returning to its childlike beginning. Later in the score, Bernstein introduces a strong piano arpeggio figure, which he repeatedly employs as a way to bind all the children together in their own world, as opposed to the world of adults.

In contrast is Leonard Rosenman's solo in *East of Eden,* played on a "tack" piano (an out-of-tune barroom upright) and echoing Alban Berg's opera *Wozzeck.* When the estranged son (James Dean) opens the door of the brothel run by his mother (Jo Van Fleet), the low-down music that assaults our ears tells us exactly what kind of a house he has entered. In this instance, it is not merely tone color that acts as an emotional signpost, but also the rhythmic style of the music.

An intriguing selection of timbres marks Richard Bennett's opening for *Secret Ceremony.* A piano, joined by vibraphone, harp, and celesta and later merged with organ and harpsichord, introduces a simple children's song that serves as the film's theme. About the music for this film, the composer said: "I tried to create a giant, music-box sound; not an actual music box but a color like it." The effect evokes a remembrance of childhood and the fantasies of children. A particularly striking scene from this film occurs inside Mia Farrow's house, where a piano is being tuned. The sound of the out-of-tune

*Music excerpt on page 316.

instrument fits perfectly her portrayal of a rich girl living in a state of mutual hallucination with a whore (Elizabeth Taylor) she mistakes for her long-lost mother. The piano tuner's jangling notes hovering over the entire sequence give a strange, tilted feeling to the images. In *The Innocents*, Georges Auric's children's song is first hummed by the little girl, later vocalized, played with one finger on a piano, and finally revealed as coming from its original source, a music box. The song appears and reappears, hauntingly weaving in and out of the story and linking the children and the specters of Quint and Miss Jessel, the adults who played an important part in their lives and who have possessed them. The song is literally a signal of this possession. In *That Cold Day in the Park,* Johnny Mandel uses a polyphone (a form of music box) behind the scene of the protagonist smoking grass. Associating this instrument with marijuana leads to all kinds of conjecture.

Different tone colors, contrasting styles and forms, and distinct tempi and rhythms set in motion contrary and antagonistic associations in John Frankenheimer's *Seconds* (1966). The background for the main titles consists of distorted facial images, and Jerry Goldsmith underscores these credits first by a piano effect produced by a bass drumstick on a bass string of an open piano and then by the sound of an organ.* The organ, with its fuzzy tones and strange vibrations, gives the blurred images their bizarre overtones and creates the film's nightmarish mood. The organ sounds fuzzy because most of its pipes produce sounds rich in harmonics. *Seconds* is a modern Dr. Faustus story about people who are given new bodies and new identities but are really controlled once they have been reborn. It is a middle-aged-man's fantasy of starting again in order to do what he has always wanted and have another chance on life's road. The composer uses the piano both as a reflection of Rock Hudson's former life and the new image of his adult youth. It accompanies scenes of his domestic life near the beginning of the film, nostalgic remembrances, and his return home to revisit the past at the film's end. The organ, on the other hand, is employed to emphasize his transformation and the eerieness connected with his rebirth.** It opens the film, plays behind the kindly-devil scene, adds a sense of evil to the nightmare sequence when a drugged Hudson believes he has ravished a girl, and lends mystery to the surgery episode. For this scene the music is lyrically dramatic and anticipates the excitement of his rebirth. The piano music arouses sympathy for Hudson, whereas the organ's ritualistic sound suggests the film's satanic theme. In between, the composer introduces a long, lyric violin line that meanders through the harmonic texture. The theme connects Hudson's old and new identities. In the commuter-train sequence, the violin line is plaintive, but during the sequence in which Hudson travels to California, the muted strings become sentimental, for, despite its horror aspects, the film is in many ways a romantic fantasy.

The kinds of music in *Seconds* are distinguished not only by tone color (piano against organ), form, and style (simple melodic song and transparent

*Music excerpt on page 317.
**Music excerpt on page 319.

outline against a complex, shifting, harmonic design), but also by tempo and rhythm (moderate 3/8 time against fairly slow 3/4, 4/4, and 5/4). The film ends with the sight of a man, a child, and a dog filling the screen and the sound of a solo piano.* At this point the instrument is revealed as the other voice—the organ's alter ego. With the blending together of piano and organ on the last chord, the two personalities fade into and are absorbed by each other in a final tragic resolution.

For *Patton,* Goldsmith also wrote main-title music built around the organ, but in a different context. In its pacing, form, color contrast, and movement, the music has a spontaneous sweep that presses forward with the same inexorable momentum as Patton himself on one of his famous armored-tank assaults. The opening archaic cries of the trumpet (triplet figure reverberated on Echoplex to a pianissimo), accompanied by ominous bass beats, are followed by a solo organ's solemn, legato line heard in relief against the trumpet interpolations and short snare-drum bursts. This prelude, called a voluntary, contains military impulses and prayerful church associations that interact with one another to delineate Patton's complicated makeup—the classic warrior, religious and irreverent. When the piccolos and woodwinds introduce the march theme, the pulse quickens; the horn's heroic announcement of the tune surges toward a joyous, full-orchestra rendition, which finally gives way to the isolated sound of the organ, in turn replaced by the opening trumpet figure fading off into the distance. This music is a paragon of objective planning.

While Francis Seyrig's lovely neoclassical music, scored for string orchestra, sets the scene, slow, romantic organ music adds a touch of elegant mystery to accompany the action in Resnais' *Last Year at Marienbad.* Film critic William Johnson, in his excellent analysis of this score, observes that the initial neoclassical harmonic style, fashionable 200 years ago, "fits in with the baroque interiors of the château and, together with the past tense of the narrator's reminiscences, establishes a sense of reflectiveness and completion. But then," he adds, "as the camera moves in among the players and spectators of the château's theater, the film shifts into the present tense, and at the same time the harmonic pattern of the music shifts to a long chain of discords, still relatively mild but persistently unresolved. While the images remain formal and baroque, the romantic languor of the new harmony helps to suck the spectator into the flow of unresolved events on the screen."[10]

The full-bodied overtones and ritualistic connotations of the organ lend themselves to melodramatic subject matter. The instrument plays a prominent role in the numerous variations of *Phantom of the Opera* and similar shock films. In Eisenstein's *Alexander Nevsky,* the symbol of the Church is placed on the side of the German knights; it is their God, not the Russians'. Prokofiev uses old instruments as a rallying cry for all patriotic Russians to fight the invaders. In opposition, the organ, which is associated with the Church, plays in the Crusading Knights' camp. Its tone in the film would seem to mock the Germans and the Church.

---

*Music excerpt on page 323.

The portable rock organ introduced into many of today's sound tracks is the organ's contemporary counterpart. Although capable of expressing lyricism and suspense, it is usually employed as a percussive instrument to articulate staccato chords and rhythmic patterns. Along with the piano and organ, the harpsichord, including the modern electric variety, has been exploited by many composers. The British school in particular has used it to delineate character traits: eccentricity, as in Ron Goodwin's theme for Margaret Rutherford in *Murder at the Gallop*, one of Agatha Christie's Miss Marple series; impudence, in John Addison's tuneful frolic for *Tom Jones;* fantasy, in *Sleuth;* and unreality, in both *The Whisperers* and the pixilated charm of Tristin Cary's score for *The Ladykillers*. In *The Ladykillers*, the composer simulates a harpsichord-music-box effect, using flute, harp, celesta, and strings.

At the opposite end of the orchestral ladder stand the pristine tones of the flute. While the instrument's timbre is effective in counteracting tendencies toward overdramatization, its most curious attribute would seem to be its chameleonlike ability to change color. Against the bleak, desolate landscape of the opening scene in *The Virgin Spring*, Erik Nordgren's solo flute sounds cold and unemotional. As background for the rainy-day opening of *That Cold Day in the Park*, Mandel's flute music is lukewarm and reflective. Following flashbacks during credit titles superimposed over stills of Alcatraz in *Point Blank*, the same composer's use of the bass flute, played without vibrato and later joined by trumpet and low strings in a kind of three-part dialogue, conveys a lonely sense of the isolated prison. In freeze-frame photography, the deserted island rock projects memories of men behind bars and their despair. For *The Luck of Ginger Coffey*, Bernardo Segáll's baroque "clock theme" on solo flute with bass-pizzicato accompaniment is heard during the main titles. As the camera travels down snow-swept streets in Montreal, the music gives a sad and lonely feeling to the early morning scene. The entrance of a solo-accordion line adds color contrast and a touch of nostalgia to this loser's story.* As a curtain raiser for *Death of a Salesman*, Alex North's fine, lyrical alto flute threads its way through the scene of Willy Loman entering the house, suitcases in hand, and sets a sympathetic mood. (It is interesting that the effect of the solo-flute opening is more dramatic in the stage production. When the curtain rises, the theatre is dark and silent, and the music seems to float out of the air.) As a dark, shady tone color that follows Michael Caine around in *The Ipcress File*, John Barry's theme, frequently played on the low flute, acts not only as a continuity factor, but, more importantly, points up the hero's shadowy personality. Georges Auric's sparse music, featuring a breathy flute in its lowest range, intermingles with whimpering voices to lend an air of mystery to *The Innocents*. (The use of a solo piccolo as a replacement for the flute might have enhanced the scene even more. In its low register the instrument has a thinly veiled, ghostly sound like that of a disembodied voice.)

As mentioned earlier, the main-title music of Hans Henze for *Muriel*

---

*Music excerpt on page 324.

speaks a musical language generally alien to mainstream motion-picture music, and for this reason alone the score is noteworthy. In the opening music the tone color of Rita Streich's solo voice soaring over the action in a high range transmits an awareness of those moments not sharply delineated on the screen where Hélène (Delphine Seyrig) is most tormented. Streich's atonal vocalization is an art song, not a theme tune, and functions as another instrument. Any composer in Hollywood who would dare to introduce this kind of a vocal line as opening film music would run the risk of being fired off the recording stage. And how many American actors would stand by and not complain about the strange, unfamiliar sounds interlaced through their dialogue?

Henze's voice and orchestra settings stylistically suggest Alban Berg. As Susan Sontag points out, "In its most powerful use, the music constitutes a kind of purified dialogue, displacing speech altogether."[11] This displacement becomes an active "structural element in the narration." In effect, bits and pieces of music reflect the characters' emotions, almost speaking for them. The vocal line segments connect disjointed scenes and imagery. Sometimes a music sound or chord stimulates Hélène's memory of something in her past. At the end of the film, the vocal lament accompanying Simone (the wife of Hélène's former lover) as she enters the apartment searching for her husband *is* the dialogue. The music at this point reaches an emotional climax of stunning proportions.

Because of the use of electronic music in many current films, it is worth examining Toru Takemitsu's score for *Woman of the Dunes* (1964), in which the composer employs electronic equipment, percussion color, and normal instruments. For the opening music, he relies on electronic chord-and-percussion accents—bamboo on wood, sharply amplified. In the first scene, a young entomologist is walking on sand dunes near the sea looking for insect specimens and taking pictures. The music consists of abrupt electronic interjections, out of which come sustained tones on the bass clarinet. The sound is eerie and desolate, as are the beach and the dunes, and it replaces the natural sound of the wind. The beginning would seem to be atmospheric comments using pointillistic vibrations. In many places, Takemitsu associates ripple marks on the sand with sound waves at a high-decibel level. The villagers persuade the entomologist to spend the night in a sand shack at the bottom of a dune with a widow whose task is endless shoveling away of sand, which is hauled to the surface by a rope ladder. The significance of Takemitsu's strange opening sounds for this bizarre allegory is not made clear until the man attempts to leave his sand shelter and discovers he is a prisoner. Now the sounds take on a threatening and ominous connotation, literally intoning his entombment.

Schlondorff's film *Young Torless* (1966) portrays a young boy's unhappy reaction to a paramilitary academy in the Austro-Hungarian empire. The youthful exuberance and rebelliousness of the boys are vividly depicted. Hans Henze often uses the classic purity of the string quartet—speaking a contemporary musical language, alternately strident and lyrical—to define the conflicting elements of poetic fantasy, bullying intimidation, and emotional insecurity of the youths, especially the diffident nature of the hero. The pristine tone color of the string quartet is the musical counterpart of unformed manhood, as yet uncorrupted but paradoxically capable of vicious acts in an environmental hierarchy where the stronger prevail. By contrast, the ensemble's contemporary sonorities sharply underscore the tensions and uncertainties of their world. The dramatic clarity of Henze's music evokes a strong response, more so than other scores for similar films, such as Lindsay Anderson's powerful *If* and Jack Garfein's *End as a Man*.

There are other good examples of dramatic associations triggered by tone color. John Dankworth snaps home the tensions in *Accident* with a harp, whose nasal twang jars the nervous system. In *The Best Years of Our Lives*, Hugo Friedhofer's lyrical cello solo conveys a feeling of open sentimentality as war veteran Frederic March returns home to his family. Paul Glass uses the dark, somber tone of the clarinet in its low register over concentration-camp scenes in *Interregnum*—a documentary on Germany between the wars based on George Grosz's paintings and drawings—to underline Lotte Lenya's narration: "They heard no evil, they saw no evil." In *So Ends Our Night* (1942), Louis Gruenberg's music for the deathbed sequence gives this tragic ending a cold detachment. A long, sustained, high violin solo that employs few notes merges into a dissonant sonority as Frederic March commits suicide. Johnny Mandel's trumpet solo is almost a bystander to the last scene in the prison yard in *Point Blank,* filling the screen with a tragic gloom and playing through to the last frame as the camera slowly pans over Alcatraz and San Francisco Bay.* In *The Bad and the Beautiful*, David Raksin's lush music accompanies a low, muted trumpet solo that brushes Lana Turner with a starkiss as she stands on an empty Hollywood stage. In *Elmer Gantry* (1960), André Previn's sassy trumpet solo played in Gantry's face tells us that he is a fraud, a Devil's disciple, not the Lord's preacher. Gantry has been exposed in the newspaper by pictures that frame him in a compromising position with a whore. As the revivalist-meeting crowd peppers him with eggs and garbage, Previn introduces an agitated orchestral undercurrent. A polytonal counterpoint to the furious sarcasm of the trumpet, it reflects Gantry's hurt and humiliation. Once again, there are differences between the two kinds of music. They are set apart not only by tone color (trumpet solo versus orchestral sound), rhythmic tempo and articulation (fast, sharp interjections against slower, measured movement), but also by form and style (jazzy, bluesy song on top of symphonic passages).

While duplicating what the cinematic image has already captured is not a creative exercise in musical imagination, it is a simple if obvious way of establishing an ambience. But, because the ability of music to create a definite mood for a specific scene cannot automatically be assumed, some composers take the safe route and resort to musical stereotypes to underline obvious imagery. Unmotivated to break the stylistic chains used to supply the audience with a simple-minded, ready-made identification, they rely on stereotyped associations that quickly invite boredom. Who can forget the early films set in the Far East (remember Charley Chan?) that made no pretense of

*Music excerpt on page 326.

establishing a far-eastern idiom. As a result, countless scores written in an occidental, nineteenth-century symphonic style had only to add the omnipotent gong to achieve the proper "oriental" effect. This representative timbre in conjunction with open fifths and the pentatonic scale gave adequate testimony and still does in many recent films to a Chinese locale. In the same way, the song "Sakura" (cherry blossom) is synonymous with Japan; characteristic rhythmic-melodic patterns, often for voice and guitar, confirm that *Viva Villa, Viva Zapata,* and *The Professionals* are part of Mexico's lore; and the calypso "Matilda" invariably reminds us that *Island in the Sun* is set in the British West Indies. In *Last Tango in Paris,* when Bertolucci surrounds one of Marlon Brando's love encounters with what sounds very much like a Hawaiian love song, the stylistic association is startling. We don't know whether or not this is supposed to be the director's musical put-on. Taken at face value, the effect is incongruous.

The tendency toward musical stereotypes can be offset by the composer seeking other means. In the Rockefeller Foundation documentary *Rice,* film-maker Willard Van Dyke directed me to create my own far-eastern style. Immersing myself in the instrumental resources of the Orient and avoiding conventional Chinese sonorities, I invented my own world of sound. Included in the score are Kabuki instruments, gamelans, assorted gongs, chimes, bells, marimbas, cymbals, and drums. For *A Man Named Horse,* Leonard Rosenman spent a great deal of time investigating the nature and language of American Indian music. Despite some familiar sounds and a style reminiscent of other Indian films, one feels the presence of an authentic voice. Scored for eagle-boned flutes augmented by a quartet of recorders, drums, and rattles, the music's contrasting rhythmic patterns give it an air of distinction.

The use of stylized music for psychological associations can be just as banal as ambient Eastern or Western music. As discussed before, jazz falls into this category. In its cinematic debut it was an exciting, rhythmic experience in dramatic communication. Today, as a background for violence, an accompaniment for skullduggery, murder, suspense, drug traffic, and a means to convey emotional instability, jazz has been worked to death until it has become an audio trademark for neurotic drama.

On occasion, imaginative uses of stereotyped associations can be an asset. In *The Bridge on the River Kwai* (1957), the British prisoners whistling the "Colonel Bogey" march represent more than a clash between British and Japanese cultures. In the beginning, when the men, marching in strict formation, arrive at the Japanese prison camp, they boost the morale of the other British captives in the camp hospital. As the film progresses, the tune takes on a symbolic note of defiance; it informs the Japanese masters that the indefatigable spirit of the British soldier can never be broken. When Japanese ships approach Pearl Harbor in *Tora, Tora, Tora* (1970), Jerry Goldsmith's music consists of ominous oriental sounds. In a scene change to an officer's dance in Hawaii, appropriate Glenn Miller-type dance music is heard. Shifting back and forth between the Japanese fleet and the officer's dance, both music tracks are played simultaneously, with the oriental music on top getting louder and louder and building to a camera cut of the next morning. The contrapuntal flow of the composer's mixed musical bag is made palatable by contrast, although the associations themselves are obvious.

The use of contrast is also important in *The Ipcress File* (1965). A symphonic band playing Mozart in the background accompanies the scenes in the park when Michael Caine meets the head of British Intelligence to receive his instructions. Those episodes with Caine in a London populated by undercover men and kidnapped scientists are marked by a kind of sinister cool jazz, scored for harp, flute, and the Hungarian cymbalom in featured solos. The seeming incongruity of using the clarity and formal discipline of Mozart as a musical bystander for intricate spy plottings is possibly explained by its style: it does not interfere with the business at hand. After the rendezvous, Caine's response to the music, "Let me know who wins," helps delineate his character. Amid the smoky haze of John Barry's incidental music the Mozart is a breath of fresh air. And, Caine's correlation of Mozart with his own world, as though both were a competitive, winner-take-all game, shows how deeply his involvement in secret-service activities has affected him. Another instance of indifference to music occurs in *Weekend* (1967). During the farmyard recital of a Mozart piano sonata, a lull in a storm of violence, Godard's antiheroes yawn with boredom. Their reactions to the music help to show how much they have become addicted to brutality. (Godard's thinking about music is revealed by the pianist's remark: "There are two kinds of music—the kind you listen to and the kind you don't. Mozart you listen to; serious modern music you don't." Amen to that.)

Two different but closely related musical styles are evident in *The Ladykillers*. A familiar recording of a classical string quartet serves as background for arch-criminal Alec Guinness and his gang as they plot a robbery. Posing as amateur musicians, they pretend to play their instruments to fool the landlady (Katie Johnson). The old woman's beatific smile as she listens to the music outside the door attests to her pleasure. While the music inside the house lends an amusing touch to the crooks' shenanigans, a light salon intermezzo follows a cheerful Katie Johnson on her daily rounds. It has always tickled my fancy to speculate on what her (and the audience's) response might have been if a Bartok string quartet had been substituted for the eighteenth-century piece. The image of Miss Johnson reacting to a contemporary work is both funny and ironic—a case where incongruity might be especially fitting.

Musical forms and styles used to evoke a period can be just as hackneyed as those setting a specific location. An early liturgical chant puts one in the Middle Ages. A harp, recorder, viola d'amore, or lute in a score captures a Renaissance flavor. A French minuet playing softly in the background conjures up the seventeenth or eighteenth century. A Viennese waltz acts as a musical backdrop for a nineteenth-century soirée. The songs "Dixie," "A Long, Long Way to Tipperary," and "Praise the Lord" identify the American Civil War, World War I, and World War II, respectively. And yet, properly spotted, a prosaic musical form or style can be effective. An example is Stanley Kubrick's choice of the "Blue Danube" to accompany the space-flight sequence in *2001: A Space Odyssey* (1968). Although many composers differ about the use of this old war-horse, and I agree that its evolvement to main-theme status is idiotic, I am also of the opinion that for this one episode, Kubrick's choice was a happy one. The waltz is Muzak—an endless flow of prerecorded, sentimental musical pap, heard in any air terminal the world over. Kubrick's point is made even more pronounced when the space traveler arrives at the space station and discovers that Conrad Hilton has living accommodations sewed up and Howard Johnson has the exclusive franchise for dining facilities.

A noteworthy sidelight is that originally both Alex North and English composer Frank Cordell were commissioned by Kubrick to write scores for *2001*. Their music was never used. Apparently Kubrick fell in love with his "scratch" track (demo records played while the film is in production) and ended up employing it instead. Considering the wide spectrum of style and musical approach represented by the two composers, one can be reasonably certain that enormous contrasting material was available and would have been infinitely superior and more appropriate for the film than what the audience finally heard. Kubrick's decision to use selective pieces from the late nineteenth- and twentieth-century concert repertoire—Strauss, Khachaturian, and Ligeti—sounds like what it is—a pastiche of odd musical bedfellows.[12] An impressive film like *2001* should have had an important composer and an original score. Having seen a portion of Alex North's music,* I am convinced that its use would have enhanced the film; if not North, then perhaps avant-gardist Ligeti from beginning to end. The nineteenth-century splashes of musical sentiment in *2001*, for the most part, reduce its emotional impact to that of romantic drama.

Moving in the other direction, a film-maker may skirt dangerously close to sabotaging a scene or an entire film with anachronistic music. Ulu Grosbard does this in *The Subject Was Roses* by inexplicably attaching sixties-type folk-rock to his film, which is set in the post-war forties. Another hazard is using music that fits stylistically but is out of aural focus, due to contemporary recording techniques. It is not specifically the choice of music that disturbs in *Land of the Pharaohs,* but the fact that what the audience hears on the sound track bears no relationship to the actual singing of the slaves as they build the Pyramids. Instead, we hear the incongruous sound of a well-rehearsed, over-100-voice, studio-recorded chorus, with everybody on pitch in unerring accuracy. In *King of Kings,* during the desert-walk scene, the audience is drenched in the sound of angel voices plus one-half the population of Cincinnatus—a choral rendition of elephantine proportions. Some may call it artistic license, but to me it is just another example of Hollywood exaggeration. The associations with the Holy Land of 2000 years ago are not just recalled but are made to seem part of the musical miracles of the Bible itself.

Yet anachronism in special contexts can produce intriguing results. In *Cyrano de Bergerac* (1950), Dimitri Tiomkin's stylistic idiom at the beginning of the film parallels the late seventeenth-century settings. Later, it assumes the characteristics of the eighteenth and nineteenth centuries and diverges during

*Music excerpt on page 330.

the battle scenes into the early twentieth century, incorporating some of the harshness of contemporary language. These stylistic disparities correspond with mood transitions. The music assumes romantic nineteenth-century elements to support the film's emotional framework. Other dramatic situations call for a stronger musical approach that gradually eliminates the harmonic basis and melodic contrapuntal design of the seventeenth century. Although Freud's life spanned parts of two centuries (1856–1939), Jerry Goldsmith's music for *Freud* expresses a tightly knit, contemporary harmonic texture and style that tells us something about the psychoanalyst's inner tensions and emotional turmoil. It also reveals, to the extent that music can, the nature of his work. In the preposterous science-fiction movie *Escape from the Planet of the Apes*, Goldsmith covers the musical landscape with rock music—in a complete departure from his earlier score for the original *Apes* film. The amplified rock sounds that greet the apes on their arrival on earth are probably not meant to be overtly funny; but, along with the screen image, the incongruous music (from the Apes' standpoint) reinforces the humor of many scenes and, paradoxically, the violence of others. On the other hand, perhaps the Apes feel right at home with rock music and it really is their bag—bona fide "monkey music." *The Sting* (1973) is a comedy that follows the activities of a couple of exuberant confidence men who operate out of the Chicago area in the mid-thirties. It has an old-fashioned, piano-rag, Scott Joplin score reminiscent of pre-World War I days. Nonetheless, the musical-comedy-patter style seems entirely appropriate and fits into the con-game atmosphere.

In his article for *Movie People*, Quincy Jones comments: "I've always wanted to see a juxtaposition of a Victorian setting with modern soul music. It would really crack me up to find, in the middle of a scene out of Dickens, James Brown screaming away as the town crier."[13] There is something to be said for this idea. Displacing time and style might tell us about a character's state of mind; especially if a story set in another century has relevance to our time, the music could be the common denominator. When Stanley Kubrick introduces "Try a Little Tenderness" for the scene of two planes refueling in midair at the beginning of *Dr. Strangelove*, he makes a harmless verbal joke in contrast to the deadly implications of the end sequence. In the climactic moment, as Vera Lynn sings "We'll Meet Again," the image of a nuclear explosion telescopes World War II into World War III and reminds the audience that despite the outwardly nostalgic and funny association of visual and voice, it is anything but amusing; indeed, one wants to cry more than to laugh. In Carl Foreman's *The Victors*, Frank Sinatra singing "Have Yourself a Merry Little Christmas" over the bodies of two dead soldiers conveys the far from subtle message. In a lighter vein is Charles Gross' music for Everett Aison's short film, *Post No Bills*. The composer utilizes variations on "My Country 'Tis of Thee" in different styles, arrangements, and tempi to accompany visuals of a man busily tearing down highway billboards that make the countryside an eyesore. The tongue-in-cheek potpourri includes a band rendition, a chorale, jazz, and rock. It is to the composer's credit that he is able to keep this obvious musical gag from becoming tiresome, so the impact of writing against the screen remains as strong and fresh at the end of the film as it is in the beginning.

Because of its potency in arousing associations, music is often utilized in films as a kind of affective punctuation to rapidly alter audience response. It can change excitement, gaiety, and comic-tragic inferences to sober reflection or genuine sadness in a matter of seconds. Thus the solemn brass-chord chorale intoning the death knell tells us soldier Wilson has died during the lull of battle action in *The Naked and the Dead*. But this powerful response-mechanism can be misused or abused by emotional exaggeration, needless repetition, or obvious musical devices. In *The Men*, Dimitri Tiomkin's overstated music constantly obtrudes, diluting the impact of many key dramatic moments and, in so doing, turns genuine feeling into maudlin sentimentality. Gerald Fried's heavily scored horror music for *Whatever Happened to Aunt Alice?* lacks contrast, nuance, and mystery. Its dramatic effects are overplayed from start to finish, including an agitated string figure whose repetition is supposedly illustrative of the killer's mad personality. Obvious musical devices tell the spectator what he should be feeling and what is happening or about to happen in Billie Holiday's story, *Lady Sings the Blues* (1972), starring Diana Ross. Following a lover's quarrel, when Billie injects heroin, Michel Legrand's incidental music surges up in a romantic swell, aimed, I suppose, at eliciting empathy, as well as informing anyone within earshot that love conquers all and a lover's reunion is imminent. In the scene between Sidney Greenstreet and Humphrey Bogart when they discuss the value of "the maltese falcon," the murky, wobbling music of Adolph Deutsch sneaks in under the dialogue to suggest overtly the gradual befogging of Bogart's mind, as if we didn't already know he has been drugged. The melodramatic rumblings and pitching movement of Philip Stainton's music during the ritualistic death-to-the-white-whale sequence in *Moby Dick* (1956) make the audience seasick and add another artificial element to a scene already as stilted and wooden as Captain Ahab's leg. In *Serpico* (1973), Mikis Theodorakis' use of Neapolitan street tunes to announce the imminent appearance of detective Serpico's Italian-immigrant parents is not just redundant; it is inane.

Up to the sixties, when film-makers had any doubts about the use of music in a scene, they rarely eliminated and often added. Robert Gessner criticizes the film version of Hemingway's *The Old Man and the Sea* (1957) in *The Moving Image*: "[Spencer Tracy] is not permitted the solitude of his rugged soul (à la Hemingway) as he sits day after day in his little boat on a greenish Caribbean Sea under a punishing sun. A hundred-piece orchestra, playing the noisy concoctions of Dimitri Tiomkin, must accompany him to be certain the audience is not lonely."[14] Drama is neither created nor sustained by the presence of this music; instead, it is thwarted. The symphonic upheaval interferes with Tracy's tragic characterization, which cries out for silence to evoke the necessary mood.

While the size of the orchestra has been substantially reduced today, the sound of film scores is still quite high because of a more amplified presence. We have replaced the number of musicians with a microphone-recording technique that gives a small ensemble ten to twenty times the volume of yesterday's larger symphonic group. Advanced microphone techniques have resulted in better balance that puts emphasis on certain instruments at particular

Woman of the Dunes. (Director: Hiroshi Teshigahara)

In *Woman of the Dunes,* the masked villagers, standing on top of the sand dunes shout, laugh and hurl insults at Eiji Okada and Kyoko Kishide below, urging them to perform sexual acts in the glare of the fire. The frenetic drive of the drum's rhythmic explosions is a musical sexual assault that accents the film's mood of terror and allegorical symbolism. (Contemporary Films/McGraw-Hill)

The Misfits. (Director: John Huston)

The mustang sequence in *The Misfits,* depicts Clark Gable attempting to subdue a wild stallion. The music (actually a ballet) kicks up a high degree of spectator excitement through its heroic, rhythmic energy.

To Kill A Mockingbird. (Director: Alan Pakula)

The attack on the children in *To Kill A Mockingbird*, is accompanied by violent nightmarish music that intensifies the viewer's feeling of fright. Courtesy of Universal Pictures.

Hour of the Wolf. (Director: Ingmar Bergman)

In *Hour of the Wolf*, Max von Sydow imagines himself killing a boy who stares at him. The accompanying electronic score sets up a rapid steady oscillation of beats that heightens the sense of hallucination.

Planet of the Apes. (Director: Franklin Schaffner)

As the astronauts sight the strange unearthly scarecrows in *Planet of the Apes,* high, exotic percussion sounds (metal twangs produced by stainless-steel mixing bowls) emit a wounded-bird shriek. The effect on the audience is spine-tingling. (Copyright © 1967, Apjac Productions, Inc. and 20th Century-Fox Film Corp. All rights reserved. Courtesy of Twentieth Century-Fox)

The Shop on Main Street. (Director: Jan Kadar)

While shopkeeper Josef Kroner argues with Ida Kaminska in this scene from *The Shop on Main Street,* introspective, dream-like music reflects a world of unreality inside the shop. In direct contrast, martial music and strident orders blare forth through loudspeakers outside on the street.

Images. (Director: Robert Altman)

In *Images*, abstract, contemporary "sound" language (percussion and Baschet sculptures) underline Susannah York's illusions and hallucinations, while romantic music (piano solo background) in the form of a tone poem accompanies her recitation of her children's story. (Copyright ©1972, Columbia Pictures. All rights reserved)

Images. (Director: Robert Altman)

Percussionist Stomu Yamashta performs composer John Williams' music on Baschet steel sculptures in *Images*. (Photo: Helene Adant. Permission granted by the photographer)

Seconds. (Director: John Frankenheimer)

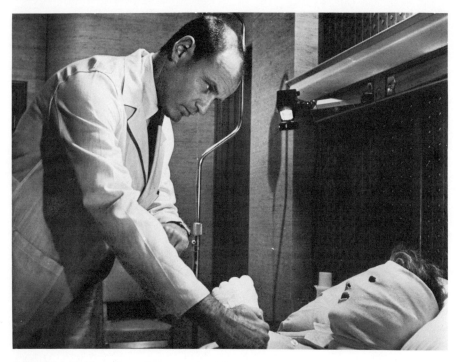

In *Seconds,* the blurred ritualistic sounds of the organ suggest the satanic atmosphere surrounding Rock Hudson's "transformation." (Copyright © 1965, Paramount Pictures Corporation, Joel Productions, Inc., Gibraltar Productions, Inc.)

Seconds. (Director: John Frankenheimer)

Nostalgic piano music reflects Rock Hudson's remembrances of his former life and his new "adult childhood" in *Seconds,* a contemporary Faustus tale. (Copyright © 1965, Paramount Pictures Corporation, Joel Productions, Inc., Gibraltar Productions, Inc.)

The Miracle Worker. (Director: Arthur Penn)

In the opening sequence of *The Miracle Worker*, Patty Duke as Helen Keller gropes her way through the yard, eventually becoming entangled in a maze of wash hanging from a clothesline. The lyricism of the music suggests both the loneliness of the little girl trying to find her way through exterior and interior darkness and the pain of her helpless mother.

Muriel. (Director: Alain Resnais)

In *Muriel*, bits and pieces of music reflect the emotions and feelings of the characters, almost speaking for them. (Courtesy Contemporary Films/McGraw-Hill)

Separate Tables. (Director: Delbert Mann)

In *Separate Tables,* the relationship between David Niven and Deborah Kerr is highlighted by lonely, gentle lyricism; more emotional, intense lyricism portrays the conflict between Burt Lancaster and Rita Hayworth.

This Sporting Life. (Director: Lindsay Anderson)

Even as Frank Machin (Richard Harris) proudly shows the check he has received for signing to play professional football to Mrs. Hammond (Rachel Roberts) in *This Sporting Life,* the music's tension-building chords and atonal language draw the spectator into their estranged personal lives; a relationship between a violent man searching for love and a widow unable to give any. (Courtesy, The Walter Reade Organization, Inc.)

Weekend. (Director: Jean-Luc Godard)

The long, funny highway traffic-jam sequence in *Weekend,* is scored for car horns creating a "Concerto for Automobile Horns." By cloaking the scene's tragic associations in comedy, the weekend of violence and death has even more impact. (Courtesy, Grove Press, Inc.)

Murder on the Orient Express. (Director: Sidney Lumet)

For *Murder on the Orient Express* (starring Albert Finney as Hercule Poirot) the waltz music serves as an "Invitation to the Dance," propelling the train down the track. (Copyright © 1974 by EMI Film Distributors Ltd.)

121

dramatic moments, so they can "speak through" the contextual flow. But the problem remains how to integrate the music and the drama in such a way as to avoid an excessive imbalance by drenching a scene in music that buries the image. In Visconti's *Ludwig* (1973), for example, the nonstop Wagner and Schumann sound track keeps the images in the background rather than in the foreground where they belong. The visuals simply can't compete. And, in Robert Wise's *Two People*, David Shire's music follows the young lovers everywhere, sometimes even obscuring the dialogue (which in this film may be a good idea). The assorted bowed and plucked strings totally submerge the visuals.

Diverse musical forms trigger various other associations of considerable scope. Banjo square-dance music effectively accompanies the madcap car ride at the beginning of Arthur Penn's *Bonnie and Clyde*. For the bicycle sequence in *Butch Cassidy and the Sundance Kid*, Burt Bacharach turns his song "Raindrops Keep Falling on my Head" into a charming, divertimento ballet on wheels for the two cavorting antiheroes. Georges Auric's more complicated choral effects for Cocteau's *Beauty and the Beast* represent the emotions of the Beast as he pores over Beauty's image in his magic mirror. In the Russian version of *War and Peace*, the waltz music in the ballroom-dance scene is carried over into subsequent shots of the battlefield, bringing the war into sharp focus by contrasting the screen violence with the happy times of peace. For *The Savage Eye* (1959), Leonard Rosenman's music accompanying the striptease is not run-of-the-mill bastardization. To understand its power and what the composer does for this scene, one must hear and compare its musical language with the cheap renditions invariably associated with burlesque numbers. Although it contains satirical elements such as a saucy piano figure, the music softens the provocative aspects of the strip act rather than accentuating its vulgarity. In jazz vernacular, the piece almost swings. The musical accompaniment modifies the suggestive movements of the burlesque queen as she slowly disrobes into a lyric ballet and removes some of the tawdry veneer that surrounds the striptease ritual without eliminating its paganism.* Stylistically related, although dissimilar in other ways, Paul Glass' nineteen-twenties cabaret-dance music for *Interregnum* is a jazzy personal statement that conveys through parody rather than exact duplication a remarkably accurate musical portrait of Germany.**

Two marches from the same historical period (the Roman Empire) but heard in dissimilar contexts mark Alex North's music for scenes in *Cleopatra* (1962) and *Spartacus*. As Cleopatra enters Rome, the composer's processional march—in which he simulates instruments known to have been in existence—combines high woodwinds and percussion color to triumphantly announce the momentous occasion. The music helps put on a spectacle that Cleopatra has cleverly devised in order to win acceptance from the Roman masses. In *Spartacus*, the death march features a tuba solo accompanying the four gladiators into the arena for their duel to the finish, a match put on to amuse the visiting Roman officials. Not only does the music introduce the

*Music excerpt on page 333.
**Music excerpt on page 335.

scene, but, more importantly, it acts as a dramatic contrast for a simultaneous scene in the viewing gallery where the women engage in chit-chat and the men plot political trickery. The sad, despairing music reflects the background violence and projects its own rhythm, which is not in tempo with the talk going on in the foreground. Hopelessness is made clear to the audience as the camera focuses on Kirk Douglas and his black opponent looking into each other's eyes while they await their turn to fight.

In Fritz Lang's *Hangmen Also Die*, when Heydrich lies dying in a hospital bed receiving a blood transfusion after the attempt on his life, Hanns Eisler uses strident, brutal music in a very high register to suggest a rat's death rather than tragic music that might denote a hero's passing. This kind of musical inventiveness says something more than is shown or even inferred on the screen. The scene itself is static, and the music supplies motion as counterpoint and contrast to visual rest. The use of a top-octave piano figure plus high pizzicatos in strings draws attention to the dripping of blood. The antithesis of Eisler's treatment is the use of the *Marcia Funebre* from Beethoven's Third Symphony for the death of Robert Forrest, a supposedly great American patriot, in *Keeper of the Flame* (1943). Using a familiar piece by a great master is indicative of the naive theory that great, tragic music goes with great, noble men. It works in this film, because it does not give away the story at the beginning. Forrest is actually an American Nazi, and the music maintains the illusion of a great loss, an important point in the movie. Other similar music would be dramatically effective, but it might not arouse the same strong responses associated with Beethoven's score.

A few years ago I happened to see Victor Trivas's early pacifist film *No Man's Land* (1931), also scored by Eisler. Music plays an extraordinary part in the mobilization scene, clarifying the transformation of simple, nonmilitant people into an army of savages. It is still vivid in my memory. In this episode, the music climbs to an exultant pitch. It is not just a background accompaniment to the screen portrayal, but it is the *essential* driving force. Were it not for the score, the scene's power and sociological inferences would be completely negated. Eisler writes about this sequence:

A German carpenter receives the mobilization order of 1914. He locks his tool cupboard, takes down his knapsack, and accompanied by his wife and children, crosses the street on his way to the barracks. A number of similar groups are shown. The atmosphere is melancholy; the pace is limp, unrhythmic. Music suggesting a military march is introduced quite softly. As it grows louder, the pace of the men becomes quicker, more rhythmic, more collectively unified. The women and children, too, assume a military bearing, and even the soldiers' mustaches begin to bristle. There follows a triumphant crescendo. Intoxicated by the music, the mobilized men, ready to kill and be killed, march into the barracks.[15]

This triumphant crescendo accentuates the druglike potency and barbaric sway music can wield. However, this musical amphetamine, in spite of its high, causes no viewer identification with patriotism, for Eisler's screaming instrumentation and unrestrained harmonic tonality tilt the musical center of gravity and threaten to send the music into utter frenzy. It has an unsettling effect on the audience.

In contrast is a scene from *Is Paris Burning?*, where the German high command in Paris has been instructed by Hitler to place dynamite charges at strategic landmarks and await final word to detonate. The music should play up the suspense and horror of this insane directive to destroy the most beautiful city in the world. Instead, Maurice Jarre writes a "military German march" as if to celebrate the occasion. He completely misreads the scene, providing stylistically incongruous music that arouses spurious emotions.

Elmer Bernstein's heavy, march-style music for *The Great Escape* (1963) has a militant spirit. It contrasts sharply with the lighter, ebullient "March of the Merrymen and Battle" from Eric Korngold's lusty score for the 1938 version of *The Adventures of Robin Hood.* Korngold's music, bursting with fun and fervor, captures the feeling of joy and pride of Robin Hood's band. Both of these examples differ markedly from the satirical Germanic march by Meyer Kupferman for the opening credits of the comedy *Goldstein* (1964).

The scene in Pskov at the end of *Alexander Nevsky* contains three dramatic sequences matched by three different pieces of music that are programmatically suggestive. As the Russian dead are brought into the city on carts following the battle with the German knights, Prokofiev introduces a dirge; when the German captives are led into the square, his music takes on an alien design punctuated by agitated, fluttery figures that imply hostility—a kind of musical hiss; and for Nevsky's entrance, accompanied by ringing bells and tumultuous shouts of welcome, he writes a triumphant, Russian hallelujah piece that is, in effect, a form of musical applause. While Prokofiev's music adds a sense of realism and continuity to the three interrelated scenes, the musical forms themselves are exceedingly simplistic and recognizable as old-fashioned signposts. They reinforce the general tone of the scenes but come dangerously close to being clichés. (In examining this music, however, one has to consider the political atmosphere in Russia in 1938, when *Alexander Nevsky* was produced. Elements of Old Russia and the rise of New Russian patriotism are expressed through Eisenstein's fusion of film and music into a single entity. With a prophetic third eye, the film forewarns of the Nazi invasion and the ensuing Russian resistance that would lead to Hitler's total defeat.)

Other associations are set off by the fugue, the most highly developed form of contrapuntal imitation. A theme stated by one part is successfully taken up by all participating parts (at the interval of a fifth), allowing each in turn to achieve a special prominence. This form is ideally suited to scenes involving a predominance of rhythmic movement, aggressiveness, and sudden dramatic twists. Or in those instances where related or disconnected scenes and activities are superimposed upon one another and the action is shared by several or more persons, the fugue can give dramatic force and support to such action. For these reasons, Dimitri Tiomkin introduces his "nose" motif as the subject for a fugue at the beginning of the fight scene in *Cyrano de Bergerac.* The strong, rhythmic syncopation of the dramatic line is marked by accents that closely parallel the thrusting motion of Cyrano's sword in the dueling sequence.

124

CYRANO DE BERGERAC (Fighting theme: Fugue).

It is the imitative nature of the fugue, with its heightened sense of climactic progression, that minimizes the apparent Mickeymousing effect. The audience sees the images and hears the busy excitement of the score without being aware of any audio-visual duplication. There are fugues for all seasons. Tiomkin's conservative musical language differs sharply from what another composer might do with a more contemporary theme. For example, William Walton's fugue for the Spitfire-construction sequence in *First of the Few* (1942) gives a sense of the urgency involved in putting the plane together. The three scenes following the opening sequence in *The Luck of Ginger Coffey* depict Ginger Coffey (Robert Shaw) looking for a job, and in each instance the building he enters is larger than the preceding one. Using a free fugue form and starting over with each excursion, composer Bernardo Segáll's music grows in orchestration and variation—he adds brass instruments to increase the size and volume—becoming more ponderous and intricate as Shaw confronts each new rejection. The composer matches visuals—larger buildings, bigger orchestras—as a dramatic device, but it is the fugue form and the resultant leaden sound that conveys the fatigue of Shaw's frustrating series of defeats. Had the composer wanted, he could have adopted a different tack for the sake of contrast by working against the cinematic context: as the buildings grew larger, the size and strength of the orchestra could have diminished until at the very end only a single, weak-voiced solo instrument was left to inform the audience that Ginger Coffey had failed again.

Virgil Thomson scores the exciting boy-fights-alligator scene in *Louisiana Story* with a fugue to convey its supercharged tension. The four-minute composition is one of Thomson's most dramatic and successful pieces on or off the sound track. The score is marked by a consistently high-level volume, strongly accented lines, interlocking crescendos, and a powerful, dynamic hammering of the short, two-bar theme made up of two quarter notes, followed by three eighth notes and finally a sixteenth triplet. The longest values come first and gradually get shorter and shorter; the entire musical idea is based on the diminished fifth interval. The fugue's thematic subject gives this music its unrelenting motor drive, and the composer's contrasting orchestral color—the transferring of the motif from one instrument to another

125

in a pyramidal progression—endows the score with an extraordinary kinetic energy and explosive force right up to the shattering climax.*

For the documentary *Of Earth and Fire,* directed by Wheaton Galentine for the Lenox China Company, I used a fugue to cover the scenes of glassblowing and ceramic making. The music's light, buoyant, but sharply marked rhythmic flow gives movement and continuity to the sequences depicting these intricate arts.

For Pare Lorentz's famous documentary, *The River* (1938), Virgil Thomson furnishes a spirited rendition of "There'll be a Hot Time in the Old Town Tonight." As with Charles Gross' variations on "My Country 'Tis of Thee," the composer first plays it straight; then, as the excitement of stripping the virgin American forests mounts and the camera focuses on shots of trees falling and of logs sliding down sluices and splashing into rivers, the music pulse quickens, rising in pitch and rhythmic tempo in variations on a theme whose associations are not apt to be missed. In *The Great Impostor* (1961), Tony Curtis stars in the authentic story of a man who successfully impersonated a number of people in such diverse professions as teacher and surgeon, among others. The theme-and-variations form strongly suggests itself. Henry Mancini uses a theme, all right, but his idea of variations is to orchestrate the tune in different ways for different scenes. He does not create imaginative elaborations that could develop the capacities of the tune. He requotes rather than invents. A more enterprising approach would not only have made the audience more aware of the impostor's amazing virtuosity but would have underscored his obsession.

The passacaglia—an old dance form that consists of variations written above an ostinato ground bass, usually of four measures—is used by Goldsmith in *Patton* to accompany the last German counterattack in the Ardennes. The heavy, repetitive bass figure articulates the enemy's despair, making the audience aware of the hopelessness of the undertaking.

In *Lilies of the Field,* when Sidney Poitier introduces an order of refugee German nuns to the chant response, he teaches them more than his music and the English language. He is, in fact, using the song "Amen" in a simple, revivalist style as a form of dialogue to establish a sympathetic relationship between himself and the sisters. And, in *Elmer Gantry,* André Previn's use of "Onward Christian Soldiers" suggests double meanings. The surface association of this Salvation Army musical identification tag is one that would be superficially connected with any American revivalist sect, while the deeper, psychological association arouses feelings of scorn and sarcasm toward the preacher.

Film and Music Relationships

If the shortest distance between two points is a straight line, the fastest emotional path to the heart is through the ear. While music is the most abstract of arts, its rhythmic, harmonic, and structural designs are readily expressible in mathematical terms. We have repeatedly noted that music has a

*Music excerpt on page 337.

126

strong physiological and emotional impact. Perhaps this is so because sound waves entering the ear hit the nervous system, ricochet, and echo through the body. (There has been a love affair between music and the medical profession for a long time, and many doctors, especially psychiatrists, display a remarkable affinity for music. In Joseph L. Mankiewicz's *People Will Talk* (1951), Cary Grant plays a physician who conducts a Doctor's Symphony in his spare time. This eccentricity is not at all far-fetched, for there are numerous amateur and semiprofessional symphony orchestras of this type throughout the world.)

In addition to its abstract elements, music is the one art form that means nothing on the printed page except to the musician. One can read a book or see a picture hanging on the wall, but without the services of a second artist—the performer or group of performers to make the written notes come alive—the sound is stilled and the composer's manuscript remains a dead if decorative piece of paper. In a sense the musical interpreter recreates the score after it has been composed. Up to a point, it is like a movie script that needs the director, actor, and camera's eye to give meaning to the narrative.

By being in the wrong place at the wrong time or with too much presence, music tilts the delicate balance that must be maintained between the blending of visual and aural images in order not to destroy the film's dramatic force. The problem of balance is further complicated by the fact that the organization and development of a piece of music—its organic makeup, impersonal linear flow, and balanced proportions of its formal elements—contrast sharply with the uncertain, often vague and desultory images of filmic reality, none of which can be expressed (as music can) in numerical symbols. Film and music are separate forms, and because they operate as distinct entities, they elicit separate stimuli. Each has an individual rhythmic pulse and structure that does not necessarily parallel the other's, and any attempts to devise an audio-visual correspondence in order to pinpoint areas of agreement (and disagreement) result in needless duplication. Simply stated, the audio components of rhythm, melody, harmony, orchestration, form, and style are only superficially related to visual components—that is, speed of movement, directional motion, scene or tangible object, environment, and image. Therefore, the interlacing of music to film is a matter of deft handling.

The films of Bergman, Kurasawa, Buñuel, and Rohmer are basically one-man shows. They exemplify the art form (verbal ideas, literature, and pictures) to which film aesthetically belongs. It is no surprise to find very little music in the works of these directors, and when it is employed, the music is usually of a literal or naturalistic kind. Bergman regards his films as compositions not unlike music compositions. To him adding the score is in effect piling music on music.[16] In Eric Rohmer's films *Ma Nuit Chez Maude* and *Claire's Knee*, the verbal exchange of ideas through excessive dialogue leaves little or no room for music. The *talk* is the score.

The basic concept of movement and rhythm for film and music is at best ambiguous. In music, movement is usually designated by the underlying metronomic time unit or, in another sense, by the overall breathing pattern of the total form, including the stop-and-go action of the intermediate musical links. In film, the concept of rhythmic movement is even more unclear and open to various interpretations. It can mean the measured tempo of people, places, and things or, from a different viewpoint, the rhythm resulting from the structure and relationships of the literary-pictorial elements. In some films, such as Rohmer's, for example, this movement is delineated by a dramatic technique that uses extensive dialogue with relatively few camera-eye variations; in other films, by short, episodic sequences connected only through content and meaning but often sharply contrasting with each other and without unity of structural elements.

Many contemporary film-makers do establish a metrical impulse through fast-cut editing techniques commensurate with a musical pulse, but its use is limited and for good reason. The cutting of sequence after sequence to a definitive musical beat would be self-defeating, not to mention the epitome of monotony. Brief episodes, short films cut to sharply defined musical accents, or parts of compositions incorporating movement synchronization can be dramatically effective, as can be seen in the experimental-film field as well as in some abstract art films, institutional documentaries, and animated pictures. Many abstract films consisting of geometric configurations and mathematically generated visual-rhythmic patterns are set to the composer's preconceived musical designs; in some instances, he constructs a musical pulse that blends its aural beats to the visual rhythms. As pointed out earlier, while many innovative abstract films have been scored by using aleatory music involving random and problematical results, little music of this type (as distinguished from planned improvisation) is utilized in dramatic feature films. Commercial interests are not apt to take a chance on the hoped-for associative responses of the audience to this kind of music.

In animated films the possibility of successfully establishing and coordinating a definitive and measurable rhythmic structure between music and film exists. This is so because the essence of animation *is* movement. In the animated cartoon, for example, music is the key to the story. At the same time, mutually articulated rhythmic patterns do not imply musical mimicry— slavish synchronization with the visual animation. There is a higher aesthetic quality of movement within a musical fabric, as exemplified by Gail Kubik's innovative and exciting score for *Gerald McBoing Boing* (1950, United Productions of America). The ten-minute cartoon is a noteworthy example of a successful, cooperative commercial-art venture in motion pictures. *Gerald McBoing Boing* is also one of the first entertainment cartoons to depart from the routine animated-score procedure. Until *McBoing Boing*, 99 percent of cartoons used such glorified super–sound effects as runs and stops, speed-ups and slow-downs, rising and falling scale passages, grunts, groans, squeaks, whistles, and explosions to follow the action as closely as a shadow trails an image. The music that did occasionally accompany all this noise generally fell into the "Stars and Stripes Forever" category or other similar absurdities.

Engaging Gail Kubik, a distinguished American concert-hall composer with experience in films, was an expression of confidence by the film-makers. Kubik was invited by the director to create the musical continuity from the script and a few colored-pencil sketches. Only after he had composed the score did the animators and narrator, ever mindful of the composer's tempo, rhythmic design, and overall musical-pictorial concept, start to work. Writing the music first gave Kubik a chance to make an independent contribution as an equal member of the film team rather than as an employee on the bottom rung of the creative ladder. The successful cooperation among director, narrator, animator, and composer is largely due to Kubik's understanding of the true function of music in films and a personal philosophy that takes the composing of a movie score as seriously as the writing of a symphony for the concert hall. This artistic consistency enables the composer to write his own sounds and maintain a stylistic rapport between his absolute and functional outputs, no matter how much his musical vocabulary is reduced or simplified for filmic purposes.

Gerald McBoing Boing is the story of a little boy who doesn't speak words; he makes sounds instead. Kubik's musical assignment was to characterize this unusual child, to depict the parents' bewilderment over their freak offspring, and to express the boy's loneliness and despair at his rejection by parents and classmates. Frederick W. Sternfeld writes with insight about the score and its cinematic relationships:

> Kubik's first job was to create the personality of Gerald in musical terms. This he did by identifying him, in rhythms and sonority, with the percussion group of the orchestra. Just as the speechless Gerald in the script is surrounded by *talking humans,* so the percussion group, with its incisive rhythms and few variations of pitch, is surrounded by the melody-carrying instruments of the orchestra. As a matter of fact, the whole score is basically a concerto for percussion and orchestra, just as Stravinsky's *Petrouchka* is a concerto for piano and orchestra, and neither the American cartoon nor the Russian ballet yield any of their dramatic punch to the music, although the music is foreground, rather than background, in both cases.[17]

The three opening percussive chords, followed by a sharply accented rhythmic motif, set the mood for the piece and introduce Gerald. These three chords parallel extraordinarily well the metrical pattern of the sounds Gerald emits, and at times the narrator relates the hero's "boing-boing-boing" in precisely the same rhythm as these three chords. Such deliberate timing, rarely used in the score, becomes immensely effective when executed.

The film's conclusion is a deliberate satire on the radio industry of the period and an equally thought-provoking comment on social behavior and Madison Avenue values. For when little Gerald's nonverbal suggestiveness on the air proves a big public hit, his sudden celebrityhood causes his parents and playmates to embrace and acclaim the former outcast. At this point, the composer takes his cue, and his ridicule of conventional radio music, with its inane fanfares and musical aridity, is deliciously irreverent.

What strikes me about Kubik's score, in addition to its dramatic validity and the marvelous use of contrasting material—from the lilting flute theme that accompanies Gerald to school to the plaintive oboe-viola music signifying his despair—is the simple directness with which he communicates his poignant musical elements in a visual context. Kubik makes his dramatic point from the very first bars and in the working out of his subsequent material manages a perfect integration of sight and sound. Sometimes the music is dominant; at other moments, subordinate, acting as accompaniment or counterpoint. There is not a single wasted motion in the entire score, from the opening phrase to the final peroration. The score has been performed many times in its concert-hall version.* In the cartoon, Gerald performs a sound-effects concerto with prominent percussive elements, whereas the Concert Suite is an outright percussion concerto.

Norman McLaren's music for his celebrated animated film *Neighbors* (1952) employs a different technique for its effects. The hard, staccato tone of his artificial score—produced by drawing or punching the sound track directly onto the film—is antiseptic and almost totally devoid of warmth. By eliminating sentiment from his brutal parable about friendly neighbors who become enemies, there is no watering down of the moral. The animated film *A Time To Live,* produced by students Sal Mallamo and Randy Brody at the School of Visual Arts' workshop, uses a human voice on microphone to create diverse sounds. This simulated percussion track was initially constructed like a piece of music: rhythmic sketches, prepared beforehand, set down patterns and beats. In inventing his own vocal effects, Brody followed his initial rhythmic design, adding echo chamber and reverberation. As a result, the sound track for this savage moral tale has a definitive musical pulse, with a startling, quasi-electronic, dry explosiveness that keeps the film free of any sentimentality.

The organic differences between music and film can be seen in various ways: for example, when contrasting motion is introduced to evoke meaningful associations. Bud Greenspan's documentary *The Glory of Their Times,* based on Lloyd Ritter's book and record album, centers around baseball players of the period between 1900 and 1920, the quiet time before the furious rush of technological progress made civilization dizzy from excessive speed and incessant sound. The rhythmic pace of the old silent-film footage showing the players cavorting on the diamond (plus their voices on the sound track) is intercut with old newspaper headlines of famous events. As the composer, I refused to score this film with the typical "Take Me Out to the Ball Game" variations or with a jazzed-up, frenetic beat. Because the footage represented a backward look in time, when things moved slowly, I chose to decelerate the tempo by using a basic movement half the speed of the fluttering silent figures on the screen. The opening theme—a harmonica solo recorded on echo chamber—projects a gossamer cobweb of sound that envelopes the flickering ghosts of the past with nostalgic sentiment.

This Sporting Life also consists of two opposing rhythmic pulses: the screen action is represented by violent movement and emotional outbursts, which are given accelerated motion through sudden cuts and flashbacks, while Roberto Gerhard's music is essentially slow in tempo. But during the football-field scene near the end of the film, the effect is reversed. The sequence begins with the camera focusing on Richard Harris on a hill away from the stadium. A howling-wind sound leads into savage football action taking place in a sea of mud and in slow motion. As they run, block, tackle, and exhibit all the brutal aspects of the game, the human behemoths literally

*Music excerpts on pages 338 and 340.

float in the air, almost becoming live sculptures on the screen. The physical mayhem, with all its hurt and anger, is doubly intensified by the music's undercurrent of suppressed violence: short, taut chords (with the wind sounds in the background), timpani glissandos, pointillistic woodwind figures, and a deep rumbling sound increase the tension by creating rhythmic sound waves that seem faster than the slow-motion visuals they accompany. Compare this kind of musical treatment with the usual jazz-propelled, upbeat score used in American films or on television for sport footage. Through its unique musical language, Gerhard's score expresses the game's built-in rage and viciousness and draws the audience into the hostile atmosphere of the players, enabling them to experience firsthand the noise and blood lust of the football mob.

An uninterrupted, perfectly balanced, rhythmic flow of visual-aural movement is present in Willard Van Dyke's famous documentary of the thirties, *The City*. During the highway-congestion sequence, with automobiles choking the road in a traffic jam not unlike today's monumental tie-ups, Aaron Copland's marvelous theme and lyric sweep makes a virtual ballet out of the cars streaming along bumper to bumper in a freewheeling parade of cinematic motion. The rhythmic projection of sight and sound is not just amusing but a clever way of communicating the irony of overcrowded mass-transit conditions brought about by man-made machines.

Music's basic constructional difference from the film can also determine the effectiveness of a score. Following a lead on their kidnapped son's whereabouts, James Stewart and Doris Day, in Alfred Hitchcock's *The Man Who Knew Too Much* (1956), find themselves outside a London church. Entering furtively, they try not to disturb the music, even making clumsy efforts to join in singing a hymn in order to keep their presence as inconspicuous as possible. The church is the setting for the scene's intrigue, but it is the organic makeup of the music and its remarkable ability to flow through a scene rather than any individual rhythmic, harmonic, or stylistic elements of the performed piece that increase the tension. This is especially noticeable when compared to other parts of the sequence. During the sermon, for example, the tension is actually attenuated. Of course, the unlikely prospect of encountering foul play in a place of worship also adds drama.

The old adage "music soothes the soul" takes on a different twist in those scenes of imminent danger or natural catastrophes where the band plays on to quiet the nerves of its audience and avert panic. In *A Night to Remember*—a film dealing with the tragic sinking of the *Titanic*—as the ship slowly and majestically sinks, the orchestra continues to play as a deterrent to passenger hysteria until the rescue ship arrives. Naturally, being a musician, I don't see that our duty extends this far, for in this film, as in the historical event, the orchestra indeed went down with the ship, gloriously playing to the end. In *San Francisco* (1936), the rumblings and screams in crescendo and fortissimo, with the shouting and the roar of collapsing brick walls, render the montage more realistic. Prior to the first rumble one hears a tune being played in the music hall. When the initial tremor occurs, the lively piano tinkling starkly contrasts with the shock, and as the earthquake grows, the music continues in an attempt to avert a stampede.

The organic differences between film and music can also contribute to a scene that stresses visual flow above dramatic action. In *Singin' in the Rain,* a musical of the early fifties set in the Roaring Twenties, Gene Kelly dances alone down a lamplit street followed by a long, tracking camera shot that catches his every movement. Insouciantly swinging his umbrella back and forth in the heavy rain—the camera angle absorbing the huge rain splashes of light on the dark pavement—he gracefully leaps into the street with an extraordinary sense of timing, splashing through the puddles until eventually, at the end of the sequence, he quiets down in mock caution as a passing cop gives him a curious, disbelieving stare. In the meantime, a charming little theme with the caressing touch of fresh raindrops accompanies Kelly's discrete yet scenically connected choreography and lightly meanders through the overall melodic flow. The exquisite blend of dance, color, and song make the entire divertimento ballet one continuous, fluid motion. In Kubrick's *2001,* when Keir Dullea is bouncing and pushing himself around the Jupiter spacecraft, sparring with the camera in motions that take him toward, away from, and through the cinematic lens in a series of distinct yet uninterrupted movements, he is accompanied by the Adagio from Khachaturian's *Gayne Ballet* suite. Moving along slowly, almost wistfully, the music's undeniable linear flow suggests to a remarkable degree the calm progress of the ship through the dark vastness of outer space.[18]

It is because film and music *do* differ in their organic construction, operation, and application that a piece of music takes on another dimension when combined with film. The effect of this cinematic coalescence can be quite different from hearing the music alone. Even a filmed concert without a scenario has dramatic overtones not present for a listener attending a concert. The camera zooming in on particular soloists during special moments of a performance gives the music and musicians a prominence and close-up dramatic presence that they would not necessarily have for anyone seated in the impersonal confines of a concert hall.[19] This can be seen clearly in films where the story calls for the performance of serious concert music within the structure of the plot—something accomplished either by borrowing extracts from the concert-hall repertoire or by composing special miniature works to fit the requirements of the film. Because it is not the usual function of films to be a visual adjunct to concert composition, these pieces can rarely be given a full-scale performance. In *Hangover Square,* by switching back and forth between the musicians onstage and the violent drama offstage, the camera heightens the delirium surrounding the piano-concerto premiere, already made austere by the onstage candelabra effects. In *The Man Who Knew Too Much,* Arthur Benjamin's *Storm Cloud Cantata* is introduced at the beginning over the title credits and plays a crucial role in the film's plot, becoming the focal point around which the finale is built. The imaginative use of the opening camera shot zeroing in slowly over the orchestra, descending on the percussion section, and finally focusing on the clashing cymbals that conclude the work—the cymbal impact fades into the sound of a bus traveling across North Africa—gives a sense of drama and tension to the music that one could not experience in the concert hall. It does more: the audience is conditioned to feel a heightened tension when the work is played again at the climax of the film, at the point when an assassin plans to synchronize his gunshot precisely with the cymbal clash. The camera movement is even more impressive during the final scene. As the killer's accomplice (obviously a musician) follows the score, the camera hits the manuscript; then close-ups the idle cymbals lying on a table near the percussionist; back again to the score; then to the percussionist picking up his cymbals in preparation for his entrance; and back again to the score, tracking the music page by page. All of this camera motion builds the tension and suspense to a maximum.

Benjamin's cantata is exactly the kind of conservative, English concert piece one would expect to find on a subscription symphony program. It was probably chosen because its climactic signpost, the cymbal clash, would be easy for the assassin to pinpoint. If, for example, the piece had been avant-garde, the complexity of the music could have made it difficult for the unmusical killer to spot his gun cue—although the strongly accented, discordant impacts of a contemporary work might have stimulated audience restlessness and given him more than one opportunity to fire his shot. On the other hand, the long cinematic and musical crescendo leading up to the explosive cymbal clash would have been destroyed, and with it all the mounting tension. In addition, I enjoyed seeing Bernard Herrmann's name on the marquee outside the concert hall, not to mention watching him conduct the cantata. It is one of the rare times a film composer has ever been visible to the public, and for this little inside joke one must thank Alfred Hitchcock.

The incorporation of concert pieces into numerous films is a hangover from early film days. Remember the old Bette Davis movie *Deception*, with Claude Rains as the composer, Paul Henreid, the cellist, and the music of Haydn, Beethoven, Chopin, and Korngold? The fictionalized lives of real composers, such as Franz Liszt's colorful story in *Song Without End*, encouraged false impressions about the entire act of composing serious music. These romantic dramas used standard, repertoire passages as dashes of emotional saccharine running the scale from the syrupy offensiveness of Chopin in *A Song to Remember* to the gross distortions of the many lives of Tchaikovsky and all the stops between for Bach, Beethoven, Paganini, Wagner, and others. To a music-loving purist the use of concert music in films of this type is offensive because the original mood and tone, organic to the composition's formal structure, are altered when combined with oversweetened narrative. Romantic, sentimental, or prosaic music becomes exaggerated when attached to films that stress an emotional overflow. David O. Selznick's *Intermezzo* (1939) and Bo Widerberg's *Elvira Madigan* (1967), an idyllic tragedy married to the Mozart Piano Concerto no. 21, are examples of the use of concert music as an integral part of what are essentially love stories. The music frequently instigates the action or acts as a transition between episodes.

The strategic placement of concert pieces in a dramatic context, however, can be effective. In Bergman's *Cries and Whispers* (1972), the short-lived reconciliation of the two sisters as they laugh, cry, and embrace, recalling happier, childhood times, is accompanied by a solo cello playing Bach. The music's sudden entrance and unexpected warmth reverses the dramatic mood and comes as a welcome relief amid the shrouded atmosphere surrounding the imminent death of the third sister. It is one of the few genuinely lyric moments in the film, and the cello's long singing line adds another, almost human voice to the scene's lyrical associations. In *Hour of the Wolf* (1968) the sound of the harpsichord (again Bach) draws Max von Sydow to the room in the castle, where an old woman takes off her hat and removes her face. The sustained flow of the music acts as both counterpoint and accompaniment, somewhat tempering the melodramatic surrealism. In this film that explores the creative artist, his work, and his relationship to society, Bergman uses extracts from Mozart's *The Magic Flute* as spiritual inspiration.

Fritz Lang's *M* (1931) has no music, but it has an expressive sound track. The murderer, played by Peter Lorre, is characterized by his whistling the theme from Grieg's *Peer Gynt* whenever his sadistic impulses compel him to pick up and kill little girls. The whistling is a dramatic device used by the director as the essential clue that eventually traps the killer. For it is a blind beggar selling balloons who hears and recognizes the whistled theme. By associating the tune with a balloon bought by the killer for one of his victims, the beggar identifies the murderer, leading to his capture. During the death sequence in *Phaedra* (1962), when Tony Perkins drives his car over a cliff, Bach accompanies him from the car radio. Dassin uses Bach for religious connotations—analogous to the ritualistic mythology that is the basis for the film's theme. Religious associations also play a part in Buñuel's *Viridiana* (1961), whose many controversial anti-Christian scenes and decadent social portraits are set to Handel's "Hallelujah Chorus" blaring from a phonograph. In *Vertigo* (1958), James Stewart, in a sanitorium after having suffered a nervous breakdown over Kim Novak's presumed death, asks that the recorded chamber music of Mozart being dispensed to him as music therapy be turned off because it makes him dizzy. Appearing after the mazelike visual pyrotechnics of the opening, which spins both the audience and Stewart around in its vortex amid Bernard Herrmann's swelling emotional-shock music, the lucid calmness of Mozart is a brief moment of respite in the film's constant, whirling motion and convoluted plot. Thus Stewart's response (comparable to the protagonists' responses in *The Ipcress File* and *Weekend*) helps reveal the depth of his obsession.

In *The Ladykillers*, the classical purity of the string quartet softens the crooks' absurdly sinister characters and imbues them with a warmhearted clumsiness that greatly assists in changing this black comedy of murder into a hilarious spoof. After all, how can hard-core criminals play or even pretend to play string quartets? In *Goldstein*, as a "doctor" ostensibly performs an abortion, his assistant goes around casually whistling Tchaikovsky in a hilarious scene reminiscent of a Laurel-and-Hardy routine.

Aside from functional considerations, my objections to the excessive practice of using concert pieces are fundamentally pragmatic and aesthetic. The marriage of a concert piece to a film is not an equal partnership. With this conjugal arrangement, the piece itself loses importance: only the music's ability to convey a mood or an association has any validity. As a result, the total blend becomes Bachlike or Chopinesque, and any number of pieces by these composers or others could be substituted without altering the effect one iota. Moreover, the shape, content, and complexity of the music—its interrelationship of parts and subtleties of nuance, balance, and detail—shrink or disappear altogether when interlocked with the visual image. A good portion of its concert-hall punch is lost.

Concert music is occasionally inserted into a film with comic results. *The Tall Blond Man With One Black Shoe* (1973), a French spoof on counterespionage, illustrates this point. The hero is a violinist selected at random by the secret service as a decoy. With his mistress (the harpist) and her husband (the timpanist), he totally disrupts a performance of a Mozart symphony in a tour de force worthy of the Marx brothers' antics in *A Night at the Opera*. Their love triangle is played out in a vaudevillian skit marked by missed cues, wrong entrances, broken strings, and complete chaos. Equally uproarious is the seduction scene, where the hero plays his own violin concerto for a blonde Mata Hari. The music is a scratchy, unattractive contemporary work. His performance elicits indifference from his bed partner and displeasure from her cohorts, who have bugged the apartment and watch the proceedings on closed-circuit television. Their reaction to the score, summed up in their request to "turn it down," expresses their obvious annoyance at having to listen to a piece of disagreeable modern music.

I am still waiting for the day when a contemporary concert piece will be used for those countless scenes where instant source material is needed. When an actor flips a radio dial or puts on a record, we hear pop regularly, classical occasionally, romantic always, but contemporary—never! In *Point Blank,* as Lee Marvin systematically destroys a car by running it back and forth against steel girders, he switches on the radio and the usual stereo pop pulp flows out. Watching this sequence, I thought of several alternatives: for contrast, the classic lines of Mozart being smashed to smithereens along with the car; or the complex harmonic texture of Stockhausen distintegrating into total splintered sound, dent by dent; or even a late Lukas Foss work where the composer takes Bach apart note by note, bumper by bumper.

Although it is not the function of the screen to be a visual aid to a concert piece, occasionally a situation demands this kind of treatment, as in *The Red Shoes* (1948). The music, the dominating factor in the film, floods the scenes with its color and song. While primarily wedded to the ballet choreography, it also establishes an atmosphere for the story and provides transitions between scenes. Professing to be an accurate inside look at the world of classical ballet, the film, to a great extent, is as counterfeit in its sentimental, romanticized narrative and theatrical artificiality as the previously mentioned ersatz biographies.

But there are some authentic portraits of composers and musicians captured on film—usually those still alive and capable of speaking for themselves. One such documentary, made for television, is Gene Searchinger's *Fantasy and Fugue* (1973), featuring keyboard artist Rosalyn Tureck, one of the great interpreters of Bach. What this nonfictionalized, noncommercial close-up conveys is how music dominates Rosalyn Tureck's entire life. Her total preoccupation is demonstrated in her mastery of Bach's intricacies. The camera's eye revolves around the music, but unlike *The Red Shoes*, in which concert repertoire also comes to the forefront, and in contrast to previously described instances where it remains in a supportive position, Searchinger accentuates music placement by toning down the cinematic structure. Although he follows his subject around—in a boat on the lake, in her home, walking in the garden, close-ups with her dog—to catch a feeling for her life-style, his camera movements and cutting are kept to an artistic minimum. He leaves the foreground stage to the music. The playing of the music created a special problem for the film-maker: what to put on the screen behind Bach and how to handle the subject in such a way as to avoid the usual pitfall of hands-face focalization. Searchinger solved this by tightly restraining the number and length of keyboard shots; he concentrated most of his attention on the judicious interpolation of selected out-of-doors nature footage: what is going on outside the house while the music is being performed inside. His intent is to depict life growing and moving around the artist as a background for her music rather than to identify Bach with pictorial light-and-shadow reflections. While the sound of Bach floods the total scene, the simple, lyrical imagery melodically contrasts with the more complex, contrapuntal musical flow. This portrait reveals a woman whose austerity and lack of warmth are the products of a Germanic musical mind just as clearly as it does a self-absorbed, dedicated artist. The film-maker has not attempted to smooth over the rough edges, and what meets the eye is an unsweetened image somewhat softened by the expressive power of the music.

If concert music loses its intrinsic force in the cinema, it is no surprise to discover that some music that is banal in its original state can still make effective background accompaniment. This is illustrated by Moras Hadjidakas' melody (hardly more than a Greek jingle) for *Never on Sunday* (1959) and the previously mentioned Karas theme for *The Third Man*. Despite aesthetic shortcomings, they do their job and set the film's mood as well as, perhaps better than, any music that might have been furnished by the great masters. In contrast to a song interlude heard in only one sequence, these theme tunes and other previously mentioned superior ones, both lyrical and dramatic, are repeated regularly throughout the picture. The associations they evoke are meant to complement or contrast with the mood of the total film. While the dramatic situations change, the theme itself remains essentially the same. It acts both as a melodic fragment, a conscience, coming back again and again in altered tempos and harmonic modulations at crucial moments, and as a chameleon, changing its color from one episode to another in order to adapt to scenes of diverse cinematic action.

In certain films, a theme tune appears in a different context to interlink disparate scenes. In *Fate Is the Hunter* (1964), Rod Taylor is an intrepid airplane pilot who constantly whistles the pop standard "Blue Moon" as a form of whistling in the dark to keep his spirits up. Rather than merely wending its way through the film or setting a mood, the song helps reveal Taylor's inner fears and anxieties in contrast to his cool outer demeanor. At the same time, the consistent recurrence of the tune establishes a sense of continuity. Dooley Wilson's piano rendition of "As Time Goes By" creates a nostalgic aura for *Casablanca* (1942) amid the danger and political intrigue of the unoccupied North African French territory during World War II and also melodically links dramatic episodes and symbolizes the destiny of the film's star-crossed lovers. But it does even more: in some ineffable way the tune projects Humphrey Bogart's live-for-today, tomorrow-may-never-come character.

The Wild One (1954) displays another kind of continuity. While the motorcycle gang congregates inside the café, fifties dance music issues from the jukebox. But as Marlon Brando moves outside, the sound follows him through the subsequent sequences. When he takes the waitress on a motorcycle ride through the countryside, the jukebox background music swells up into a full-scale sound track as a romantic accompaniment for the scene. What actually happens in this bridging of sequences is that the music continuing without a break smoothly shifts from ambient café sounds to incidental score.

Contemporary theme tunes—often just another version of Muzak—have been used abundantly to sustain a mood. John Huston's *Fat City* (1972) has the usual up-to-date rock ballad on top of the titles, contributed by Kris Kristofferson. The remainder of the score fills the screen as ubiquitous room tone, filtering into the ear the well-worn money rhythms of today's pop scene.[20] This is also evident in *They Only Kill Their Masters* (1972), where Perry Botkin, Jr.'s room-tone pop-dance beat accompanies the film's "in" dialogue with highly illustrative, "now" sounds.

Although Mickeymousing is usually associated with films of an earlier period, this technique still crops up in isolated instances. It can be found in Cornel Wilde's *The Naked Prey* (1966), in which the actor also stars. The movie is interesting musically because it involves cinematic motion and speed rhythms: Wilde runs almost continuously from beginning to end as he tries to elude the pursuing African-native hunters. His decision to use native music and instruments is commendable if predictable, but the musical application is a failure. An almost nonstop drumbeat with little or no variation dogs his movements through every inch of dramatic footage. When Wilde slows down from physical exhaustion, the drumbeat retards, and as he or the natives pick up the pace, the drumbeat quickens. Rather than heightening tension, the illustrative music tires out the audience long before Wilde's final physical collapse. Because there is so little rhythmic and instrumental contrast, the authentic African music is wasted and seems strangely antirhythmic and flat. Its endless drumbeats add nothing to a film dominated by visual movement and out-of-breath sequences. The best music in the film by far is the contrapuntal rhythm created by combining natural sounds made by insects, birds, animals, and hissing snakes.

In *Images,* Yamashta's percussion interjections frequently anticipate, announce, and comment on screen action and camera movement in an excessively illustrative way. In particular, when the heroine is violently thrown on a bed, the scene is accompanied by a violent, sound-amplified explosion, as if to make certain the viewer recognizes the obvious sexual urgency of the moment. And, at the end of *Tony Rome,* when Jill St. John walks away and bends over with her shapely derrière facing the camera, the jazzy gutteral mouthing is as blatant as a burlesque joke.

The slithering serpent music that slides up, down, and around as it accompanies a snake moving across the floor toward James Bond (Roger Moore) in *Live and Let Die* (1973) represents a current form of Mickeymousing related to the put-on. Part of the brassy, foreground film-music track that frequently inserts cues for no meaningful purpose, the musical put-on says nothing, does nothing (except to accentuate the obvious), and progresses nowhere. It is a kind of doodling that utilizes the latest galvanizing, pop-sound equipment to increase the amplification level while eliminating subtlety. It is essentially music to be consumed quickly with no aftertaste; its only lingering strain is its omnipresent title song. The put-on is not really a joke, nor is it satire or irony. Halfway between gag and serious, it is over before you are aware of it. There is no payoff. (This kind of scoring is not to be confused with the tongue-in-cheek use of silent-film-music footage to parody a scene.) The Bond films, exercises in tinker-toy idiocy, and other current spy diversions that feature black and/or white supermen are clearly put-ons. In these films nothing occurs except the passing of time. While the big-city sets seem real, the film's atmosphere is a sales-pitch con game with everything ludicrously exaggerated. The music gives the audience a free bandwagon ride from one sexual episode to another or from one violent sequence to the next. In truth, some film and concert music is merely put-on doodling, and the art of doodling—the writing and nature of unfinished sketches—has been raised in our time to the stature of serious creativity.

Continuity music, compared to personal dramatic statement, is perhaps the easiest kind to write. The composer has to tie up all the loose, dangling ends without betraying his, and the film's, thread markings—and to accomplish this without running afoul of Mickeymousing, although he may often sail close. He can best do this by exercising restraint: by holding down the tragic inferences and carefully measuring his musical solemnity; by keeping his romantic utterance from degenerating into sentimentality; and by using lyricism without allowing it to become overrich and sticky. It is a matter of balance and contrast, of being in the right place at the right moment with the right touch. An example of continuity music that helps bind together the film's characters marks Georges Delerue's score for Truffaut's *Jules and Jim* (1962). At the beginning the music is gay, but as the film progresses and the dramatic circumstances of the triangular love affair close in and engulf the three principals, the music assumes a songlike plaintiveness, tender and sad yet restrained. While Truffaut's lovers outwardly laugh and play, the music mirrors their inner feelings and helps the audience to understand the depth of emotional drainage wrought by their *ménage à trois*. The nostalgic lyricism that recalls the happy days of youth gradually changes to a mood of quiet somberness, marking the dark tones of tragedy. The expressive cinematic flow, with its light-and-shadow interplay reflective of gaiety and sadness, is subtly paralleled by Delerue's musical shading, which underscores the tone of the film yet has its own independent, fluid, and uninterrupted movement. An especially pointed binding together of characters occurs during the letter-writing montage between Catherine and Jim. As the camera switches back and forth between writing, receiving, reading, and replying, a low flute reiterates a back-and-forth lyrical phrase. Far from being illustrative, this is an inventive musical association, a sensitive nuance that flows behind both characters and acts as an emotional link between them.

For *Separate Tables* (1958), David Raksin's lyric composition flows expressively through scenes and creates a long, musical line of continuity. Underscoring specific dramatic moments without heavy illustration, the music's warmth floods the screen with compassion. The opening sequence at a summer resort hotel on the English coast is accompanied by an intimate and plaintive musical statement: an oboe sets the mood, quietly eavesdropping on the initial dialogue between Deborah Kerr (the timid spinster) and David Niven (the shy, phony major). Raksin's ability to interrelate various lyrical shadings to the cinematic context is extraordinary. For Niven and Kerr, the music is primarily lonely and gentle, taking care not to frighten them, and becoming tender during the scene at the end of the film when she confronts him with her knowledge of his indiscretions. For the young lovers and the domestic interludes in and around the hotel, the music is warm and glowing; and for the episodes between Burt Lancaster and Rita Hayworth, it is emotional—intensely so at times—and quite passionate during their moment of truth. Raksin treats Hayworth throughout the picture with a kind of restrained elegance befitting her movie role. The music's texture (winds and strings) imparts a sympathetic association to all the characters. Its lyric flow helps bind together into one family these people who sit at "separate tables." Musical continuity is also present in Friedhofer's score for *The Best Years of Our Lives* (1946); Newman's, for *A Letter to Three Wives* (1948); and Raksin's, for *The Bad and the Beautiful* (1952). Each film involves three central characters, whose integrated lives are followed separately and in connection with one another. The music functions as emotional glue, keeping disparate scenes—some in flashback—from falling apart and thereby maintaining an uninterrupted narrative flow. As with *Jules and Jim* and *Separate Tables,* the music is the stitching that binds the characters together.

Sometimes a single chord can be the thread that links people and places. The opening montage for Sidney Lumet's *Murder on the Orient Express* (1974) consists of twelve separate shots (filtered through a blue light) in sequence to introduce the characters and events important as clues for the subsequent solving of the train murder. Richard Bennett's music track reiterates the same, sharp chord with each changing episode. It serves to bind everyone together as intricate parts of the whole.

The way music can tilt the audience's emotional equilibrium is one of its most powerful applications. In *Wuthering Heights* (1939), Alfred Newman's "Cathy" theme is played in a strange, haunting, altered tempo when Lockwood is alone in the cobwebbed room once occupied by Heathcliff's bride. As the shutters bang and Cathy's ghost appears, Lockwood becomes terrified. Newman's ghostly music for this scene immeasurably increases the viewer's apprehension. There is a similar moment in *The Innocents.* During the scene between Deborah Kerr (the governess) and Flora (the little girl) on the water porch at the pond, the girl hums a children's song as a strange apparition—the ghost of Miss Jessel—appears across the water, standing transfixed as though caught in a photographic landscape. Simultaneously, Georges Auric introduces a distorted version of the tune as counterpoint to the humming. The effect is chilling.

An equally potent effect of music is its capacity to evoke memories.

Hoagy Carmichael's playing of "Among My Souvenirs" sets in motion nostalgic thoughts of homecoming in *The Best Years of Our Lives.* Snatches of "Souvenirs" run through the film, evoking warm remembrances; its melodic strains remind the returning war veterans of the meaningful things of life made dearer by the violence and death of war. Stronger, more dramatic memories are recalled in two related scenes: as Dana Andrews tosses back and forth in the throes of a nightmare, Hugo Friedhofer's restless music helps convey his battle fatigue and the agony he is suffering as he relives an air tragedy; and when he visits the flying fortress graveyard, where the old planes are to be broken up for scrap metal, and climbs into the bombardier's cabin, the music vividly recalls his wartime experiences, allowing the audience to share his memories.

Although the usual function of music is to be an aid to the development of the sequential screen action, as already indicated, it is most impressive and effective when it says something *not* shown on the screen. Music can suggest a state of mind or, as the case may be, what is hidden behind the naturalistic imagery. Film itself is not real: it depends on the fusion of its intellectual and emotional components to produce the appearance of being real. Admittedly, within the cinematic frame of reference, music is the most unnaturalistic element, and yet it is, frequently and paradoxically, the affective power of the musical statement that gives the film its semblance of reality. By entering directly into the film's plot, music adds a third dimension to the words and images. This intrusion alters the apparent visual associations—the naturalism of the images—causing the audience to resee, to perceive them differently. Jean Cocteau referred to this new musical dimension as dramatic counterpoint—making the music provoke the audience by seeming to let it run counter to the apparent mood of the action.[21] The music then creates what Leonard Rosenman has called a *suprareality,* from which the audience can glean new insights into the aspects of behavior and motivation that are not discernible through the cover of naturalism projected on the screen. Thus the actual image seen can also be perceived subjectively and interpretatively.

A striking illustration of this precept occurred in the film workshop of the School of Visual Arts in 1972–73. The problem concerned the scoring of an opening scene for a short film by Robert Goodrich. The image is a close shot in sharp detail of a large city—in this case, New York. The camera focuses on a man and follows his movements walking and crossing the streets in and out of the congested stream of traffic. He is seemingly oblivious to the moving vehicles, crowds, and hustle-bustle around him. Although nothing is revealed about the subject, his apparent lack of concern with his environment suggests a preoccupation with personal matters. But this is pure conjecture and not clearly delineated on the screen.

In scoring a scene like this, the composer has several choices: he can write the usual big-city music—strong, ostinato, rhythmic accompaniment, typical commercial tune, and lots of percussion; he can elect *not* to score the scene and allow the sound effects of horns, whistles, and other street noises to give the sequence a naturalistic atmosphere (these options, which are frequently combined, do absolutely nothing to stress, add to, or say anything new about what the eye and ear already perceive); or he can revert to the old literalistic approach by supplying composed and orchestrated big-city noises and substitute, in effect, one form of sound effects for another.

But this is an excellent opportunity for the composer to make a personal contribution, to write against the scene, by injecting his music into the plot in order to give the audience a totally different, keener perception of the image. What influences him to choose this inventive approach is the need to make a musical comment that adds something not on the screen; in this case, something that reflects the protagonist's true state of mind. For, in fact, he is on his way to rent a hotel room for the express purpose of committing suicide. In his despondency, he is unaware of the traffic or any other outside influences. He does not hear the city hubbub, nor does he actually see the people around him. The composer can help the audience recognize that something is amiss by blocking out all the things the protagonist does not see or hear: no traffic noises, no distracting big-city music, no sound effects—real or artificial. The musical solution might be to score this sequence with a solo instrument—flugelhorn or bassoon in a high register, for example—playing a long, plaintive line; or perhaps a group of solo instruments using extended phrases and disjunct intervals; or even one sustained chord, slightly tilted out of focus and hanging unresolved in midair, tipping the scales of emotional balance. Now it becomes clear that a city, for all its outward appearance of movement and activity, can be a lonely avenue of despair.

Hypothetical, but no less striking, are the possibilities open to a composer in this scene: it is the aftermath of a holocaust such as an Indian massacre or some other battlefield slaughter. Everything is deathly quiet—no movement, not even the rustling of a tree, is heard. As the audience views the desolation, the strident shock of brutal, explosive, fast music helps him to imagine what has happened, to reconstruct, with or without flashback action, the violence that has occurred. The contrast between the calm horror of the image and the loud, frenzied music arouses not sorrow or pity but anger and indignation at the monstrous waste of human life. Conversely, it is possible to score a scene of stark desolation with grim, slow-moving, deliberately painful music. In *Survival-1967*, for the scene in the desert following the short-lived tank battle between Israel and Egypt, I made no attempt to shock, but tried instead to horrify by emphasizing the madness and futility of modern warfare. The austerity and forceful tension of the musical language—played softly in slow motion—intensifies the sense of devastation portrayed by long, continuous lines of burned-out trucks, tanks, and equipment endlessly passing before the camera in a parade of death and destruction, even as it magnifies the ghostlike instruments of mechanized armies standing like half-buried castles in the sand.

There are other examples of composers entering into the plot of the film. In *This Sporting Life*, Frank Machin (Richard Harris) lies on a football field bleeding from an injury. As the camera pans in on his face, Gerhard's dissonant sound of pain fades into dance music during a crosscut to a lively celebration held in honor of the city football team. Outsider Machin, a violently aggressive miner who aspires to a place on the team, attempts to cut in on a dancing couple. The composer's taut, stretched-out, tension-building chords boldly intrude into the gay party scene and express Machin's inner rage better than words or images. Later, as he, Mrs. Hammond (Rachel Roberts), and her children play soccer in the park, the image is that of a seemingly happy family on an afternoon's holiday. In this situation, it would be easy for the composer to write light, airy music—perhaps a bouncy fugue—as simple accompaniment, playing the scene as it appears to be. But this would be redundant and would say nothing about what is really going on. Instead, Gerhard writes athematic but poignantly lyrical music consisting of a long, violin-solo line on top without vibrato, accompanied by shorter clarinet phrases and intermittent beats on a single drum. With this sparse, poetic, and essentially somber music, he draws the audience's attention away from the evident pastoral elements and into the estranged personal relationship between the violent man searching for love and the widow unable to give any. As the camera closes in on the widow watching the children and Machin splashing around in the pond, the music reflects her frame of mind and dramatizes the unresolved conflict between them, even as it contradicts the simplicity of the scene's action. Here is an example of music that fits into the scene's subconsciousness while at the same time accompanying it with deliberate detachment. But the unrelatedness of the music to the naturalistic setting is justified by the meaning of the whole, and the contrast evokes a special associative response that preserves the scene's structural unity.

A simpler, more direct intrusion takes place in *The Bad Seed* (1956), which is based on the Broadway play about a child killer. As the young girl (Patty McCormack) prepares to leave on a picnic where a boy is subsequently murdered, Alex North's music is not lighthearted; its subtle suggestion of evil reveals something about the girl that is not on the screen. Besides being used to substantiate the dramatic action, Henze's music for *Muriel* occasionally adopts a different tack. When Bernard (Hélène's stepson) displays a crude film showing soldiers in Algeria cavorting about, the music is harsh and jolting, in complete contradiction to the surface innocence of the image. And for good reason; the laughing soldiers have remorselessly murdered Muriel.

Leonard Rosenman's score for *The Savage Eye* contains several noteworthy sequences. In one scene, divorcée Barbara Baxley lies on a bed, alone and anxiety-ridden over past events in her life. At this point the music literally replaces dialogue—not an unwelcome relief, for the film's stream-of-consciousness narration is so pretentious that it destroys whatever potential the movie possessed. The scoring for chamber orchestra consists of a piano, ostinato figure two octaves apart, agitated solo-string passages, and a florid bass-clarinet design with crescendo and decrescendo dynamic markings—disjunct phrases and disconcerting sounds that mirror perfectly the heroine's perturbed mental state. There is no need for words. The music says it all; by interpreting in explicit emotional terms what the screen image can only imply, her personal distress is made poignantly clear to the audience.* Later the composer introduces a delightful touch: he has "Auld Lang Syne" performed in a slow, mournful, minor key over a New Year's Eve party. By nature sad and nostalgic, the traditional song for the New Year is first

---

*Music excerpt on page 341.

performed in an upbeat manner. Within its own melodic limitations it promotes a festive spirit and allows the audience to join in the excitement. But by slowing down the tempo and projecting a dirgelike somberness, a different light falls on the party celebrants, many of whom are trying desperately to have a good time. The screen depicts gaiety, but the music reflects sadness and the utter despondency of the heroine.

In scoring a sports-action scene, a composer has more than one option. He can write rhythmic music of driving, brutal force that emphasizes both the savage violence of football, boxing, wrestling, and other contact sports and the raucous, bloodthirsty participation of its spectators. The result will be an increased level of sound and excitement. Or he can alter the perspective by going against the screen image and creating, in the process, a new picture. For example, what happens if he substitutes a tinkling toy piano for pounding rhythmic shock? The entire cinematic perception of the image is now changed. Hammerlocks, gouging, blocking, tackling, hitting, and concussive impact take on an innocence that suggests "boys will be boys." An adult sport is now given infantile associations, and the effect is to de-emphasize the brutality. The childlike timbre of the toy piano calls attention to kids at play and sharply contradicts the violent action of high-priced athletes beating the hell out of each other for the amusement of paying customers.

It is Ron Goodwin's addition to the screen images in *Those Magnificent Men in Their Flying Machines* (1963) that relaxes the audience. The gay, spirited, cartoon style of his music recreates the atmosphere of a pre-World War I carnival. Frolicking along, never heavy-handed or ominous, it confirms the film's fairy-tale romanticism and reassures the viewer that it is all good, wholesome fun and that airplane crashes never involve fatalities. For how can anybody be seriously injured in a land where banjos twang, trombones slide, whistles whiz, and jostling, brassy instruments bump each other around in a merry gaggle of musical vaudeville? A different kind of fantasy occurs in *Far from the Madding Crowd*. In a panoramic country vista, Julie Christie and Terence Stamp make love. In the visual superimposition she imagines him as a charging battalion of cavalry, sweeping his saber around in flashy swordplay. Richard Rodney Bennett's music—a rhapsody based on an original English folk tune—alters the scenic naturalism and enables the audience to perceive the image interpretively.

Although it deals in violence, *Hard Contract* (1969) is really a nonviolent adventure story about a professional killer (James Coburn) who has conflicts about the nature of his job. Alex North's music is quietly romantic and, for the most part, understated as emotional accompaniment. Only occasionally does it rise above the dialogue. It is moody, sparse, and uncomplicated, giving no hint of evil. As a result, the score becomes, in a sense, an interpreter of Coburn's conscience.

For Caesar's assassination scene in *Cleopatra*, North attempts to interpret the killing through Cleopatra's eyes. His music probes beneath the surface to reflect *her* feelings, and triggers associations other than the obvious violence of the staged event. As Cleopatra watches, a fire divination depicts Caesar's assassination. North utilizes different musical elements to make the scene work. The bassoons growling in the low register paint a dark, brooding color and, together with the haunting sounds of the strings plus percussion sparks, work up to a shattering crescendo for the assassination moment. Pounding hysterically with anguish and shock, the music ends on a note of ineluctability (chimes and cymbals) that imparts a signal of resolution to what has occurred.*

For *Who's Afraid of Virginia Woolf?* North uses small touches of color supplied by strings, solo woodwinds, and occasionally a harpsichord. The plaintive score is held together from beginning to end by its lyricism. Gliding through the picture, it gently rocks the dialogue, which growls and shouts its own musical climax. There is great compatability between the words of Edward Albee and Alex North's music; you can't divorce one from the other. While action and dialogue snarl, bite, scream, and snap, North subtly interpolates little abrasive intrusions into his warm, lyrical flow. It is quite effective, almost like musical breathing marks between the bitter verbal exchanges.

To Kill A Mockingbird is a portrait of life, drama, and racism in a small Southern town. Elmer Bernstein projects the images as seen through the eyes and ears of the children. By creating a special perceptivity—the aforementioned suprareality—he enables the audience to see and comprehend the children's responses and behavior patterns in both their own and the adult environment. The score mirrors the children's warmth, curiosity, vibrancy, secret conspiracies, and freedom of spirit. It is full of surprises and changes of pace—alternately gay and moody, inhibited and extroverted, exactly as a child's world often is. When the children crawl on hands and knees toward the haunted house, their fear is made real by the music's nervous starts, stops, and intermittent breathing that rises and falls with the same dynamic shading as the children's own fast-slow heartbeats. The filtered, ghostlike sound scored for small groupings of solo instruments—piano, flute, clarinet, bassoon, and strings—is scary in just the way a child might hear it, as part of the strange nighttime sounds of the dark. Even when the adults intrude into their world, the music takes the children's side and remains part of their games, dreams, and fantasies. Sometimes the camera also views the scene from their vantage point, as in the final dramatic courtroom confrontation, which is shown sans music as it appears to the children peering down from the balcony at the proceedings unfolding below. Bernstein's entire score has an underlying tenderness and lyric expressiveness that keeps a sentimental film from becoming maudlin. The end, for example, would be ineffective without the music, which gives meaning and emotional nuance to the narrator's nostalgic recollections and helps the audience to reflect on their own childhood remembrances.

In *Men In War* (1957), during the scene when the soldiers are walking through the mined forest, Bernstein uses woodwinds to suggest the sound of birds instead of playing up the obvious danger. His approach is naturalistic, not suspenseful, and is designed to bring out ambient sound that is implicit rather than explicit. The viewer can see and feel the danger without it being reinforced. By taking a detached view and immersing the music into the

*Music excerpt on page 342.

scene's atmosphere, the composer emphasizes the tension more than if the music had directly followed the action.*

For the night scene in *The Desperate Hours* (1955), the image shows Frederic March outside his home, where his family is being held captive at gunpoint. He is trying to get inside but hopes to keep the police, who have surrounded the house, from disturbing the criminals and possibly incurring their wrath. The composer's problem is how to write night sounds to heighten the suspense of the visual action without resorting to the usual clichés associated with this kind of dramatic scene; in essence, to compose innovative, atypical music that still fulfills the cinematic functions. Gail Kubik's music is pointillistic. He uses fragmentation, silence, and sudden musical interjections coming from strange, unexpected sources at staggered moments to exaggerate the mystery and accentuate the tension. The score features diverse soloistic elements (woodwinds and brass interlaced with piano and various percussion colors), alternate staccato attacks and slurred phrasing, and sharply accented forte dynamics contrasted with piano markings. Anyone who examines the music for this cue will be struck by its inventiveness and sense of drama. Unfortunately, its novelty so disturbed the powers that be at that time that they deleted it from the film. Thus, the picture's climactic moment, which had been made visually exciting by an imaginative scoring approach, became just another prosaic suspense sequence. In a happy ending of sorts, Paramount Pictures, which produced the movie, later published the full score, entitled *Scenario for Orchestra*, under the aegis of its music corporation.**

In *Louisiana Story*, during the scene when the boy floats his boat under the low-hanging trees, Virgil Thomson's music quietly reflects the lapping water, gradually growing in wonderment and awe as the boy watches the incursion of modern civilization (in the form of an oil-drill rig) into his private world. Thomson's score creates an aura of allegorical fantasy more pertinent to director Robert Flaherty's intentions than would have been a realistic interpretation of life in the bayous. Natural sounds are used extensively in other places, but in this particular scene, Thomson says something extra.

Sometimes, intruding into the plot of the picture by using out-of-context music produces comedy, satire, or both. As the Russian people's army routs the German invaders in *Alexander Nevsky*, Prokofiev gives his folk theme a Mack Sennett-Keystone Kop treatment, perfectly mirroring the silent-film movie-music chase accompaniments. And, in so doing, he sardonically pokes fun at the Germans by portraying them as mechanized robots instead of iron-masked supermen.

In that popular staple of motion pictures, heavy-action war scenes, it is not always necessary or desirable to have music accompany violent slaughter. Sometimes realistic effects are quite enough. Again, in *Nevsky*, as the opposing armies rush headlong toward a collision, the rhythmic crescendo builds to a shattering climax. At the moment the forces collide, the music cuts off abruptly and is replaced by the sounds of steel blades on steel shields and

*Music excerpt on page 345.
**Music excerpt on page 346.

helmets, augmented by the exultant shouts of the combatants. Of course, in those days the sounds of war had a percussive clash and physical immediacy in its hand-to-hand fighting not associated with the deafening, long-range aural assault of modern warfare. Usually, in war footage, battle music merges with realistic sound effects into a bombastic hodgepodge of blurred noise. But other possibilities exist. A composer can treat the scene with music that isolates the loneliness of the fighting soldier in the midst of violent combat, emphasizing by contrast the sadness of human beings destroying each other. With humor—for example, in the previously mentioned singing of "We'll Meet Again" in *Dr. Strangelove*—he can stress the futility and utter stupidity of war. Or, he can use frightening and brutal music instead of actual sounds to tell the frightening, brutal story of cannons, rockets, jet planes, and bombs. This was my intent in scoring a two-minute attack sequence for *Survival-1967*. By taking a quick stab at victory, neither heroic nor predestined, I let the music's discordant, organized hysteria suggest the sudden devastation of war and its dehumanizing impact. Jerry Goldsmith's music for *Patton*, on the other hand, is a complex war characterization. Frequently lyrical, heroic, and grandiose, it helps delineate the joy and supreme confidence of a general who really loved the idea of doing battle.

The Sounds of Film Music
Because modern technology has opened up new avenues of experimentation in the science of sound, the entire subject of *sounds*—musical ones and others—is extremely relevant to the visual experience. Anyone who ever speaks with a film composer is immediately struck by how often he will remark, "I've found a new sound" or "It's an interesting sound." This new-sound preoccupation is not only musically directed but also covers the entire spectrum of sound effects and acoustics. While other composers outside the film medium also seek ingenious tonal combinations and colors, the film composer has a special pragmatic as well as aesthetic interest in them. Film composers compete for job assignments; they know that their adroitness in coming up with new sounds increases their market value and betters their chances of getting assignments. It also enables them to give a different shading, a new point of view, and a distinctive personal dressing to tired, old film situations—and this is what really counts. In addition, film music revolves around the *sound* of the music rather than the specific aesthetic value of the notes or formal structures that produce the sound. Of course, when someone does unearth a novel sound or instrument, for self-preservation everyone else incorporates it into his own musical design. In this way, jazz and rock were new sounds harnessed for motion pictures. Jazz flutes, walking basses, electric organs, electric guitars—with *wa-wah* and fuzz-tone attachments—percussion colors, ring modulators, and amplified effects established a new language; and the Moog Synthesizer with its available electronic combinations has further extended the pathways of discovery. Despite new instrumental resources, Hanns Eisler's comment is still valid: "The task is not to compose ordinary music for unusual instruments; it is more important to compose unusual music for ordinary instruments. This refers not only to the

structure of the music, but above all to the particular gift of 'inventing' in a specific instrumental sense."[22]

That sounds do not always make music is hardly relevant in films: they don't have to. It is their dramatic-visual aptness that matters. The composer who is skillful enough to integrate his musical sound effects into his conceptual flow so that they become real music displays his artistry. But this is an aesthetic by-product; for, as pointed out in Chapter 1, the craft of sound manipulation is commonplace today, in and out of films, and does not necessarily make one a composer. It can, however, produce an effective, if somewhat limited, background score to cinematic action. In short, some music sounds function as musical sound effects. They may or may not make music. Realistic sound effects primarily describe natural noises. These carry-overs from the early silent films and radio are the familiar doors slamming, horses' hooves, gunshots, chimes ringing, trains whistling, and brick walls collapsing. Depending on the imaginative resources of the director, they can, however, make a kind of music that turns the effects into an organized, created score.

In constructing the film's sound track, the film-maker can select from a multitude of combinations that include the human voice, natural and artificial sounds, electronic effects, and music. What will be effective varies from picture to picture and director to director. Of most importance is deciding what will be *excluded* from the sound track, for the final amalgamation is arrived at via the elimination process. In life we hear and see what our ear and eye discriminately perceive, out of either necessity or curiosity. The film's artificial sound track has the ability to filter out all the extraneous noises that interfere in everyday experience, which we turn off by concentrating on what we *want* to hear and see. And because the sound track is man-made, recorded sounds can either be distorted and overemphasized or sprinkled around like exquisite raindrops, whether or not they belong to the scene by nature. Usually sound effects are heard at excessive volume and length rather than underplayed. But the dynamic levels can be adjusted, analogous to musical gradations—extra soft, very soft, soft, moderately soft-loud, loud, very loud, as loud as possible. If utilized, these different tonal shadings can greatly contribute to the affective power of the total pictorial concept.

The use of sound effects as an extension of the cinematic possibilities paralleled the introduction of speech and the addition of music to the great film revolution. For an astute use of natural and/or artificial sounds can induce the same response as music. This counterform of film music was, and is today, in many instances more effective than composed scores and often more sophisticated, complex, and inventive. Two striking early illustrations are the caterwauling of the animals in *Trader Horn* (1931)—an active ingredient in the film's excitement—and Reuben Mamoulian's unidentifiable, convoluted sound—actually pre–musique concrète—for the transformation scene in *Dr. Jekyll and Mr. Hyde* (1931), where his own heartbeats are used in conjunction with artificially devised high-and-low frequencies and the reversed-time vibrations of gongs. The total effect on the viewer is one of unsettling disorientation.

From vintage films to recent output, directors have frequently relied on unusual, ambient sounds to reinforce the tension of their images. Some other noteworthy examples are: the scream dissolving into a train whistle in Alfred Hitchcock's *The Thirty-Nine Steps* (1935); "Marie," spoken in rhythmic meter inside Frederic March's head in the John Cromwell-William Menzies film *So Ends Our Night*; the unearthly, electronically generated whirling sound for the Martian spaceships in H. G. Wells' *War of the Worlds* (1953); the aforementioned vertiginous drone created for Orson Welles' *The Trial* (1962); the symbolistic fusion of an excruciating musical chord with the violent impact of Richard Harris' fist smashing a black-widow spider on the wall, nerve-shattering after an interval of silence in *This Sporting Life*; Charlton Heston's "scream" of shock delineated by the sudden hissing-sound intrusion of high-pressure water forcibly ejected through the open hatch in Franklin Schaffner's *Planet of the Apes*; the startling substitution of electronic "gunshots" for revolver firings in *Hour of the Wolf*; the disturbing, high-pitched whine of the electric moon beacon in *2001*; and the jet-plane noise that obliterates the telephone conversations on political machinations in Luis Buñuel's *The Discreet Charm of the Bourgeoisie* (1973). Especially effective is the penetrating terror of Takemitsu's electronic sound for the sand quakes in *Woman of the Dunes*. The sound-wave accompaniment for the sand cascading down the dunes vividly projects the sensation of being buried alive. The drifting sand and electronic waves inundate the house and the audience's ears, producing a kind of super-sand track. The last entrance of the sandstorm is treated naturalistically. The sudden injection of a realistic wind sound, heretofore electronically associated, is unexpected and striking.

While screening *Secret Ceremony* for a film-class workshop, a dramatic effect was inadvertently produced by running the projector at half speed during the priest's incantation in the opening church scene. The resulting slow-motion, artificial sound suggested the supernatural. Incredibly effective, it fit into the picture so perfectly that everyone assumed it was part of the score's planned sound.

Certain unidentifiable sound effects have been extraordinarily impressive in heightening the sense of drama. In the German film *The Bridge* (1960), during the final days of World War II when manpower was in short supply, a group of young German boys defend a strategic bridge crossing against the expected arrival of Allied troops. At the beginning of the scene a strange, indeterminate sound is quietly introduced. Slowly but resolutely growing in volume until it fills the screen with sound, it stretches suspense and nervous anticipation to the breaking point. At that moment a tank appears in the near distance and for the first time the audience realizes that the source of the sound is the armored vehicle's motor. At the start of the Czech film *The Fifth Horseman is Fear* (1966), everything is hazy and undefined. The viewer, not sure where he is, hears an odd, intoned sound effect. Gradually it becomes apparent that the scene is a depot used to collect the personal belongings of victims seized by the Nazi government. Shoes and other paraphernalia are piled high everywhere. Only at the end of the main titles, as the camera comes in for a close-up, does the audience discover that the sound effect emanates from a confiscated piano in the process of being tuned. *The Getaway* (1972) opens on deer grazing outside the walls of a penitentiary. A conspicuous but indistinguishable sound effect continues through the expositional sequences until it finally reveals itself as the hum of a machine-shop lathe being worked on by Steve McQueen. Despite the recognizable setting, the source of the sound is puzzling to the viewer and arouses curiosity. As *The Wild One* opens, the sound of motorcycles is heard softly in the distance. Growing louder and louder as the gang of riders approaches full screen, the sound of the motors explodes into a roar of revved-up engine noise. Here the sound is always identifiable but nonetheless impressive, for, added to the excitement stirred up by the oncoming cyclists in military formation, it creates an image of potential violence and destructive power.

Some films contain sequences "scored" by the director exclusively with sound effects. For the first section of *The Getaway*, Sam Peckinpah organizes naturalistic sounds to portray a sense of solitary confinement. Cell doors clanging, bolt latches slamming, chains clanking, shuffling feet on cement floors, machine-shop sounds, and human voices tell a story of lonely, frustrated lives. The emotionally debilitating prison routine is dramatically set against the omnipresent threat of riot and jailbreak. Added to the images, the natural sounds, themselves violent, convey the pent-up energy, smoldering hostility, and potential explosiveness that surround a place where men are forcibly caged. The sounds have an underlying rhythmic-dramatic charge that music cannot match or transmit. The sudden intrusion of Quincy Jones' music is almost anticlimactic. And yet, its entrance, while destroying the realistic setting established by the sound effects, serves to jolt the viewer back to the mundane world outside. For the long, funny, highway traffic-jam in *Weekend*, Jean-Luc Godard "composes" a "Concerto for Automobile Horns." The music track consists of the orchestral sound and rhythmic pulse of car horns. By ingeniously scoring the horn effects with sustained tones, short toots in diverse rhythmic patterns, and fast and slow blasts simultaneously sounded in contrasting counterpoint, Godard's percussion "concerto" evolves into a dissonant, unmercilessly hammering, avant-garde composition. But the scene's tragic associations are not lost; by cloaking them in situation comedy, his weekend of violence and death has even more impact. In *Muriel*, Resnais' sound effects provide an auxiliary, second music track. His abrupt cuts to loud, realistic sounds (ambulance sirens, city street noises) are jarring, and, in one scene, when the family is having dinner, the unexpected movement of pulling the curtain room dividers is a startling intrusion.

In *The Discreet Charm of the Bourgeoisie*, Buñuel eliminates all music and relies on limited sound effects—jet-plane noises, bells ringing, rain, thunder, and wind—to achieve his dramatic results. The question remains whether or not the addition of music would have helped the film. In the surrealistic dream sequences, for example, when Buñuel strips his characters of their urbane facade, music might have pointed up, through contrast, how his people really felt as opposed to how they acted. But this is conjecture, for the film manages to communicate its power while firmly anchored on nonmusical legs. In *The Man Upstairs* (1958), Don Chaffey also uses no music and depends for dramatic strength on the judicious placement of natural sounds—Big Ben striking, fire-engine bells, police cars, ambulances, ship and fog horns. And in *Pickpocket* (1959), Robert Bresson methodically records and orchestrates the noises of the city to give his film an extra dimension of sound resonance. During the over-thirty-minutes-long, detailed jewel-robbery sequence in *Rififi* (1955), Jules Dassin uses no sound whatsoever; he removes music, effects, and dialogue. Suspense and tension are sustained as the audience's eyes and ears focus on the action and the characters without any distraction. The scene works beautifully and is in large measure responsible for the film's international success.

In *Blow Up* (1967), Antonioni surrounds his fashion-photographer hero, David Hemmings, with the sights of mod London and the frenetic sounds of its rock beat. But it is the pantomimed tennis game sans ball and music at the end of the film that has the strongest *musical* impact. The stillness and color of the landscape, the dance movement of the players, the visible pendulous swing of spectators following the ball's imaginary flight, and the total silence create a kind of music pitched too high for the human ear to hear. At the very end, the rock over titles interrupts the scene. Fade-out—back to reality—picture is over.

Occasionally, an isolated musical or naturalistic sound adds a special touch to the screen image. The only sound in John Houseman's *Executive Suite* is an infrequent, churchlike clock chime that marks the passing of time; Humphrey Bogart's clicking of steel balls in his hands in *The Caine Mutiny* is a nervous quirk that signals his psychological disorder; and in *If*, Mick (Malcolm McDowell) shaves off his mustache, grown during his school vacation, to the ringing of school bells that announces the end to the time of his freedom and individuality. Bergman is especially fond of using a few sounds like a soft brushstroke on canvas. A single gong stroke precedes *Wild Strawberries*. The opening of *The Seventh Seal* is a series of hollow drumbeats separated by long intervals of silence. This musical sound of death combines with symbolistic images of waves breaking on shore; for *Cries and Whispers*, he employs sparse bell sounds wafting through the atmospheric opening sequence into the house, changing into the wall clock's ominous tones of impending death.

Sometimes, sound effects are integrated into the film and form, with the music, a part of the dramatic action. In *C Man* (1949), Gail Kubik uses the sound of airplane motors during the in-flight sequence as an ostinato, harmonic drone against a solo trumpet recorded several times, seconds apart. These staggered tracks create a strange, extra sound dimension that heightens the suspense. In *Louisiana Story*, the driving, rhythmic energy of the oil-drill rig contrasts with Virgil Thomson's lyric music. The natural sounds of modern machinery vibrate with power and come alive at night with the derrick lights dancing on the water, contributing a visual excitement to the sounds. They enhance the poetic beauty of the bayous as expressed through the composer's distinctive voice. Laslo Benedek's interpolation of motorcycle horns blasting into Leigh Stevens' pounding, rhythmic chords in *The Wild One* adds a defiant, rebellious note of anger and frustration, building the scene to a dramatic crescendo. While inside the house, in *Point Blank*, Lee Marvin becomes enveloped in a tidal wave of sound flowing from electric kitchen appliances and electronic equipment—stereo, radio, television. Everything in the house capable of making a sound is turned on and buries him and the audience in a flood of loud, disorganized noise that produces an intriguing musical piece à la John Cage.

On occasion, vocal tracks are added. In *The Innocents,* Georges Auric combines voice tracks—crying, laughing, humming, whispering, screaming—and natural sounds—wind, door closings, window rattlings. In one scene, while Deborah Kerr holds a candelabrum, the camera swirls around her from above. The overlapping voice tracks made up of distorted screams and hysterical laughter cascade on her head in mounting frenzy, enhanced by echo and reverberation, for a stunning, terrifying, dizzy effect. And in the final, tragic moments of Carol Reed's *Odd Man Out* (1947), when his girl friend finds political terrorist James Mason near the docks wounded and dying, William Alwyn's intensely emotional music combines with speech and the natural sounds of a ship's whistle, gunshots, and the chiming of a clock, which literally ticks away his hours of agony. This climactic scene still remains a powerful example of total sound-track integration. In the *Exorcist* (1973), director William Friedkin uses an electronic sound track made up of vari-pitched voices rerecorded at slower speeds, animal noises, and musical effects. The organized sound is an integral part of this frightening tale of a young girl possessed.

Three celebrated examples show how intriguing musical effects often add dramatic stress to the cinematic action. In the World War II film *Desert Victory,* William Alwyn scores the scene prior to zero hour for the British forces' nighttime assault on General Rommel's Afrika Corps with ingenious simplicity. Camera shots of military equipment poised for action and close-ups of the men's faces reveal the tension of silent vigil as the officers' eyes remain riveted to their synchronized watches. Alwyn's music consists of a single, persistent note ascending octave by octave, giving the sensation of stretched nerves that finally snap when the barrage breaks loose in wild, fortissimal explosion.

During the love scene in *Woman of the Dunes,* Takemitsu's sound of passion is a high-pitched, electronic tone that frequently wavers; sliding up and down, its increasing-decreasing decibel levels subtly suggest emotional ardor. In this context, it is the epitome of sensuality. What is interesting about this musical effect is that behind different imagery the sound could easily transmit terror, evil, or even horror.

Impressive illustrations of inventive and exciting musical sound effects are part of Goldsmith's score for *Planet of the Apes.* One is a gong scraped with a triangle beater plus horns blowing air through inverted mouthpieces on echo and reverb, which sound like sand swooshed into a bucket. The effect is introduced at the beginning of the film, enters later when the marooned astronauts cross the desert in the forbidden zone, and again at the end when it coincides with the waves breaking on the shore. Another is the previously described use of tuned mixing bowls for the frightening post-scarecrow sequence. These effects, along with timbres of rarely used instruments—ram's horn, friction drum, bass slide whistle—and avant-garde techniques such as pizzicato and col legno (tapping the wood of the bow on the strings), reverberation, and the clicking of woodwind keys on microphone increase the sound scope of the film. The score also features fast-changing tempos and alternates extremely high, shrill pitches with low grunts and soft resonances. The sounding of a pristine tonic chord to denote the triumph of Man, when Charlton Heston says, right after his capture, "Take your filthy paws off me, you damned dirty ape," is a touch of comic relief that invariably prompts the audience to applaud. The sound reproduction of the music track in the theater is extraordinarily high, and its maintenance behind dialogue contradicts the heretofore golden rule that music must always be toned down in order to hear the words. But what is really striking and something that rarely happens is that Goldsmith's sounds make music. The composer has skillfully integrated them into the musical flow as a logical extension of his formal structure, not as detached effects that attract attention out of proportion to their importance. The music enters the narrative and supplies that extra dimension of supreality, in this case of other-world echoes of sound—whatever they may be.

Despite recording techniques that give sounds an electronic presence, the musical effects in this film are produced by normal instruments without benefit of electronic devices or the Moog Synthesizer. It is *not* electronic music.

Assorted musical sounds frequently repeated throughout a film serve a variety of dramatic purposes, both positive and negative. Ennio Morricone, whose alternate lush musical statements and bizarre orchestrations created a melodic style for many Italian films of the sixties, especially Italian Westerns, scores *Without Apparent Motive* (1971) with a repetitious, melodic tune fragment embellished by a distorted effect that aims to heighten tension and add to the mystery plot. It does neither. The music track is essentially a long-playing record with the needle stuck in the groove, incessantly intoning the same melodic passage. Incredibly monotonous and tiring, whatever contribution it makes to the film's mood or continuity is accomplished at the audience's expense. In *Klute*, (1971) Michael Small repeatedly relies on a short, pungent chord to attach a sinister quality to the psychologically disturbed killer. Also serving to tighten the chords of suspense, the repetition here is less objectionable and tiring because it is one chord hanging in midair, making its point quickly and dropping out of sight. In addition, it acts as a bridge. Similarly, in *The Last of Sheila*, (1973) Billy Goldenberg employs abbreviated chord punctuations primarily to span dramatic sequences and help move the audience along through the narrative maze.

For Claude Chabrol's *Le Boucher* (1969), Pierre Jansen's imaginative score opens with a soft, chimelike, out-of-kilter bell sound. The subtly distorted phrase floats and vibrates to hint that the image of a peaceful French village is not that peaceful. The sound, entering the plot and repeated at various times in dramatic and tranquil circumstances, is not offensive, probably because it is light and soft rather than heavy or obvious. The composer's writing against the images is analogous to Chabrol's cinematic concept. The director has a penchant for juxtaposing placid scenes with horrifying intrusions, such as a peaceful moment in a pastoral setting that is suddenly violated by the discovery of murder.

In contrast, the scoring—if you can call it that—for *The French Connection* is decidedly gauche. I suppose Don Ellis' quarter-tone meanderings are his idea of how to musically connect the dope theme with the film's sinister overtones. But they are naive, repetitious, and, after the initial impact, tiresome.

Rock music, courtesy of the youth pop culture, has itself been the subject of films, such as *Woodstock, Gimme Shelter,* and *Let the Good Times Roll.* With elements of folk and jazz, it has also been used to score numerous other films, such as *A Hard Day's Night, Easy Rider, Shaft, Superfly,* and *Pat Garrett and Billy the Kid* (starring Bob Dylan and Kris Kristofferson). In *O Lucky Man!* Lindsay Anderson employs rock music in an innovative and adventuresome way. The music, written and performed by British rock musician Alan Price, functions like a Greek chorus to explain and connect the screen episodes of the Candide-like story. At crucial moments, Anderson cuts from the narrative to a rehearsal hall, where Price's rock group performs songs that reflect what is happening to the luckless hero (Malcolm McDowell). Eventually, McDowell joins Price's rock group, which then enters the film action. After a series of misadventures, including a prison sentence for a crooked business deal, our hero becomes a movie star, and the film ends with everybody rocking and rolling on the set during the final day of shooting.

The propaganda message of this simple-minded, anti-establishment film is that no matter what we do or how we attempt to get ahead in life, it's all a question of luck as to whether we end up at the bottom or the top of the ladder. Price's title song makes this point immediately and does so with a gay, cheerful, witty style. His music is honest and sparkling. The rock beat is not harsh, but the songs have a rhythmic vitality and immediacy that is the basic appeal of this kind of pop music. Price performs the title song behind the opening credits and contributes a second version at the end of the film. *O Lucky Man!* is not a musical—the cast neither sings nor dances—but it is the music and not the dramatic action that binds the film together, gives it a sense of direction, and conveys its philosophy better and faster than Anderson could manage in nearly three hours of belabored effort.

Rock music depends on the inspiration of the performer, and its creation cannot be separated from its performance. Each rock piece has its own unique aural experience as interpreted by each group or soloist, as is clearly demonstrated in Anderson's film. The nature of rock—its performer syndrome—has directly influenced many film producers and directors, and with the successful merger of rock and film in *O Lucky Man!,* we can expect future duplications.

I think it was Beethoven who once said that there is music in a pause. This is true. The ear seems to sustain a sound longer than it can actually detect aural vibrations; it briefly stores the sound waves in a memory chamber. The exploration of sound can thus lead to silence, and this paradoxical idea is applicable to both film and concert music. Pauses, rests, and moments of silence can be as effective as sound if objectively planned as part of the whole. Of course, silence is not always golden. If silences, dead moments, and taut seconds are scored with arbitrary or simple-minded heterogeneous music, the result is valueless. This kind of scoring cannot camouflage a poverty of ideas or lack of genuine imagination.

Music is not a free-flowing, emotional faucet to be turned on and poured over a scene like running water. The effectiveness of sound and/or music is intensified when contrasted with no sound; loudness is only relative to softness. Contrast in all forms and degrees sustains interest. It is the absence of music that makes its presence more powerful. A perfect illustration is *Hour of the Wolf*. In the first half of the film there is little or no music—a few natural sounds and voices form a kind of vocal collage. When the electronic score does appear, its dramatic entry is stunning and its presence electrifying. I believe that it is not underscoring (emphasis) but underscored (de-emphasis) that is the crux of the matter. Film music's greatest asset is its economy of means. Just a few bars lasting only a few seconds but aptly fitted to precise cinematic footage—for example, the opening of *Planet of the Apes*—may express as much as the entire slow movement of a concert piece. In the concert hall, Webern's compositions—short, succinct, totally organized and developed works—prove the point that length is not necessarily indicative of or a prerequisite for strength. Sometimes a touch, a brush or soft stroke, a short phrase or solo line, a shade of color or nuance, a brief fermata, a subliminal sound, a suspended tone, or a quiet passage that fits the action or wends its independent way through or against the image can do wonders for a film.

In *Wait Until Dark* (1967), actor Alan Arkin, who plays a psychopathic killer, enters a room where Audrey Hepburn is alone. She is blind but capable of detecting the presence of an uninvited stranger. Henry Mancini's music track at this point contains one isolated note played on a piano, immediately followed by the same note produced out of tune. The tonal distortion convincingly delineates Arkin's disturbed psychoneurotic personality; it does this by an economy of means infinitely superior to the illustrative sounds and ominous musical announcements usually associated with this type of dramatic scene. For the opening of *The Cat People* (a film made expressly for television), Leonard Rosenman sustains a taut chord for an inordinate length of time. The shock of his initial statement jolts the nerves, gradually increasing the tension and suspense by stretching out the musical tones like a rubber band. The chord has a bulldog tenacity, relentless and unrelieved, and the effect creates an aura that helps launch the film on its unearthly course.

And yet there is always room for thunder and lightning, sparkle and shimmer, trumpet call and lyric sweep.

Economy of means implies modesty and restraint, not taking film music too seriously—at least, not in the same way as autonomous music—but at the same time seriously enough. In composing for films I believe a composer actually expends about one-tenth of his creative capacity. This does not mean that the composer refuses to take his composition seriously or that writing film music is a breeze but refers rather to the ratio of creative energy expended to total capacity available. The film-music composer's prime asset is his versatility, a term frequently disparaged in concert-music circles as a jack-of-all-trades but master of none. This pejorative attitude toward someone capable of stylistic flexibility is snobbish and grossly unfair. Versatility does not mean an abandonment of individuality. There is such a thing as style.

Music's role is not meant to be an extra in the cinematic casting of parts, but rather to be a meaningful supporting player. If the real melody is the visual image, the composer represents the bass line. When the film image occupies the foreground, expressing salient ideas, persistently conspicuous forefront music will only blur and counteract these ideas, neutralizing their dramatic power and hindering motivation. While parallel motion between image and music is not desired, there must be some area of correspondence, however indirect. Each picture should determine its accompanying music or vice versa. No matter what kind of music is written, it must fit into the given scenic frame of reference, even if the music contradicts the image by going against it. A structural unity must be preserved.

In *Murder on the Orient Express,* for example, Richard Bennett deliberately rejects playing the obvious—in this case, the train moving from a standstill position to full-speed ahead. Instead, he starts the train wheels in motion by composing a symphonic waltz of elegance and style. Here, the music serves as an "Invitation to the Dance," propelling the Orient Express down the track with a lyrical sweep that anticipates high adventure, setting the stage for the charade that ensues.

Nina Rota achieves total integration of his scores into Fellini's *La Dolce Vita* (1959) and *8½* (1963) by playing against the picture and not piling similar textures on top of one another. In *8½*, for example, the stylistic difference between Fellini's abstract images and Rota's romantic language enriches the picture: the music supplies ingredients missing from the multilevel cinematic context. Rota's score gives a kind of formal structure and continuity to a film whose brilliant staging and shooting techniques often seem undisciplined and desultory. Many of *8½*'s cues stand on their own as pieces of music (divertimenti) that can be performed apart from the screen: in particular, the opening carnival music, "La Passerella di Otto e Mezzo," and the charming "Carlotta's Galop," which is a marvelous parody of Khachaturian's *Sabre Dance.*

To recap, time is of the essence in films. Visual and dramatic elements must be summed up quickly, without any effort wasted in musical verbiage. Climaxes, for example, must sometimes be precipitated with a minimum of preparation and few or no crescendos. Musically, this presents a problem, for there is considerable difference between a simple forte or a very loud passage and one that has the effect of a climax, the latter usually resulting from a gradual building-up process. In the same manner, concluding passages must be dispatched with celerity, bringing cadences to a sharp conclusion minus any preceding musical elaboration. The character of endings must be found in the structure of the music itself, in the inherent nature of thematic material that lends itself to immediate crystallization. Of further significance is the fact that modesty in design and total compositional approach go hand in hand with the knowledge that film music is really not listened to carefully. Most people associate the music with the picture to the extent that if they like the picture, they probably will feel the same about the score. And, if they don't like the picture, they will probably be apathetic toward the music. This attitude carries over to directors and producers, who, if their film is successful, consider the composer partly responsible, even though success may have been attained in spite of the score. Conversely, the director or producer never forgets for one minute that a particular composer was part of an unsuccessful venture or outright dud—and, in some cases, resents the good reviews he receives in the midst of generally adverse criticism of the film.

People may listen inattentively, but correctly conceived film music can still fulfill its function and assist the viewer in grasping the desired associations without detours or emotional roadblocks. The composer's task is both challenging and frustrating and, in some ways, almost impossible. He is asked to produce something unusual, offbeat, and unique; to make sense; to justify the music being there in the first place. And at the same time, he is expected to compose music that can be perceived by way of a sidelong glance that makes its point and fades out of sight. Although everyone connected with a film enterprise—producer, director, scriptwriter, cameraman, actor, and editor—faces limitations and technical difficulties, the composer's world is distinct and apart from the rest of the film team. He labors in a special domain, with his own vast resources and potentialities of form, style, vocabulary, and associations; and how effectively he uses the musical elements he has selected defies precise measurement or evaluation in concrete terms of time, length, volume, or sound.

Film music should scintillate, regardless of style or duration; when possible, it should surprise by framing the unexpected. It must stay abreast of the cinematic flow and maintain its position without lagging. Unfortunately, by displaying a tendency to evanesce as soon as it appears, a film score almost renounces the claim that it exists. And yet the blatancy of many of today's music tracks is notorious. The music is there too much, and this is its cardinal offense. The composer must find the delicate balance between presence and reticence, simplicity and complexity, warm and cold musical elements, the overtoned in relation to the undertoned; between the freedom to create inventively and the restrictive chains imposed by the script and its visual interpretation. All this he has to accomplish even as the music moves closer to the screen image and at other moments backs away from it.

1. Hanns Eisler discusses this same point in his book *Composing for the Films* (New York: Oxford University Press, 1947), p. 50.

2. William Johnson, "Face the Music," *Film Quarterly*, Vol. XXII, No. 4 (Summer, 1969), p. 3.

3. Pauline Kael, *Kiss Kiss Bang Bang* (Boston: Little, Brown, & Company, 1968), p. 261.

4. The multiple-stereo sound track for this film was the most complex ever conceived. At the world premiere more than 150 speakers were placed in every part of the theater, including the floors.

5. In general, television suffers from the same disease as feature films. Its situation comedies, action shows, and specially produced films duplicate themselves to an obnoxious degree. The same holds true for its jazz scores or other music, which is used up faster than it can be produced. As a result, each series has its own library of reusable cues, repeated from week to week behind different dramatic situations. In this capacity it welcomes the viewer as an old friend with a familiar voice. And yet, paradoxically, more controversial sounds come through the TV speaker than one might expect to hear, especially in proportion to the quality of the dramas.

6. Lan Adomian, "Viva Zapata," *Film Music Notes* (March–April, 1952), p. 7.

7. Honegger also used the Ondes Martenot in his striking score for Bartosch's animated film, *L'Idée.*

8. Excerpts from a letter to critic Charles Boyer ("Page Cook"), published in *Films in Review* (October, 1971).

9. Johnny Mandel, original motion-picture sound track, *The Sandpiper,* music composed and conducted by Johnny Mandel (MGM, 1965).

10. William Johnson, "Face the Music," *Film Quarterly,* Vol. XXII, No. 4 (Summer, 1969), p. 5.

11. Susan Sontag, *Against Interpretation* (New York: Dell Publishing Co., 1969), p. 243.

12. I daresay there are many people who connect Richard Strauss' *Thus Spake Zarathustra* only with the opening of *2001,* and I wouldn't be surprised if they believe Strauss wrote the music with Kubrick's film in mind.

13. "Quincy Jones On the Composer," *Movie People at Work in the Business of film.* Fred Baker and Ross Firestone, eds. (New York: Douglas Book Corporation, 1972), p. 159.

14. Robert Gessner, *The Moving Image* (New York: E. P. Dutton, 1970 [paperback]), p. 377.

15. Hanns Eisler, *Composing for the Films* (New York: Oxford University Press, 1947), p. 23.

16. From Ingmar Bergman, *Four Screenplays of Ingmar Bergman* (New York: Simon and Schuster, A Clarion Book, 1960), pp. 16–17.

17. Frederick Sternfield, "Kubik's McBoing Score," *Film Music Notes,* Vol. X, Number II, (Nov.–Dec. 1950).

18. William Johnson makes the same observation also using *2001: A Space Odyssey* as an example, *op. cit.,* p. 8.

19. Anyone who has ever watched a television Young People's Concert conducted by Leonard Bernstein will recognize these effects. Aside from the Maestro's magnetic presence, which rivets the attention of the children—and adults—at the concert, through the magic of the camera's eye the individual contributions of different members of the orchestra are magnified in their full-screen musical solos, not to mention the extra tension and drama the camera movement gives to the music itself.

20. Room tone is usually considered to be the sum total of the acoustical characteristics or the natural tone (not pitch) of any given environment.

21. Roger Manvell, *The Film and the Public* (Harmondsworth, Middlesex, England: Penguin Books, Ltd., 1955), p. 67.

22. Hanns Eisler, *Composing for the Films* (New York: Oxford University Press, 1947), p. 108.

6. Closing Music Cue

A fact of life for the film composer is the recent trend toward the use of prerecorded music in motion pictures. The current growth of music libraries is astounding, and an infinite variety of material is now available on commercial records and tapes. The musical stockpiles include rock, folk, country music, progressive and experimental jazz, and soul. They also include contemporary avant-garde concert-hall music, twelve-tone compositions, and electronic-synthesizer pieces. This gives the film-maker an inexhaustible new source whose use is not necessarily determined by budget. Films such as *Easy Rider*, *Alice's Restaurant*, *The Yellow Submarine*, *Paper Moon*, and, of course, *2001*, among others, have employed recordings for their sound tracks. Even eight seconds of avant-garde composer George Crumb's score from *Black Angels* was snipped for use in *The Exorcist*. The music is there and can successfully be made to fit the image. If this tendency were to continue, the film composer could become obsolete.

On the brighter side, today's development of new electronic sound-producing equipment—multiple stereo, echo chambers, reverberation and distortion techniques, feedback, staggered tracks, multiple overdubbing, compression, high-speed tape effects, filtered sounds, and the electronic amplification of all types of musical instruments—gives the composer a limitless world in which to enlarge his musical spectrum. In addition, electronic sound-producing instruments utilizing white noise, sine waves, square and sawtooth waves, and oscillators capable of alternating pitches and microtones enable the informed composer to reproduce any known sound and create myriad new ones.

The orchestration of musical sound and sound effect makes me think about the formation of a new kind of music for films: a totally athematic, nonmelodic language that would use organized sounds and/or clusters instead of traditional melodic designs to support background and foreground dramatic action. These nonmelodic sounds, fusing with image, motion, and speech patterns, could break down the established associative concept-communication principles between film and music and create, in the process, a new aesthetic. It could also end the stranglehold on film music maintained by the overuse of upper-voice, melodic phrase structure. In this way, film producers' love of theme tunes would be discarded in favor of strategic *musical-sound* placement. Of course I can already hear some producer saying, "How are we going to get any record sales out of *Organized Sound #1 for Dramatic Situation Part 3?*" But this is not a problem. With the addition of a lyric and an ingeniously packaged promotional campaign, *Organized Sound #1* is a definite candidate for a top spot on the record charts.

During my interviews for this book I talked at great length with many film composers. My experiences were extremely informative. Setting aside my natural pro-composer bias, I was greatly impressed by the composers themselves. As a group they are the most articulate, artistically curious, literate people in the film medium; and, as several have remarked, "We are the ones that should be making the films." They could be right.

Personal Appearances:
Interviews with Composers

It was my intention in these conversations to ask similar questions of the composers in order to compare their responses and equate their answers. Although the transcribed notes have been edited for readability, nothing has been altered in the text; the composers speak for themselves.

The interviews with Bernard Herrmann, John Barry, and Richard Rodney Bennett were taped by Ms. Pat Gray (London office of Van Nostrand Reinhold) from questions submitted by me.

Space and time prevented me from interviewing many outstanding musicians I would have liked to include in this section. Those selected represent in my judgment an excellent cross-section of composers writing for films.

I.A.B.

Elmer Bernstein with wife Eve and daughter Emily. (Photo: Patricia Layman)

Leonard Rosenman. (Photo: Patricia Layman)

Jerry Goldsmith. (Photo: Patricia Layman)

John Williams. (Photo: Patricia Layman)

Richard Rodney Bennett. (Photo: Clive Barda)

Alex North.

Lalo Schifrin. (Photo: Patricia Layman)

Bernard Herrmann. (Photo: John Engstead)

David Raksin (right) with the author. (Photo: Patricia Layman)

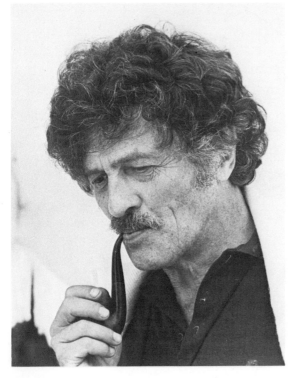

Bernardo Segáll.

166

Laurence Rosenthal. (Photo: Patricia Layman)

Johnny Mandel. (Photo: Patricia Layman)

Paul Glass. (Photo: Patricia Layman)

John Barry.

Gail Kubik (right) with the author. (Photo: Patricia Layman)

INTERVIEW with ELMER BERNSTEIN

Irwin Bazelon: In the context of defining a composer as a person who knows how to put a piece together, do you think it's necessary that one be a composer in this aesthetic sense to write film music, or can someone function in films without really qualifying as a composer?

Elmer Bernstein: Obviously, people who are completely unqualified to do so have become recognized as composers. To answer the first part of the question, my answer would have to be yes. I don't think that a person who does not understand structure, who cannot put a piece together, can possibly write a score.

IB: But you agree that there are a lot of people out here who can't qualify as a composer in this context but still get jobs writing film music?

EB: Well, yes, because the root of the problem is that there are more film-makers making films who are not even qualified to make films. There are people with very poor or no artistic judgment, and basically they are not looking at the difference between a score and a nonscore, but they do understand the economic value of getting a song in the top 40.

IB: How do you feel about the title-song mania and the current influx into the film scene of record companies paying music-production costs and creating hit records and instant composers?

EB: The funny thing about that is that it's been a very long-time thing, and in a very strange sort of way I've always felt partially responsible for that situation, although I must say that my responsibility is partly accidental. I suppose it first started, as far as I can remember, with Dimitri Tiomkin in *High Noon*. That was the first big blast. And then a few years later I came along with *Man with a Golden Arm*, and really after *Man with a Golden Arm* people began to realize that music has a certain commercial value.

IB: The line is, "Everybody hates canned music unless they happen to be playing his tune."

EB: Yes, well, that's sort of the human nature of the composer, but I think it's gone far afield from where it first started. I know that we all got to the point—I mean, I got to the point very quickly where I resisted the idea of having to write a title song. Because I can only think of addressing myself to the overall problem, the demands of the picture in terms of creating a score. But I think it's simply reduced itself to the crassest kind of commercialism, in that all the producer's concerned with is whether the song is going to be a hit. I don't think he's particularly concerned with whether it has anything to do with the motion picture. I mean we've seen case after case where songs are grafted onto films where they have no function, where they don't belong. And unfortunately, I think a few composers have given this technique a certain respectability. As pretty as, let's say, a theme from *Love Story* is (it may be considered as sort of a small piece) and as pretty as some people might think it is, it basically results in a nonscore in terms of the fact that it is not serving any particular dramatic function; it's a graft. We can get into the philosophy of what film music is all about. But certainly the repetition of a pretty theme is not what the function of a film score is. Unfortunately, these things lend a certain respectability so that, strangely enough, you'd be surprised at how many people—people whom you would consider people of substance—consider that a score.

IB: Why do you think there are so few contemporary concert composers who are given the opportunity to score mainstream feature films? Is there a problem of director-composer communication or ego involvement? Is there such a thing as commercial-mindedness that influences film people to avoid so-called serious composers? By and large the big names, the people who have reputations as contemporary concert composers, have rarely been hired.

EB: Well, I think there's no one answer to it. I'll answer the question in several ways. One thing that's gone out of the making of motion pictures in this country is respect for art. There is, I think, no respect whatsoever right now, especially in the Hollywood area, for the artists. There are very great reasons for it. I think that the enterprising people of the forties, who hired people like

Copland, may not themselves have been great intellects, but they were people who had immense self-confidence as showmen, and they had enough respect for a person in another field to feel they wanted to buy the best. And they were willing to take that risk because they had confidence in themselves as showmen, if nothing else. I think today that you have motion-picture people on the production end who are a group of individuals who have no confidence in themselves whatsoever as anything. And a very low level of intellect. Basically, I think, they're really quite scared of composers. And I think this goes not only to the joke about producers, but I also think it extends to young directors who basically are afraid of musicians, because we speak a language they just don't understand. And I can only assume (one must be pragmatic about analyzing these things) that their level, their intellectual level and cultural development, is at the level of rock and roll, because it's the only thing they feel comfortable with, and it's the only thing they trust. In order to get a young contemporary composer to do his thing, you have to have enough confidence in yourself as a director to respect the fellow for what he does and let him do his job. Because, obviously, there's no way, except on a certain intellectual level, that a director can tell a composer what to do. They can discuss concepts, but the fellow in command has got to be willing to let the composer do his creative work and trust it. Now they don't trust the composer, because they don't trust their ability themselves. I think—this may sound too extreme, but I really think that things have descended to such a point here where basically, I have to say, the largest percentage of film-makers really don't know the difference between a good score or a bad score, haven't got a clue of what the hell the score is supposed to do in the first place. And furthermore, and even more damaging, I don't think they really care. I think the only thing most of them really care about is the possibility of a commercial adjunct to the picture. The big companies, of course, have these big music companies and are very interested in how much money they can make from the music-publishing companies—it's as simple as that. As you know, we are involved in a Federal antitrust suit against the studios right now, and the whole practice of demanding the copyright as a condition of employment. Now if we win this suit, I think it's going to raise the level of music, because the minute we deprive the studios of a pure profit motive in the exploitation of the music, then, at least, the composer will be on his own to make his own decisions. I'll tell you something—the real reason that a person gets employed to do a picture today is that the companies feel that if the composer has a "track record" in the commercial field and sticks these copyrights in their company, and if they get lucky with one of the tunes, they may make as much money or more money from the music than from the whole picture. That's happened to me on one occasion.

IB: Now you understand one of the reasons why I've been giving this course on "Music for Motion Pictures" to potential film-makers, most of whom want to become directors. I got so tired of having such difficulty communicating with people who hired me that I thought I'd do a little proselytizing and try to influence young people to understand that when it comes time for music, not to go to their local discotheque and hire the bongo player or guitar player.

EB: There's a great deal of that. I used to do a lot of work for American Film Institute, where you run into some of this problem, and what I've done on occasion is actually do the music for one of the student films. To work with one of the students so that they learn something about the problems of communication with the composer. You see, one of the problems is that there's a tendency to blame the composers for what's going on now. A couple of years ago a reviewer, Page Cook, wrote an article in which he took me to task for a score I had done that he thought was not up to par in terms of my own standards, and in the same article he lit into a lot of writers, notably, people like Michel Legrand and Quincy Jones. I could name more; it's not important. I wrote Page a letter at the time and said, "Listen, if you want to be rough on me, that's fine, because there's a certain personal standard against which you're comparing, and if you don't think that I'm doing my best, have at me by all means. But don't flog Michel Legrand and Quincy Jones, because they're not goofing off. I mean, they're doing what they do best. If you're really angry about this situation, attack the producers, attack the people who make films." You can't blame Burt Bacharach or Michel Legrand or Quincy Jones for what they're doing. They're simply doing their thing and doing it well. They're applying their craft; they're conscientious. They're doing what they know how to do and what they think is best for them to do. The problem is that the people who do the hiring are thinking more of the 'chart' than the art. The ignorance is at the film-making level."

IB: What percentage of producers and directors that you have worked for know anything about music or even how to communicate on a simple dramatic level with a composer? How would you grade their overall native musicality?

EB: Well, I'd have to do it in terms of about ninety pictures, which is very difficult, and I think it's changed a great deal. I think that up until about roughly ten years ago, a lot of the producers and directors had learned a sort of "pidgin-music" way, if you wish, to communicate with composers. At least, you sort of understood what they were talking about, and, if they felt that you were working in some mysterious world of shades and sounds, they could at least tell you, "Well, I would like it to be 'like something'." I find that in the past ten years there's been a tendency to be more and more ignorant, and I find it very difficult in recent years to communicate with people, because the only thing they know how to say is, "Talk about a new sound." And everything must have a new sound, which is obviously simply a reflection of the poverty of their vocabulary and also their total lack of knowledge of what the hell a film score's all about. So there's nothing to talk about, really.

IB: This is a very interesting thing you're saying, because in many ways you're refuting the contention of a lot of people that with the new influx of directors willing to try things, the scores and the communication are getting stronger. And you're saying in reality this is not really so. We agree that just because something gets brassier and amplified doesn't mean that it's better than something in the background that doesn't have this kind of projection.

EB: You know, you just have to be related to the whole cultural ambience in the country. This is not a problem that exists here alone. It exists in painting, it exists in concert-hall music. You know, the minute you begin to have a poverty of content or you don't develop techniques to deal with form, you begin to look for gadgets. Art constantly is going through this kind of situation in times of stress, and I think all the arts are going through that right now. You find a lot of that in serious music, a lot of gadgetry. But when you say directors are ready to try anything—yes, they're ready to try anything, but I'm not so sure that that simple level is necessarily creative. Because by trying anything, what they mean is, "Try the latest electric gadget." That's what they really mean; they have no concept of form. You know, I always ask myself when I score a film or when we look at a film and they say, "Well, we'll have music in this scene." My matrix for whether the scene should be scored or not is, "Well, what the hell is music going to do in this scene? What is its function? Why is it there?" That's what the important thing is. It has nothing to do with the sound. A new sound per se means nothing. The question is, why should a scene be scored, what is the music going to do, how is it going to function?

IB: A great deal of my book deals with this element. Just what does music actually do for a film? How and why does it enhance or detract from a spectator's involvement?

EB: Yes, and you get into the whole thing of whether it should be unobtrusive, which is another thing that is happening that I think is part of the cultural ambience— that there's a tremendous amount of fear of passion in art right now. Anything that's passionate is very suspect. After the fight that we made for all those years to try to create a certain kind of acceptance for writing music for motion pictures as, God forbid, an art, we've now gone back to the thing where it's only appreciated when it's unobtrusive or it's delicate or it's small or it makes no statement. If it makes a statement, everybody gets terribly suspicious. There's a time when you really have to, you know, get in and do the job. *The Magnificent Seven* is no place to get sparse. You've got a big, outdoor film that was a bit on the slow-moving side, and it needed a kind of vigorous score to get in there and really fight.

IB: When you are not writing for films, you function in many ways. You have your own orchestra, don't you?

EB: Yes, I conduct a community orchestra called the Valley Symphony, which I might say, immodestly, is probably about the best community symphony in the country, I think.

175

IB: I'd like to ask you a little bit about your working habits. You are a pianist, but do you use the piano a great deal when you compose?

EB: Less and less as time goes on. I basically think it's an insecurity syndrome. I generally do better when I do not use the piano, because it frees the mind. When you're working at the piano, you have those ten dumb fingers to think for you. That's inevitable. I think it's much better if you can get away from the piano and let your mind do the thinking.

IB: I know that different people work in different ways. Some of the composers, I've been told, sketch out everything from beginning to end at the piano.

EB: What I do now is, I make a real shorthand sketch, such a shorthand sketch that nobody but me would be able to work from it. But I do it as a way of organizing my thoughts before I go to score paper. And I do all my own orchestrating.

IB: There's such a mystique about the business of orchestrating. I wanted to ask you, do you use an orchestrator upon occasion, and, if so, how much does he actually contribute to your score?

EB: I must say that I've covered the whole range of relationships between a composer and an orchestrator. When I first came here, I enclosed in my contract that they could under no circumstances assign an orchestrator to my work, because I was brought up in the strange and old-fashioned and quaint tradition that composition and orchestration are inseparable. Nevertheless, as you know, the practice in this town has been, and was until recently, that composers are separable and work separately. Now, as I say, I've used orchestrators on pictures, and I think they've contributed a great deal in situations where a score is straightforwardly symphonic and conventional. For instance, in a score like *Hawaii* or a score like *The Magnificent Seven,* which is quite straightforward in terms of tutti, conventional, orchestral, symphonic writing, orchestrators have contributed a great deal, I would say. On the other hand, in terms of pictures where the sound is still much more transparent—take a score like *To Kill a Mockingbird* or *The Birdman of Alcatraz*—there were orchestrators on those pictures, but the orchestrators in those instances were much more like secretaries. I mean, I wouldn't say that the orchestrators contributed in any way to those types of scores. In recent years I haven't used orchestrators at all.

IB: What do you consider your best score or your best-scored scene from a film? I realize this is difficult, as you've done an awful lot of films, but you must have one or two favorites.

EB: Well, first of all, as you very well know, I always suspect a composer's opinion of his own work, because the things you like best about your own work are based upon unreliable things. Personally, *Mockingbird* would definitely be one of them, because that was a very difficult one to solve. It took me six weeks to even get off the ground with that score. And so I really scared myself until I realized that the whole point of that score finally became in mind—what is this score doing here? What kind of ambience is it creating? And, what I got to realize was that its real function was to deal in the magic of a child's world. And that was the whole key of that score, and it accounts, for instance, for the use of the high registers of the piano and bells and harps and all, things which at least I associated with child magic in a definitely American ambience, and I have tremendous feeling for that score. I think that if, perhaps, I were to pick a score that I want to talk about in terms of its function in a film—ideal function in a film—I'd probably pick one that very few people know, a very early one, a score for a film called *Men in War*. I think that it probably is, of my work, the best integrated. It dealt with a lost platoon of men in the Korean war. Robert Ryan and Aldo Ray—United Artists. There are a couple of sequences— one in particular—that I remember very well. A scene where men are walking though a mine field—and once again, it's a very interesting thing, because it involved the decision of what to play as they were going through these mine fields, and it suddenly occurred to me that they were going through this mine field in basically beautiful country. There was a forest, you know. And I was playing a lot of my forest sounds and bird sounds and that sort of thing against the terror of walking through the mines. The scene worked very well.

IB: You really interpolated yourself into the plot, and, by doing that, music changed the perception of image.

EB: Yes.

IB: Do you think there's too much music in films today or that they're overscored?

EB: I think the way things are going today, most of them are overscored one hundred percent.

IB: Did you always want to write film music or did you have other musical ambitions? I know the kind of pianist you are, and you've also talked about the conducting that you're doing, but how did you get into films—did you stumble into this medium?

EB: I stumbled into it completely. My background in music, as you can guess, is very conservative, and I was going to be a concert pianist. I think when I was eighteen or nineteen, if someone suggested I was going to write music for films, I would have been insulted at that point. It was a total accident; actually I was in the army, World War II, and I was writing some arrangements of American folk songs for a singer, for some radio shows they were doing. And one day one of the composers who did music for the dramatic shows went over the hill—AWOL, that is—and their director of the unit called me into the office and said, "Do you think you could write music for a dramatic show?" Being a young kid, I said, "Sure." So that's how I got started.

IB: I remember *Saturday's Heroes*. Was that your first feature?

EB: That was my first feature, yes; that was in 1950.

IB: What other film composers do you admire? What scored segment from somebody else's film is your favorite?

EB: Well, I would say the first that jumps to my mind would be Jerry Goldsmith. It's a funny thing—Jerry has a consistency. I wish I were as consistent as he is. I really admire his consistency, and it isn't because he doesn't work a lot—he works more than I do. He's really the consummate film composer. I mean, he is so right and so interesting and somehow so integrated. I must say one of his scores stands out as a fantastic achievement, simply because it was so difficult to do, and that was *Patton*. The whole concept of that score and the way it was executed I think was just extraordinary.

IB: *Patton* has almost two levels of sound. One is barely perceptible, with another level on top of it.

EB: I think they were electronic trumpets at the beginning of the film—and you wonder what the devil was that all about, but as the film goes on, you begin to understand what the film was all about. I also like the works of Leonard Rosenman—for instance, the score from *Fantastic Voyage*. If I were going back in history, I'm a great admirer of Bernard Herrmann, of his early works, which I think are very important achievements. I certainly think some of David Raksin's scores are superb.

IB: How often are your scores thrown out, if ever, and what's your reaction to it?

EB: Well, I hate to say it—it's the jinx—I've never had a score thrown out. I just recently barely escaped. Unfortunately, there's a tremendous thing going on now about that. I mean there's so little respect for music, the whole art, you know. But people throw scores out very cavalierly. It's a very complex problem, because they're the buyer and American society gives the buyer the right to do anything he wants with the score presumably—but I think that it's been a power very greatly misused in recent times.

IB: Do you believe that bad music or controversial sounds can kill a film and cause people to leave the theater or blame the composer for the film's failure?

EB: Well, I would be willing to compare how our legitimate composers' ability stands against the film-makers' ability anytime. I think that more people walk out on bad films than bad music.

IB: I have a standing bet in my class that there is no film that has ever been killed by music.

EB: Well, I want to tell you, if bad scores hurt films, they couldn't get anybody into the theater.

IB: Of course, this is one of the arguments that these people have used through the years, also claiming from the other side that avant-garde film scores would do the same thing.

EB: You know what happens? As it will come out in the book, of course, the score is the last thing that gets into a film. By that time the producers and/or directors have an impending feeling of doom, because they know they've got a turkey on their hands, they want the score to save it, and, of course, the score will never save it. That's one thing—I always say that the most brilliant score in the world will never save a bad film, never. It can help divert attention from it, but it's not going to save it.

INTERVIEW with LEONARD ROSENMAN

Irwin
Bazelon: Do you have to be a composer to write film music?

Leonard
Rosenman: I feel that the answer is no, that you don't have to be a composer to write film music. Because first of all, a little goes a long way in films. By that I mean that certain kinds of sounds are really quite as applicable as developed scores for certain kinds of scenes. I personally know many people who are called composers who really aren't composers, who organize sounds and put them in films. You mentioned a film which had kind of a low drone—I think it was *The Trial*—well, it really wouldn't take a composer to figure that one out. Stanley Kubrick got together a bunch of records for *2001* and it worked quite handsomely. The answer to your question is definitely no. All you have to have is a sense of drama and a sense of sound. You have to, perhaps, appreciate music to some degree—or you don't even have to appreciate music: all you have to do is appreciate the relationship between sound and visual media to organize music for films.

IB: Has the position of a composer in films changed much during the years that you have worked in Hollywood?

LR: I don't think so; I think it's basically the same. Regardless of new techniques, twentieth-century techniques being used suddenly, and, parenthetically, there are a few innovations of serial techniques, but basically they've caught up to Bartok and Stravinsky of the twenties and thirties. Regardless of styles, I think the business of composition for films has not basically changed the role of the composer. Because to the film-maker he is still a kind of a mystery-magical person who is capable of doing something absolutely abstract, i.e., unknown to the film-maker. And he is capable of establishing certain kinds of relationships which mystify the film-maker. The relationships of analogue—that is to say, the image becomes an analogue to the music, the music becomes an analogue to the image, and thus changes our perception of both. And this is why the composer is regarded with tremendous ambivalence by the film-maker because of the lack of knowledge about what he does. And in that sense the role of the composer has not basically changed.

IB: Do you think that film music tends to mirror the pop-music culture of its time? Do you think that these two relationships—pop-music culture and motion-picture music—are commensurate? Or do you think that they follow divergent paths?

LR: Well, I think that they are commensurate to each other, and I think that they are put in juxtaposition to each other. After all, the commercial film is a very expensive gadget, which has a great deal of technology connected with it, has a great deal of money connected with it, which means that they have to take in a great deal of money. In order to take in a great deal of money, a lot of people have to buy tickets, and that means a lot of the pop culture. And movies are kitsch to begin with; there really is no reason why the music, which is another small manifestation of a larger production, shouldn't be kitsch also. It is another manifestation of the general values of films. I don't regard anything that happens in the music department of the great studios to be any different than what happens in all the other departments of production —cutting, directing, everything else.

IB: How much leeway are you given to compose novel and interesting, offbeat scores? Now I realize certain films dictate certain kinds of relationships, and it's obvious that science-fiction films might give a composer an opportunity to use unusual sounds that he might not other-wise have a chance to use. But, just from a practical standpoint, are you given specific orders or are you allowed to write what you want to?

LR: Well, of course, that varies really with the person you're working with or the studio you're working with and with the individual project. I'd say there's more implicit pressure than explicit pressure. Now I've done three television series: I've done *The Defenders, Combat,* and now *Marcus Welby.* Now with *The Defenders,* I had a very explicit direction by the director and producer, Herb Brodkin, who said to me, "I want a theme for *The Defenders* that exemplifies the law." Well, I said, "I can give you a theme that will exemplify certain laws of music, but I don't really believe that music can exemplify the law any more than Strauss can exemplify the laws of the dinner table in *Sinfonia Domestica.* I feel that music cannot express certain literary things without direct literary association. Of course, he really thought I was a wise guy, and I really was at the time—I was being very facetious, because he just didn't understand the function of music. But this was kind of an explicit and an implicit limitation, because what he really meant by that was that he didn't want any wild stuff, he didn't want any different stuff, he wanted something majestic and kind of nineteenth century. *Combat,* on the other hand, in which I wrote Germans sneaking through the bushes for four years, was sort of a different score, because there existed a kind of general tension and general mayhem and, you know, 1600 people got killed in every one of these shows. There were gigantic machines, there were tanks and machine guns and God knows what all—and I had absolutely no stylistic limitations, except for a kind of a march theme which they wanted for the series—a kind of World War II-type march. Well, of course, that's a limitation in itself. But generally, the scores in *Combat* were very experimental situations for me, because I really was able to try out all kinds of avant-garde situations in that. *Marcus Welby*—the material itself is so circumscribed —there are really a limited number of ways with which you can score it—family doctor, small town stuff. It's very individual. If a composer wants to write really avant-garde music, he would pick projects—he could do the science-fiction projects, tension, mystery, suspense.

IB: Why do you think so few serious American concert composers have been hired to do films? What do you think is the reason that they've never been given an opportunity to bring a new kind of imagination or extend the horizons of motion-picture music?

LR: Well, the answer to this question is very complicated. First of all, the aegis under which films are made in Europe is much different than here. A certain amount of money is subsidized by the governments of various countries, and therefore it's only natural that people in government want to use what are considered the natural resources of the country—the intellectual natural resources of the country. They don't depend on the kind of box office that we need here in order to make ends meet, because films are cheaper. They're a little more practical, and, of course, their standards of living are lower; the union situation is different. They also, don't forget, have subsidized radio stations, so many of their composers' works are played constantly, and so they're better known. So therefore, it's not as much of a luxury for them as it is for us to use some of their serious composers. They make more serious films than we do here; they make many more experimental, interesting, imaginative films than we make here. It doesn't cost them as much; they can afford to use their best talent, and they don't depend upon the kind of returns that we do to make ends meet. Now, on this side of the fence we have certain problems; aside from this unstructured freedom that we have here, we have films that are part of the pop culture. In order for them to make money, they've got to be part of the pop culture—it's not an art. As a matter of fact, it's kind of interesting to look at films, because people speak about film business, show business, the film industry—and then there are other people who speak about the film art. Well, it's not art, we know that. And it's not industry, we know that. The function of art is to be artistic; if it's not artistic, it's not art. As industry—the function of industry and business is to make money—it doesn't even make money. It's not even good on that level, so basically it's a kind of dying, cancerous leviathan—as I pointed out the other day about the city of New York; it's constantly buying new clothes, although it has terminal cancer. The whole relevance of the big commercial film is nearing its end.

IB: In other words, if a so-called concert composer, even if he had won the Pulitzer Prize, came into competition with a successful songwriter to do a motion picture, the chances are that the songwriter would win?

LR: The chances are that they never will have heard of the concert composer, even if he had won the Pulitzer Prize—or for that matter, of the Pulitzer Prize.

IB: If you had to give a yes-or-no answer, would you say that Hollywood film music is really, in many ways, a haven for the second-rate musical talent that perhaps can't make it in the competitive world of so-called serious composers?

LR: No, I would say it has nothing to do with that at all. I think it's a totally different world. It's as different from the concert world as the pop world is. I think they have different goals in mind; they have different training, background. A lot of them are refugees from cool jazz. A lot of them are from the pop-rock kind of thing, people who have never even thought of competing in the concert field and people who have no interest in competing in the concert field. And likewise, on the other side of the fence, the people in the concert field have very little interest in films, although that may be changing now. But, certainly, ten years ago they had very little interest in it.

IB: Now I'm going to ask you to talk for a few minutes on this whole music scene in which you've been involved for the last fifteen years, namely, writing music for Hollywood. I'd like to hear your comments as to what it has been like to be a composer in this scene, what some of the advantages are, and how you have managed to function in the midst of this kind of a culture.

LR: Well, when I first arrived on the Hollywood scene in 1954, when I did *East of Eden,* and up to comparatively recently, I felt that these people, the Hollywood people, were intruders in my culture. And recently, as I began to grow older and assume a certain aspect of sanity and reality, I began to realize that I was an intruder in *their* culture! And that I was damn lucky to be alive and making a living, and if they didn't see through me, then I really had something else going in the background; and I was allowed somehow to continue with my camouflage of being a Hollywood composer, despite the fact that I was doing serious music on the side and getting a certain amount of performances. And so I'm thankful to the culture in one sense for allowing me to make a living writing music and for allowing me at times to actually express myself in my own style to a certain extent—close to my own style. And I've used film music as a sort of laboratory, which has helped me enormously. I've become, thanks to Hollywood, a fair conductor, because I've learned how to put together the pieces very quickly, rehearse an orchestra, hear an orchestra—get it in my ear—and to write for the orchestra and smaller combinations too. And to make do, to have a kind of pragmatic contact with music, which the film musicians really have. Also, I've developed because it's like a marriage—let's say you're married to someone for sixteen years (which is the time I've been married to Hollywood)—either you hate her, or you're ambivalent to her—fighting all the time. If you have a close relationship with somebody for sixteen years, something's bound to rub off, and you're bound to find love somewhere, you're bound to see the good parts of it, and you're bound to grow from it, to derive something from it. And I've developed for myself in the last few years, just based on observation of images and music and how they go together, and experienced a set of aesthetic-dramaturgic values, which I hope will help me in writing mixed-media work, utilizing film for the concert stage. So I think there's another place where it can be a help. Negatively—oh, let me say one thing, aside from the fact that you can make a great deal of money in Hollywood, these are the more positive sides of the life as I've seen it in my sixteen years. But the negative aspects are also quite overwhelming. Although you can use the orchestra as an experiment—an experimental laboratory—you really are not writing music, basically. You are using all the ingredients of music: counterpoint, harmony, etc. But basically it doesn't function as music, because the propulsion is not through the medium of musical ideas. The propulsion is by way of literary ideas.

IB: Would you say that movie music is almost composing?

LR: Yes, as a trombonist told me about a piece of mine, "You know, it almost swings." And it's almost music, but not quite. It smokes, but it's no cigar. It's the difference between a marvelously wrought wallpaper—you know, interior decoration—and, let's say, a Jackson Pollock. And they have different functions. I'm not, again, disparaging any of the media—they have different functions, as a table and chair have different functions. And what happens musically is that the material becomes very truncated as opposed to, let's say, all other literary musical forms where we call it a musical form, because the composer takes the libretto and bends it to the music. The libretto fits the music; it has to have holes in it and so on and create certain requirements, certain circumscriptions to the music. It's just the opposite in films. The film goes through a projector at ninety feet a minute, and it just doesn't go any faster or any slower, and the same scene takes exactly the same time every time, and your music simply has to fit. And the minute you squeeze in music under this aegis and you write in a procrustean fashion, cutting off the beat or stretching it out to fit, then you are dealing with extramusical evaluations, extramusical values. The result is the overall picture of Hollywood music as a series of truncated little phrases, very often making do to fit a scene—not being complicated under dialogue, under sound effects, punctuating this, punctuating that. The composer who wishes to use films as a laboratory for any length of time, unless he really has his wits about him and becomes a real schizophrenic and divides himself right down the middle and knows what to draw from what medium for what purpose, will become very, very confused in his serious work and will begin to write these same truncated phrases, which indeed most of these people write. So there it has caused me a great deal of burden in the writing of my serious music. Also, the people you're dealing with don't know too much about music. Of course, I must say, I've dealt with people on the university level who don't know too much about music either.

IB: In all the years that you have been writing music for television and films, what percentage of directors and producers that you have worked for knew anything at all about music or how to communicate with you on an elementary level?

LR: I would say less than one percent.

INTERVIEW with JERRY GOLDSMITH

Irwin
Bazelon: In light of so many young musicians getting music credit for films and contributing sometimes just a little guitar singing and songs, what are your feelings on whether or not one has to be a composer in order to write motion-picture music?

Jerry
Goldsmith: Of course you have to be a composer to write motion-picture music. You have to be a composer to write any kind of music.

IB: Are there an abundance of films today that are scored by unqualified people?

JG: I think the thing is that today there are a lot of films being made that are of a very high caliber, and certain people come along to do music for them who are quite unfit for the job, and they can make some funny noises, and the strength of the film is so much that it can survive the funny noises. That's almost like the old axiom that I sort of coined, "No music has ever saved a bad picture, but a lot of good pictures have saved a lot of bad music." And I think that much of the rubbish that's being written today is really disgraceful, and this sounds like sour grapes, I'm sure, but nonetheless, I am sort of upset with it all.

IB: In all the years you've been in Hollywood working in films and television, what percentage of producers and directors that you've worked with knew anything about music at all, or if they didn't know anything about music, at least knew how to communicate with you on any level whatsoever in any dramatic way?

JG: About one percent. I worked with one director, who did *Planet of the Apes* and *Patton,* who was an incredible man musically. His instincts are so correct—there was once a very funny story: I didn't realize what his knowledge of music was, and we were dubbing *Patton*—you know, the funeral scene, which was underscored. We were going to lunch, and he had his car radio on—it was playing the funeral march, the *Eroica* Symphony. He'd just turned the radio on, and it played about three bars, and he said, "That's what we should have used in the funeral scene."

And I said, "That's really a very smart-assed way of trying to tell me that you know what that piece of music is." But that's the kind of man he is, and that's his knowledge of music, but I can't speak of any others like that.

IB: It's been a bone of contention in my classes when I've screened *Planet of the Apes* that a lot of the music that you used was done electronically. Let's clear this up—there was no electronic music or synthesizer in that film, right?

JG: That's correct. That was the whole object. Because there was a great deal of thought on my part on how to approach it, and the obvious way would be to use electronics and all sorts of synthetic means of reproducing the music, and I feel, without trying to sound pretentious, that the resources of the orchestra had just barely begun to be tapped, and I felt it an exercise for myself to see what I could do to make some strange sounds and yet try to make them *musically* rather than effectwise.

IB: You've functioned almost all of your musical life in film. Is there a difference doing something for television and something for movies—I mean as far as the media are concerned—or is it on the same general level?

JG: Well, I think there's basically a great difference in approach: forgetting the pragmatic thing such as lower budgets and less time to do it in, you're dealing in a much more intimate medium. You're dealing with a screen that's nineteen or twenty inches and you also have terrible sound reproduction. The sound of the orchestra is coming out of a little three-inch speaker and to score a program with fifty or sixty men is sort of ludicrous. But mainly, the fact is that you're dealing in a smaller scope, and you must, I think, write music of a much more intimate nature. The same scene may be done one way for a theatrical motion picture and another way for a television picture. I think that the pictures themselves should be made with these thoughts in mind. Unfortunately, they're not. They try to make films too many times for television with the epic proportions of those that are shown on the wide screen, and it just doesn't come off. Television's biggest success in the dramatic sense has always been the intimate drama.

IB: How do you feel about today's opening-title music? In one film after another, we seem to be part of a guitar-washed culture, with somebody singing a title song that may not have anything at all to do with the film. In fact, in one film, *The Prime of Miss Jean Brodie,* the title song first appears at the very end of the film for no apparent reason. How do you feel about this title-song mania?

JG: Well, many of us composers are upset about this, because we get requests from producers that we've got to write a hit song. It's a real pain, because they forget what we're really supposed to be doing. It's a completely commercial device to try to promote the film. And if the song came at the end of the picture in *Jean Brodie,* it still made it eligible for the Academy Awards. And if it gets nominated and wins, it sells more and more copies, and, after all, the studios do own the copyrights on the music, and so they're making a proft off of that, and if it's really successful, it may promote the picture a great deal. It has nothing to do with anything dramatic in the picture, and this is a great annoyance to us all, but it's one of the syndromes of the business, and there isn't very much we can do about it.

IB: Tell me what your ideas about film music are and whether you enjoy writing film music. How do you feel about your life in California working in this field? Just talk in general about how you feel about film music. Are there things that you'd like to see changed?

JG: Well, nothing really should be changed as far as I'm concerned personally. I don't care what anybody else does; it's just what I do. What I do, I do to the best of my ability. I love writing music for motion pictures. I love drama, and that's why I like to do this. You happened to refer to my life in California. My life is not necessarily in California—movies are made all over the world. I'm spending a lot of time in Europe now—there's a whole different approach to doing films than we're used to doing in Hollywood. We seem to be much slicker about it. We worry much more about music fitting a scene tighter and catching things, and music being more sophisticated, whereas in Europe it's sort of a catch-as-catch-can process, although England is becoming a little bit more aware of what we've been doing in Hollywood over the years. Not necessarily that our way is the right way, but it's the only way I know how to do it that appeals to me.

But it's been interesting observing composers in Europe and discussing their attitudes—the thing that upsets me the most is that I don't find too many young composers coming into the motion-picture-scoring business.

IB: Would you say most of them are coming from a jazz-and-rock background?

JG: Most of them seem to be coming from pop backgrounds. And the difference between an arranger and a composer is quite great. But there are so many gifted composers in colleges and universities throughout our country that don't seem to be getting the opportunity. The producers don't seem to be interested in these people. They want something that has commercial value to it.

IB: I think you might agree that it isn't just the producer's or the director's fault for not being interested; some of our talented composers on the concert scene also have to make an effort to meet some of these people and influence them a little bit. You can't expect it all to be on one side, and a lot of these composers have taken refuge in the colleges.

JG: There's a marvelous line George Bernard Shaw said while being interviewed during his last years; the interviewer asked, "Isn't it a disgrace that serious composers have to lower themselves doing motion pictures?" And he replied that he thought the possibilities for film music were unlimited, and he would much rather like a piece of music from a film than an academic cantata that is performed in mothballs and never heard of again, which I must say endeared the old man to me for life.

IB: Also, don't you think it's quite conceivable that many composers who have earned rather large reputations in the so-called serious concert world, even the late Stravinsky, would constitute quite a problem in working in a film, where you're not being hired for your ego and you're not being hired to write a concerto or a symphony—you're part of a team, you have a function and a job?

JG: Well, that's a rhetorical question—you just answered it. That's exactly what happens. I feel that, without mentioning any names, the so-called concert-hall composers have their own egos to overcome, and to sublimate that to the demands of the film sound track is just too much for them to cope with. And also it seems that they have a preconceived idea of what film music should be, so therefore they're writing on a synthetic basis. I think the only concert composer who is eminently successful in films is Aaron Copland.

INTERVIEW with JOHN WILLIAMS

Irwin Bazelon: In the context of defining a composer as a person who knows how to put a piece together and understanding the structure of films and the nature of the music written for them, do you think one has to be a composer to write film music?

John Williams: No. Not in the sense I think you and I would define the term "composer." I think one could take a primitive with pie tins and bows and arrows and good recording equipment and make a wonderfully effective sound compilation of a mélange of noises. It might be very effective dramatically if it was timed correctly, if it suited the style of the film; if all these things seemed wedded to the grain or fabric of the film, I think it could be wonderful. Some people say this is composing, this is a composer—it may be, I don't know. But not in the kind of European, eighteenth-, nineteenth-, early twentieth-century sense of the word "composer" and the skills which that would designate.

IB: In other words, there are people who have learned to manipulate sounds, even though you and I know that sounds don't always make music.

JW: Some people have wonderful senses of aural design—sometimes better than composers, better than highly crafted and trained and skilled composers. There are some working in films very effectively. I think Quincy Jones is a wonderfully gifted man who has in his best work demonstrated a very keen ear. Perhaps not so much for composition in the academic or legitimate or serious sense, but composition in the sense of putting aural effects and images and noises together that make dramatic sense. I think Quincy's a good example of that breed of musician.

IB: Did you always want to write film music or did you have other musical ambitions or did you just stumble into the medium?

JW: I stumbled into films. The first compositions I did as a kid—I was a music student, a piano major and composition was second—but I wrote a piano sonata at the age of nineteen—you know, this kind of thing.

IB: Where did you study?

JW: UCLA here, later at Julliard. But in those years always mainly with piano in mind, and I did some writing, but I never dreamed I would write for films; I was thinking in terms of a piano career. I was a pretty good jazz pianist as a kid, and because of that I was able to get easily available jobs and recording-session work, sort of gigging around in New York. And when I came back to California because my family was here and the film business was here, and I was a fairly good sight-reading and jobbing pianist, I found myself working in film-studio orchestras. So I was exposed to it really through piano. I was playing piano for a lot of composers—you were one of them; Jerry Goldsmith was another. Earlier on, Alfred Newman was one of the composers I played for, one of the ones who impressed me the most. He was a genuine conductor, an interpreter of music; he brought things to other people's scores that the composers themselves didn't seem to be able to. He seemed, of that older generation, the best interpreter of the lot. From the piano vantage point, I became interested in this business of writing for films, and because of my entré into studios, because of my early piano abilities, one thing followed another.

IB: Do you believe that film music must necessarily mirror the pop culture of its time or what's currently the popular dance-music style? Do you think there's a natural tendency for the music of the pop culture to infiltrate into the films?

JW: I think there is a natural tendency for that to happen. After all, films, cinema, is a popular art; not totally, but in the main it is, commercially speaking. I admit that with some unhappiness. I mean, I think it is the opera of the twentieth century. It's what Meyerbeer and Bizet—whatever they were to popular upper-middle-class entertainment in France in the nineteenth century, so films are in this century to a segment of the population. But the promise that film music held out when sound in films developed has not been fulfilled. The greatest composers of music in the last forty years have not turned their attention to film. Many of the pop artists have achieved some very good results. But part of my own unhappiness about the development in film is that it is, to such a large extent, a pop-entertainment medium.

IB: How do you feel about the title-song mania and the current influx into the film scene of record companies paying music-production costs and creating hit records?

JW: Well, it has been overdone. God knows, it's a practice that I've been involved in on a few occasions myself. Not very happily, ever; some people seem to have a better touch at that than I do. Again, there I have mixed emotions. It's a practice that can be vile, obnoxious, and awful—very often. On the other hand, the commercial part of me says something has to do some business, and the music-selling business is not altogether a bad thing. It makes me think of Columbia Records; so many of their pop artists keep the masterwork catalogue going. You know, in the musical community there is a little bit of tit for tat. (I wish there were more tat for all the tit.) The broadest base in music publication, in music exploitation, does all of us composers some good. The idea of music earning money, whether it's yours or Stravinsky's or mine or a pop composer's or a troubadour's off the street with a guitar who doesn't know a C from a G—the idea of some of that music selling and accruing revenue and creating a broad base for the publishing industry is a healthy thing. So on the positive side of it, this business of title song and popular success from film music is both a good thing and a bad thing. It isn't a great thing for the art of music, vis-à-vis film scoring. But it does help the sort of general health of the music-publishing, revenue-creating areas of the music business—and the music "business" affects us all.

IB: Why do you think that so few contemporary concert composers in America are invited to score mainstream feature films? Do you think there is a commercial-mindedness that influences film people to avoid these composers?

JW: I think at the base of this thing is the fact that the American film industry is different in its character from the Russian, German, Italian, etc. Part of it has to do with language itself: the English language is the Esperanto of the present time. American film producers have always had the largest audience. An Englishman would say, "Why do you have so many millions for your film and I only have pittance; what is this American wealth in films?" It has to do with the number of theaters, the numbers of bodies coming to the theaters.

It's changing over the years. We could go back to the Fred Astaire-Ginger Rogers days—it was a commercial, popular entertainment medium, and commercial to a far greater extent than it ever was in France, than it ever could be in Italy, than it ever could conceivably be in Russia—and therefore, the whole sort of aesthetic tone of film-making was on a broader point on the bell curve, at a broader base aesthetically, and therefore, in some sense, a lower aesthetic base, closer to the common aesthetic ideal. I don't like to use the word "lower," because I believe in democracy in the arts, but let me put it this way—closer to a popular base—and the result has been that we've had more popular composers—Cole Porter writing for films. Not only songwriters; composers: people like Alfred Newman who came out of the theater—popular American music—and Max Steiner the same way; Franz Waxman was something of a jazz musician. I think this has something to do with it. I also think it has something to do with the American suspicion of serious-mindedness and high-mindedness. Thomas Mann, Aldous Huxley, Schoenberg, Stravinsky—these people came to California. But the interesting thing I noticed in Thomas Mann's letters was the great excitement when he got to California. It looked like the Côte d'Azur to him when he got here—and the great, naive excitement of movie-making, you know. And his great disappointment after the war—the McCarthy era—how it drove him back to Switzerland, and in his wonderfully articulate and aristocratic way, he described his disenchantment with the American sensibility. The director who was arty was suspect. Not only were his politics suspect, but his box-office magnetism was suspect.

IB: But don't you think it also has to do with the composers themselves; they're not willing to go out and meet some of these people and express an interest?

JW: Well, I think a lot of the finest musical minds in the country have concluded, "Well, Hollywood film music—that's simply kitsch—I'm not going to lower my standards and get involved in that," rather than take the positive attitude and say, "This is a great challenge in the twentieth century; this is the real art medium in the twentieth century; this is where I can really contribute something."

IB: You're quite right.

JW: And now we're coming to an era where, in serious music as well—you were talking about avant-garde and serious music growing closer to pop (in the younger generation), to noise music, electronics, and mixed-media kind of idioms of expression that suddenly become visual. Well, musicians are talking about audio-visual correspondence having nothing to do with pure visuals in the entertainment sense, in the movie sense, so there may be some hope that the Maxwell Davies of the world (he has a wonderful theatrical flair in his music anyway and probably could direct a fine film) suddenly seem to be saying to all of us, "Hey, I can take this seriously even if it's on the level of parody," which I think in Max's case it is; only until now I don't think he's really come face to face with the problem.

IB: I'm a great believer in writing your own sounds, even though we all know there are dramatic functions involved in films, and not every film has the excitement of another. Some are very prosaic and don't call for it.

JW: Right. Some films, on that point, seem to demand tonality.

IB: Sure. The other extreme would be out of place. But you still believe that pop songwriters and pop-music talent in today's scene have an edge in getting composing assignments over other types of composers?

JW: I think quantitatively they do, yes. I think more Hollywood producers, maybe London producers as well, would tend to say, "I want a pop-type noise for this picture," or "I want an exploitation song and a pop score." He's less likely to say, "I want Max Davies; I want Bud Bazelon." There are fewer things the producer probably feels that you can do or Max can do, you know.

IB: A special kind of film.

JW: That's right. And they're rare; they're very rare.

IB: I know you're a pianist, but I'm curious about your working habits. Do you use a piano to work out your ideas?

JW: Yes, I do use the piano—not all that much.

IB: Do you like to improvise a scene in the beginning, to sort of feel your way through it as far as style and form are concerned?

JW: Every score I find is different. To use an example of a kind of score where I don't use a piano—except in the rarest kind of instances where I'm writing a six-percussion kind of affair, a piano isn't very much help anyway; whereas other, more romantic things are very pianistic, and I find myself playing whole two- and three-minute sequences as almost romantic piano nocturnes, writing them down in that fashion and then scoring from that. So I think the answer would be, depending on the kind of music it is, my own habits would include a lot of piano or very little, but never none.

IB: Do you ever write music between assignments other than film scores?

JW: Yes, I do. Writing music is a pleasurable (so far) experience for me, and what little time I have, I do spend working on pieces.

IB: What percentage of directors and producers that you've worked for over the years know anything about music or even how to communicate on a simple dramatic level with a composer? How would you judge their overall musicality?

JW: My experience varies. I have worked for one or two who were terrifically well informed on music, and some were better musicologists than I am, but that's very rare. That might represent maybe five or ten percent. I'm thinking on a scale of maybe fifty people that I have worked with; I can think of two who are really quite knowledgeable.

IB: When I say simple level, nobody expects them to be musicians or to write our notes, even though I bet you find most of them think they know their business and yours.

JW: Yes, there is a lot of that. The old musician's joke, "Everybody's a musician when it comes to scoring films." And that's true, you do run into a lot of that. I feel this about directors: the best directors are musical; I think part of what they do is musical. The art of editing film in my mind is a musical art. I find sometimes when I work with editors it's a thing of —one finds a cut in the same way that you prepare an orchestra, or you breathe with them, or it's a quicker tactic (your lungs diving into cold water). And directors who are good with actors and good with editors I find in general are musical. My complaint about them is that they listen to a fairly narrow range of music. Most of them don't have very broad tastes where music is concerned, so their picture may require a kind of music (or I may think it requires a kind of music) with which they are totally unfamiliar, and there's some education necessary there, and that's always dangerous. You're trampling on egos right away. But I think the better they are, the more musical they are. Once in a while, there's an Eisenstein, you know, an immensely cultured man who knows music—maybe he plays chamber music or something.

IB: Can you name one director?

JW: I can name Delbert Mann—he's very knowledgeable in music. Another one is George Roy Hill, who plays Bach on the piano and knows music. Another one is Mark Rydell, who's something of a pianist and knows music, and he's very musical. So perhaps I'm a bit kinder to the directors in that respect. I think the central thing here is musicality, and I think musicality has to do with everything in theater, everything in dance, everything in all of these arts. I think at the base of the whole thing is rhythm. Rhythm is the key to intonation, the key to vibrato, etc.

IB: It's also the key to the physiological response of audiences.

JW: Exactly. In the whole sort of visceral way of a film—the way music affects an audience, how one attacks the tempi. I think if you're dealing with a first-class director, you'll have less problems.

IB: Do you think that music can really describe anything, or do you think that it suggests through visual imagery? I realize we've inherited the romantic tradition.

JW: I was about to say it's largely cultural association. But what I think Kubrick has shown so wonderfully well is that the associations can be dispelled. Take a thing like the Strauss waltz in *2001*. The whole thing about a waltz is grace, and you see that the orchestra can achieve this. Kubrick takes what is the essence of courtly grace, the waltz, and uses it to accompany these lumbering but weightless giants out in space during their kind of sexual coupling. And even though the Strauss waltz in my mind, probably in yours too—it's the Danube, it's Viennese awful chocolate cakes and ghastly Viennese coffee. You know what I mean? But Kubrick says to us, "Watch the film for more than five seconds and forget those associations, and it will stop being nineteenth-century Vienna," and in the hands of Von Karajan the music becomes a work of art that says "look," that says "air," that says "float" in beautiful orchestral terms, and if you go with this film, the film helps dispel all of these associations, and we're into a new audio-visual world. Zarathustra too, but it's a less startling example.

IB: You're quite right about the visual thing.

JW: In any case, how anyone goes with that, I think that the film, which is the key element here, serves to cause hints in association with that music. The audio-visual coupling is the key to your original question, I think.

IB: What about music behind dialogue? This is a tricky thing. Do you like to work with single lines or solo instruments, or do you avoid writing behind dialogue entirely?

JW: It is a tricky thing. It's become a somewhat dated practice. Back in the old Warner Brothers days a picture was scored from beginning to end. I do find myself scoring dialogue scenes every now and then, and they can be very effective. I think a composer should think of the dialogue as part of the score; he could write it as accompaniment for a violin concerto rather than compose a score to exist on its own. There are a few little tips, for example, low strings—I find that in underscoring dialogue, if the dialogue has a low string sonority underneath it, very often it gives the dialogue something to sit on—the listener seems happy with that. This isn't to say that one can't have high frequencies as well, but I think the choice of textures under the dialogue, the register of the speaking voices, and also the tempo of the dialogue—if a man says a line, and there's a pause, and the woman says the next line after another pregnant pause, it may be possible to color the music somewhat differently. If the dialogue is very tight and fast, it may create another kind of problem—you may have to go against that—a long-note-score kind of music rather than a congested, "notey" score. I think here is the thing of practice and, in the end context, style of the picture, etc., has everything to do with it.

IB: Do you think that there's too much music in films today, that films are overscored, or do you think it's the opposite?

JW: As a musician, I kind of think there's generally too much music everywhere—in the elevators, the office, everybody's car. I go to someone's house for dinner, and what do they do but put on records during dinner and right away my whole evening is interrupted—my mind is saying what key they are in, it's too slow or too fast.

IB: Airports, hospitals, everywhere.

JW: So that its effect has been lessened. That probably goes for films too. There's too much trashy music everywhere.

IB: Do you think that the tracks are too loud or too prominent?

JW: Sometimes, yes. I think all of this exposure to films has made the ways of the gentle art of music harder.

IB: How much control do you have over your score before and after the recording stage?

JW: It's a very difficult aspect. Again, some directors are very disposed to listen to a composer if they like him, if they respect him, if they've had good luck and good fortunes with him before and they trust him. Very often you will shrink with pain to hear what everyone regards as our work, and we know it represents about fifty percent of what we've done or less. This may also be one of the

201

answers to your question as to why so few contemporary composers will do films. That could be one of the reasons and a very good one, for it is most frustrating. A public exhibition of one's work, and very seldom does it represent faithfully the composer's work.

IB: What other film composers do you admire? Do you have any favorites?

JW: I have a lot of favorites. Jerry Goldsmith is a great favorite of mine. He's very versatile. There are some other older ones. Herrmann I admire; I think we all do. Maxwell Davies is a favorite composer of mine, not so much for his films—I don't think he's worked that successfully in films as yet, but he might if he chooses to and if he's interested in films.

IB: Leaving aside *Images* for a minute, what do you think is your best score or your best-scored scene from a film?

JW: The best score musically (not from a particularly good film) I think I'd have to say was *Jane Eyre,* which was a two-hour film for TV. The music is very much in a late nineteenth-century style and purpose, but the quality of the scenes and the number of them and the variety of them.

IB: You got the greatest satisfaction from doing that?

JW: Yes; as a piece of music, I wouldn't mind playing that in public. You couldn't really, because it's a pastiche of another style, necessitated by the Yorkshire atmosphere in the film. But I think that and *The Reivers*, which was the Faulkner film.

IB: Let's turn to *Images*. The credits on the screen say music by John Williams and sound by Stomu Yamashta. I don't know whether he improvised these sounds or whether he composed them, but you get the feeling that there were two composers involved in this score. Who wrote what?

JW: Well, there's a long and interesting history to this music. It was a Robert Altman film—script by him. Altman had been talking to me about this script for years. It was one of those rare things where he said, "Write a piece of music first, and I'll film the score." That didn't happen. I didn't have time to write the music, and he went off on another picture, and the whole thing matured a couple of years later. But I'd been thinking about it and thinking about the schizophrenic quality of this film and this character. Here was a girl who one moment was in touch with reality and the next moment went out of touch altogether. And it seemed to me that the music should be done in two parts and it should have a duality for those reasons. So two or three years went by, and I went to see another of Altman's films in London last February. And when I looked at the film I instantly remembered the sculptures of Baschet. He had his sculptures here at UCLA about six years ago, and he had his associates and his family with him, and they performed on the sculptures. He played things like Viennese waltzes and *Flight of the Bumblebee*—it wasn't very interesting musically, but the noises these instruments made.

IB: Were they metallic?

JW: Well, most of his sculptures (Baschet is a serious sculptor, not a musician) are made to look at, they're made to see. And the noises they make are a kind of adjunct to them. They're stainless-steel surfaces sculpted like floral petals. Some of them are sixteen feet high; they're prominent visual works, and he has attachments of sawed-off glass rods that vibrate, and the vibrations go through a wire and activate these planes of steel, making the most unearthly sounds, wonderful noises. Dissolve. Two or three years later at the Museum of Modern Art in New York, I walked in one day and there was the whole ground floor covered with Baschet, and if one put a dime in the little machine, he could pick up a headset and hear these noises created by Baschet. I forgot all about this, but when I saw in Altman's film exactly this thing, I thought now is my chance to put the music and his sculpture into a musical thing like a score. So I called André Previn and asked him about Baschet—he said, "Oh yes. Yamashta (the Japanese percussionist) plays them." And I knew Yamashta because he'd done a film for Ken Russell, *The Devils,* and he's a very great percussionist—American trained. So I rang up Yamashta, who lives in Paris, and he said, "Come over; we'll talk." So I went to Paris and asked him if he'd like to perform the percussion in this score. And he said yes, he would.

And he showed me his percussions, his Japanese bells, etc., and there's kind of this zanylike quality in this film anyway, and the whole thing began to take shape. For the other side of it, I knew I wanted to do a kind of pastoral, bucolic—something or other with lutes and strings.

IB: There's also that piano background in the opening. Are you playing that?

JW: That's right. Yes, I played all the keyboard, and Yamashta played all the percussion. He agreed to play, and we went to Baschet's studio; Yamashta was tremendously skilled even on conventional instruments, but he gave the most wonderful demonstration on these Baschet things, and I thought, "Aha, that's terrific." So I picked out two large instruments and one or two smaller ones to rent from Baschet, and that was the end of it. We shook hands, and Stomu showed up at the session, so to speak, as a playing musician, and he brought his gear with him. When I was in Paris, I made little notes for myself about the instruments: what they would do; what we would call them; a little, simple method of graph notation to time out these percussion effects with either the conventional music or the film action it was to correspond with. Where the credit business comes in—I was so pleased to have Stomu; he's such a well-known percussionist. I wanted to give him credit, to say, "Percussion played by Stomu Yamashta," and he said, "I'm trying to get away from the percussion; I want to expand my activities; I'd rather it be 'Sounds produced by. . . .' " So I think, perhaps, it was a kind of contractual agreement with him. He wanted that screen credit, and I wanted to give it to him—in the same way as if you wrote a violin concerto for somebody in a film, you would say, "Violin by so-and-so." I felt in this case, in a sense, that I was writing a percussion concerto with strings. So at Stomu's request, the idea of "sounds" was put on the film, and when you're doing things people don't usually think all that much about, who's going to take notice? It just seemed natural; that's what he wanted; we agreed. Stomu functioned as a percussionist; if it would be a concerto for percussion, this is how it would be described and perhaps should have been.

IB: But there were other percussion instruments. I heard chimes, wind chimes, bells, also blowing air through the flute.

JW: That's right. It wasn't all on the Baschets. We had the Inca flute and Kabuki percussion instruments. Then there were the Baschets—principally the four larger pieces of sculpture and few smaller pieces—plus all the conventional gear, which included timpani, hand drums, blocks, bells, marimbas—all these things, as well as a few tricks of his own—little shaking things, little sticklike Kabuki noises.

IB: But he did not improvise anything to the visuals?

JW: There are a few sections that are improvised within the context of a prepared timing—almost if one would do an aleatory bit of music. I might hit a chord with the orchestra and the score might indicate dashes for ten seconds on such and such an instrument—crescendo into double forte—that sort of thing.

IB: I never thought it was improvised. I always thought it was very well organized.

JW: Now, the way it was accomplished is of interest. I wanted to use all textures and strings and nothing else—the only thing added would be Stomu's voice. He does it in his concerts of some of Henze's pieces. So it was the Japanese style of the percussion, the resonance of the instruments, and his chest—he might even say "ouch" in Japanese. What I have on the score is just an aural noise, so his voice is a contribution. So there is, in fact, an immense creative contribution, because his performance is outstanding, I think, and deserving of every credit he has. I don't want to detract from Stomu's participation, but I felt very strongly that we have the discipline of the written symbol, timed to the film in its dramatic application, and that, I think, is what gives it its unique sense, rather than haphazardness, of taut discipline. So I reckoned percussion, keyboards—which I wanted to play all myself—and string orchestra. We began by recording—I wrote the score in the normal way—the string orchestra here, the keyboards here, and the percussion here. And the keyboards—I might play one particular section piano or piano twice, banging here, improvising something here, or playing something written here. The keyboard might be on three lines, which would require—since I was going to play it all—three overdubs on the piano; the percussion is almost always four or five lines. You would hear Japanese woodblocks, you would hear Baschet-sculpture percussion, you might hear timpani, etc., in one sequence. My idea was to make the most personal, idiosyncratic thing, have one man play everything, rather than have four percussionists, which I could have done—let Stomu play everything. So the first thing I did was record the string orchestra for a whole day—all the traditional music, all of this material, and to time it exactly when the legitimate orchestra stopped and Stomu and I started with either our written notes or whatever we were going to do. And then we would select one, i.e., the woodblocks and the piano first. It was done on sixteen-track tapes, so we put the string orchestra left, center, and right; that left me thirteen tracks of tape to play around with. And we proceeded in that way. Stomu would take line one and play that, then line two, putting on the earphones to hear what he just recorded on line one. Then on line three he heard lines one and two back. And I drew on the score—where, if you play pa pa, I play ta tee; I'm taking my notes from your cue. In this case he would just follow the arrows, which are indicated on the percussion production notes. And he followed himself with his own timings and made a wonderful effect.

IB: Also, the instruments have tremendous presence, as though they're amplified and reverbed and echoed all over the place.

JW: Yes, some of these Baschet instruments—I wish you could see them—instantly make wonderful noises. A lot of these noises Stomu pointed out to me; if you put your ear on the right place on the plane, the buildup would be most beautiful or the sonority would be the most attractive.

INTERVIEW with RICHARD RODNEY BENNETT

Pat Gray: In the context of defining a composer as a person who knows how to put a piece together and understanding the structure of films and the nature of the music written for them, do you think one has to be a composer to write film music?

Richard Rodney
Bennett: I think a well-equipped musician could very well do film music, but I think a composer is more likely to have an extended field of imagination and to respond in a more interesting way to the visual challenge. There are lots of people who could do film music, but I think composers probably do the best film music.

PG: How much leeway are you given to write your music, especially in regard to controversial sounds?

RRB: This depends completely on the film. I think all composers get typecast at one time or another. At one time I was typecast for doing horror films. In horror films, one can do anything. You can have a marvelous time. But in romantic films or comedy films, I think the director is more likely to know what he expects to hear. It depends entirely on the producer and the director. I have worked for some directors, for example, Joseph Losey, who give you complete freedom and trust you. This is marvelous. The hardest director to work for is somebody who thinks he knows a little about music and who has preconceived ideas about it. Then you're in trouble. It is hard to get from a director what he really wants in musical terms, because he doesn't often know how to talk articulately about music.

PG: Do they talk about music during, before, or after the making of the film?

RRB: I don't like to be involved during the making of the film, let alone before it, because if I read a script I get a very strong idea of what the film is going to be like, and then I start thinking in musical terms. And when you see the film, it is totally different, because you see it through somebody else's eyes. I prefer to work rather clinically, to come in at the last minute and see a fine cut and work on that. I don't like having to go on location on films,

207

because usually I can be of no help at all. Directors think you can absorb the atmosphere or something, but I get the atmosphere from the screen.

PG: Is there much pressure on you to play it safe when you are writing film music?

RRB: Yes, I suppose there is; they like to have a nice, cozy, acceptable score, and the more I work in films, the less I want to do that. And the less I want to go along with the film, which, of course, is the easy way. In other words, just to interpret musically what you see on the screen. There are all kinds of other possibilities, such as going against what you see on the screen and trying to add an extra dimension to the film. This can be extraordinarily interesting, but, of course, it's more risky. If you write a piece of music that goes directly contrary to what is being seen on the screen, people can think you've just gone mad.

PG: Why do you think so few contemporary concert composers, especially in America, are invited to score mainstream feature films?

RRB: Well, I think in America it's geographical. There is also a kind of snobbery both ways. I think that film-makers in general tend not to stick their necks out. For instance, they think it is terrific to get Leonard Bernstein for a film, but otherwise they would rather play it safe and use a commercial film composer who will just turn out "film music." But I think in England and on the Continent there is always more of a tradition of using what I would call proper composers—serious composers. And I think in England all the serious composers, almost without exception, have done film music. A few names occur to me—Britten, Bax, and, nearer my own generation, myself, Don Banks, Peter Maxwell Davies. And, of course, on the Continent the list of composers who worked between the wars on films is staggering, and I really think that the greatest progress in film music was made during the 1930s—not since then.

PG: Do you mean in Europe or America?

RRB: In Europe. There were some wonderful things done in the late thirties in America, but I think the biggest strides forward in creating a true film music were created in the thirties in Europe.

PG: When you are working, do you use the piano or a Movieola?

RRB: I work at my desk. I hardly use the piano at all, and I never use a Movieola. I detest them. I have quite a good visual memory. I see the film twice, separated by a short period of time, because I can't take in two screenings of a film at one time. I have my measurements, and I just remember what I see. Sometimes I go back and see things again if they seem to be problematic. I work entirely using metronome timings, where one can work out very precisely how long each bar of music lasts. I set up quite a tight structure for the section, guided by those timings that are important; that is to say, in the average film section there are only four or five points that you actually need to keep to, and in between you have a certain leeway. Once I have that basic skeleton, I can compose very freely around it.

PG: Do you have a stylistic problem to reconcile as far as your two musical worlds are concerned?

RRB: I think my own sounds are used very little in my film scores. I can only think of about three films where I have been able to write what I could call my own music, and so there really isn't a stylistic problem, because the two things are quite separate. I try to keep the same standards in both worlds. For instance, certain standards of musical construction and clarity of sound and so on. But I cannot say that my film music is representative of my serious music.

PG: Do you think your film music is distinctive? Listening to it, would one recognize your handwriting?

RRB: Yes, I would hope so. I try to keep a definite style—with exceptions, because every film demands a different treatment. But I know certain scores of mine do belong together. They really don't have anything to do with my serious music. Apart from anything else, the creative impulse is so different. In writing film music, one is really using only a sixth of one's musical mind, because

209

so much is given to you; and if one were to write film music with the same intensity as, say, writing a string quartet, one would lose one's mind. It is simply not conceivable, because the amount of music you've got to write for a film is so gigantic—a symphony's worth.

PG: Can music really describe anything, or does it tend to suggest through visual imagery and dramatic context?

RRB: I don't think music can describe anything at all, except in such a primitive way that one would scorn to use it as such. I mean the thunder does it much better itself—if you want thunder. But music can interpret emotions and can stylize certain ideas. You can often take up a cue from sound effects. I did a picture for Joseph Losey called *Figures in a Landscape,* and when I saw the film before it had music added, I noticed that through whole passages of the film you could hear rain falling or you could hear, say, crickets chirping; and that gave me an idea that the music could work in the same way, that it could make a continuous pattern through parts of the film. But I wasn't imitating rain or crickets chirping. In every film I try to look for some cue within the film. For example, I did a film which was set in Finland, in an icy, frozen landscape. That suggested my orchestration. And the color of the music. But I wasn't imitating anything.

PG: How do you feel music enhances or detracts from the spectator's involvement in a film?

RRB: I think it can do a very great deal—an enormous amount. But I certainly find I can be very distracted by music, particularly if the composer is trying too hard—trying to show off. That irritates me terribly. I don't know if it would worry the average listener if he wasn't involved in the business.

PG: How do you handle music behind dialogue?

RRB: I try to use as little music as possible these days in films. In fact, I just turned down a very big film because I didn't think it ought to have music at all. It was based on an Ibsen play, and I thought it impossible to put music behind Ibsen's dialogue.

PG: Is this *A Doll's House?*

RRB: Yes. One of the two versions. I tried to persuade the director not to use music. I find it quite a technical challenge to do music behind dialogue—music that doesn't have to be faded down too much and that is an acceptable background to speech. But naturally, one tries not to put music behind dialogue at all. Yet sometimes you have to, and you do your best.

PG: Do you use single lines or solo instruments as dramatic communication?

RRB: Every film I do, I try to use quite a different instrumental color. And nowadays, one is getting away from the conventional symphony orchestra. For instance, in one film I used only instruments like harpsichord, harp, piano, celesta, percussion, and so on. Another film I did entirely with strings. In *Lady Caroline Lamb* I have a solo viola with the orchestra. It's a sort of viola concerto. If I choose an orchestration I have never used before, I am much more liable to write interesting music.

PG: How do you feel about the title-song mania and the current influx into the film scene of record companies trying to create instant hits and composers?

RRB: It's very depressing. It is depressing artistically, and it is depressing also because one has to throw away half one's royalties to some publishing company that wants you, above all, to write a theme tune. And even if you don't write a theme tune, they're still going to take half your royalties, whether or not they do any promotion. That's infuriating and disgusting from a material point of view. If I get a good theme tune out of a film, it pleases me no end; of course, I make a bit of money, but I won't sit down, as I'm afraid many composers do, not only with a theme tune but with record albums in mind. It's such a moronic approach to film music if all you can do is write a theme tune.

PG: What do you think makes good film music? Entering into the plot, writing to the picture, or understatement of scoring?

RRB: I couldn't be precise about that. I try to add to the film something that wasn't there before; if one is just copying what is on the screen, one is not adding anything. One tries to write a personal thing that belongs with what the director is doing, that is in keeping with the director's approach to the film.

PG: What percentage of directors and producers that you have worked with know anything at all about music?

RRB: It is purely individual. Joe Losey, for instance, is intensely responsive to music. John Schlesinger is even more responsive. On the other hand, I have worked with directors who were very pretentious and thought they knew quite a bit about music. Those are the worst. In a sense, I like to work either with somebody who is very responsive and really knows about music or with someone who doesn't know anything about it at all. Then your hands aren't tied. I have worked with some really, really stupid producers, and it was all right, because they left one alone and regarded one as somebody who could do something for the film that they couldn't possibly do themselves. You'd be surprised how often one is just thought of as somebody who comes to paint the walls of your house.

PG: What is your best score or the one you like the best?

RRB: I don't know. I have about four films I am very fond of. They're not all necessarily good films, but they are ones that gave me pleasure. There is a picture with Bette Davis called *The Nanny*. It has quite a small music score. There are two Joe Losey pictures, *Figures in a Landscape* and *Secret Ceremony,* and I like *Lady Caroline Lamb*. In *Far From the Madding Crowd* there was a scene set in the open country—a scene where the heroine, Julie Christie, visualized her lover (played by Terence Stamp) as a charging battalion of cavalry—and that was an incredibly hard sequence to do. I nearly went crazy trying to get it so that both John Schlesinger and I were pleased with it. After it was finished, I think it really did something for that scene, which was a sort of fantasy. Often in films one goes through fantastically traumatic times and experiences doing music, and then it is not worth it. You just end up with a mess. When the director wants this fiddled with and that fiddled with and something else pulled around, you can end up with nothing. But every now and again you really slave your guts out, and it is worth it.

PG: Can you have too much music in films today?

RRB: That was more so in the past. Music is tending to be used with better reasons now. The old Hollywood tradition of swamping everything with music has gone. If one sees an old movie on television nowadays, it is incredible how much music there was. The first feature I ever did, which was in 1956, had about an hour's music; and the last picture I did, *Caroline Lamb,* which is twice as long, only has twenty minutes of music. And yet, people notice that twenty minutes more than in any other picture I have ever done, because it is there for a reason. If you have Muzak going on all the time, you don't notice it, but if you sit down to a gramophone record that you have chosen to listen to, you really appreciate it.

PG: How often are your scores thrown out? What is your reaction to that?

RRB: I have had two scores thrown out: one was very, very long ago when I was just starting in the business, and I tried to do something rather pretentious and arty. It was wrong because they wanted a commercial score. Recently I did a score for a film where I didn't really understand what the director wanted. He wasn't able to put into words what he wanted, and so I didn't know what he was getting at at all. It was a frightfully hard picture to do; what I did was my interpretation of the film, and it wasn't in keeping with what he had in mind, so he finally got somebody else. It was one of those films that should never have had music.

INTERVIEW with ALEX NORTH

Irwin Bazelon: In the context of defining a composer as a person who knows how to put a piece together and understanding the structure of films and the nature of the music that's written for them, do you think it's always necessary that one be a composer to write film music, or can people who really aren't composers manage to do film scores?

Alex North: Well, let me say that I think one should be a composer, because you're dealing with an art form in which music should be one of the chief ingredients, just as the photography, costumes, lighting, etc., but I also find it advantageous to be a composer, a schooled composer, so that if you're scoring a particular kind of scene that has a certain conflict of characters or interpersonal relationships, you can manipulate your material and make a form out of your piece, whether it's a thirty-two bar or a sixteen-bar piece that has a beginning, a middle, and an end. I think it's unfortunate that there are composers who are not really composers in the aesthetic sense as we know it. And a lot of that is not the fault of the guy who's actually doing the music but the producer or the director, who should know better.

IB: I think you're right, because, in a sense, he's doing his thing, isn't he?

AN: Right, and they don't know for the most part whether this piece that's being written for the screen is music that can stand by itself—which I don't think is absolutely necessary. But as a schooled composer, I think it's essential to try to accomplish both results.

IB: Well, I wasn't asking you that as a trick question, but I am constantly seeing films all the time, and I hear so many scores that seem to work, because there's a certain dramatic flair present, but I'm perfectly aware that this person is just not a composer. I feel that there are all kinds of people who are doing film music, and some are composers and some are not.

AN: Yes, some of them are former arrangers. And this is not putting them down; they may have done a lot of self-study, you know. But I think if you're doing a serious film and you use a certain approach—say, for example, a film that I did, *Death of a Salesman,* where you establish the character with a single alto flute, which is pure and simple, slightly textured. The technique that's involved in the development of this story is, I think, a composer's job—to try with this material, as you would in writing a serious piece, to create tension and relaxation within the story line.

IB: It's interesting that you should bring up *Death of a Salesman,* because in my book I compare the effect on the audience of the music from the stage play with the effect from the film. I found the flute opening in the stage play had more intimacy to me, sitting a few feet away from the stage; it set that scene and the whole theatricality. Somehow, when it got on the screen, I found that the flute, the opening, didn't have the same power—the screen was too lifelike, was far too large.

AN: Well, sure, in the sense that the screen depersonalizes, I prefer writing for theater, because it's, I think, a greater challenge, and you're dealing in a film with something that's a lot more synthetic, in a sense.

IB: Was the music for the opening of *Death of a Salesman* almost the same opening as it was for the stage play, or was it changed?

AN: No, it was the same. It was an alto flute solo, but, of course, the director of the film approached the film much differently from the way Kazan had directed the play.

IB: What was that opening scene again?

AN: Willy Loman coming into the house late at night with the two suitcases. And of course later in the play you couldn't see him driving the car to commit suicide. This gave me an opportunity in doing the film music to write a rather exciting kind of a scherzo, which had form and reached certain peaks and dropped; and, in that sense, writing for the film was a chance to elaborate.

IB: How much leeway are you given to write your music, especially in regard to the use of controversial sounds?

There's been so much difference in opinion about it—producers and directors tell you, "Don't give me that dissonant stuff," and that kind of business. Is part of this myth, or is it true?

AN: Well, it may apply to some directors and some producers, but fortunately, the composers are the last ones that are brought in, so that's a blind thing in terms of the end result. When the piece is actually being recorded and the director is there, he may take issue with a certain piece, and if you go along with him, if he makes sense and has good reason, then you make the change right there on the spot.

IB: I think that's also one of the differences between what we call the serious concert composer and those who have the ability to do dramatic work. I have a feeling that many of my compatriots would be absolutely lost if they suddenly had to change something immediately and rewrite something on the spot.

AN: I think it's a question of professionalism and experience. Having done, as you've done, so many documentaries— I'd done perhaps fifty to sixty documentaries before I came out here—gave me a kind of technique for writing for the films that was much more difficult, because in documentaries it's usually wall to wall. In writing a film score, I spend a lot of time charting out the whole course of the score. But I must say I've been fortunate; there have been experiences that aren't necessary to go into where directors have taken issue with what I've done.

IB: That brings me to my next question. What percentage of producers and directors that you've worked for over the years know anythng about music or even how to communicate with you on a simple dramatic level?

AN: I'd say about one or two percent, actually. If they are musically inclined and if they know music, I will listen to what they have to say, whether it's awkwardly stated or not, and try to translate what they want me to do in terms of the score. I must say I've been very lucky in that sense, having the freedom of choice in material and instrumentation.

IB: Why do you think that here in America so few contemporary concert composers are invited to score mainstream feature films? Do you think it's a problem of director-composer communications, the egos involved, that influences film people to avoid so-called serious concert composers?

AN: Well I think that's one of the reasons. I think Hollywood more or less has been and possibly still is a place where you need a sponsor. Kazan sponsored me.

IB: Kazan sponsored Leonard Rosenman, too.

AN: Right. And Benny Herrmann was sponsored by Orson Welles, you know. Unless someone has a sponsor, unless someone has the strength—a director who says this is who I want—that doesn't exist today. It's more the choice of the producer—he says I want this guy or I want that guy. They will occasionally go after Leonard Bernstein, who asks $250,000 per score. But I think it's unfortunate that more serious composers aren't asked to score films. I do think it takes a certain flair, but I won't mention names.

IB: Well, even someone like Stravinsky, I'm sure it would have been very difficult to work with an ego like that.

AN: Yes, you have to have a flair for the functional music. I've been working in functional music for most of my life. A composer came out whom I respect very much, and I know a good bit of his work. He didn't relate his music to the film, didn't tailor it to the film. I don't mean tailor in the sense of Mickeymousing it.

IB: He didn't have that dramatic-visual instinct.

AN: Right. Getting something that's the essence of the scene; or playing with a scene or playing against a scene.

IB: It is true, isn't it, that pop songwriters and pop-music talent seem to have an edge in getting composing assignments over people with the kinds of backgrounds that we have?

AN: No question about it. That's an unfortunate situation today, and hopefully it will improve.

IB: How do you work? Do you use a piano when you work on your films?

AN: I use it about half the time.

IB: Do you improvise and try to catch a certain flavor, a certain feeling about what you're going toward?

AN: Well, I think, as with most of us, it's pacing the floor before I start putting anything down on the blank page. You know, those are the toughest moments—getting started, getting an approach—an overall approach, not just writing a scene. I've been accused of writing too many ideas in many of my scores, and composer friends and musical directors have said to me, "Alex, why don't you just repeat this theme, repeat this theme, repeat it, so it will be effective as far as the audience is concerned," but I don't look at it that way. I have never put down the whole leitmotif idea, but it's not giving me satisfaction as a composer to do that, to write variations of the whole thing.

IB: Do you think there is too much illustrative music in films today?

AN: Oh, I think so. There are so many mistakes that are made where one can anticipate a particular moment of action because the composer telescopes the oncoming scene.

IB: How do you feel about this title-song mania and the current influx of record companies into the film scene, where they are actually paying the music-production costs and creating hit records?

AN: It's a commercial field, let's face it. And the producer's interested in a song, whether it's about rats or whatever, that becomes a hit; it may have nothing to do with the content of the film, but it's there, and it enables the producer to promote the film and accumulate some extra money advertising the film in that sense.

IB: Are you writing much music between film assignments other than film scores?

AN: As a matter of fact, I've been writing a piece for the University of California, and I'm reworking the music I did for *2001* into my Third Symphony, so I try to keep the juices going. I won't do a film that has violence in it, and I won't point out examples. But I do keep myself busy, as I say, just to keep the technique going.

IB: I find a tremendous versatility in your approach to films, because you've done a great many films of a very intimate nature and also some big spectaculars. For instance, I remember recently seeing *Spartacus* on TV. I found the music in the sequence where the gladiators are training a marvelous contemporary intrusion into a scene that is taking place in the Roman Empire period. And then the music is expanded and developed in the scene where the gladiators form an army and train the citizenry to join them. It's a real dance.

AN: Well, my training has been in dance, having worked with practically all the modern dancers in the thirties, and there again, with *Spartacus* I had a lot of time; I had close to a year to write that score. I had an opportunity to get a bit more—how should I say—not complex but intricate in the musical material.

IB: How often have you had a score thrown out, and what was your reaction to it? I know it happened in *2001*. You were asked to write this score, but wasn't there also someone in England who was asked to do it at the same time? What was Kubrick trying to do? Was he trying to protect himself?

AN: I think he was trying to protect himself. The man who did part of the score didn't do anything originally. He took Mahler's Third, which Stanley had planned to use in the film, and recorded part of it. Then Stanley called me in New York at the Chelsea Hotel and asked me to come over and write a new score. And I did half the score. I was very, very frustrated by it all. I really knocked myself out. It was the greatest opportunity to write a score for a film—where there are no sound effects, or hardly any sound effects.

IB: How much music did you actually write?

AN: I wrote fifty minutes of music in three weeks. I was taken to the recording in an ambulance, because my whole body was tied up in knots from having to work day and night; but I'm glad I did it, because I have the score, and I did some very fresh things as far as I myself am concerned. In many cases, a director who uses a "temp" track and takes it out for preview gets so latched onto this temporary music that he can't adjust to a new score. Now Stanley's very musical—we worked together on *Spartacus* —and I had the greatest experience with him. I had the good fortune of writing a temporary score for two pianos and two percussionists to fit the battle scene, for example, so that the cutter, Irving Lerner, could cut the scene to fit the music, which is unusual. But that was not the final track!

IB: Do you think there's too much music in films today or that films are overscored?

AN: Absolutely. I think in many cases one accommodates the director who feels that a certain scene doesn't come off—a dialogue scene, for example.

IB: Yes, how do you handle dialogue? Do you like to depersonalize the background; do you like to use a single line or soloist?

AN: Yes, it's very fragmentary. In most cases I try to avoid anything that's thick texturewise and all doublings, and I try for a more-or-less transparent score, depending on the scene.

IB: Did you always want to write film music? Did you have other musical ambitions?

AN: It's one of those things—starting out wanting to be a serious symphonic composer and sending scores out, and they come back with the pages unopened. You know that. Well, the one gratifying thing, which I'm sure the other composers have said, is that at least your music in films, if it's properly balanced and projected, reaches a mass audience.

IB: What about this business of using orchestrators? Now I realize that those who do film music or have to do a lot of music in a short amount of time can sketch things out, and that what we call an orchestrator is nothing but a glorified copyist. But without naming names, aren't there occasions when some of these people turn something over to an orchestrator that is really very scanty?

AN: That's true. There's no question about it. But I think in my case the orchestrator more or less executes my orchestration. And very often, if the orchestrator is a creative man, naturally, if he has an idea and if it's a good idea, you give him the satisfaction of using it.

IB: When you get a film, does a director ever say anything like, "This isn't going too good; save me!"

AN: Oh yes. Very often you're against writing music for a certain scene. But the director hasn't got faith in the film, he feels it hasn't come off, and he says, "Please help me out. I need your help."

IB: Do you believe what producers have tried to foster on the film public through the years—that bad music, dull music, or even controversial music can actually kill a film?

AN: No. I think the film kills itself. There are occasions where the wrong music is written for the wrong scene—is not written correctly for a particular scene.

IB: But even then it doesn't kill the scene, really, because it's married somehow to it.

AN: Exactly. And there are many different ways of approaching a scene. As you pointed out earlier, producers and directors are looking for the so-called new sound.

IB: I want to ask you about that. This constant searching for a new sound. I find the scores sound so much alike that I can hardly differentiate between them.

AN: Some of it has nothing to do with the scene. And some composers write for an album—not some, a lot. They may write a piece for a scene that lasts two-and-a-half minutes, let's say, and they write a three-minute piece for the album and just dial it out at some point, and that's that.

IB: What other film composers do you admire? What score or segment of any particular film has impressed you?

AN: Well, I like works that Leonard Rosenman has done, specifically, parts of *East of Eden*. And Jerry Goldsmith has a great range for writing something that's fragile and delicate. Also Larry Rosenthal—the score for *Beckett* and the score for *The Miracle Worker* are favorites of mine.

IB: Now about yourself. What do you think is the best score or the best-scored scene that you've done of all the films that you've worked on? Would it be the assassination scene from *Cleopatra?*

AN: Well, that's one of them. There's a scene from *Viva Zapata*—the gathering of the forces where Marlon Brando is to be executed—the peasants are tapping their stones together to call everyone out of their hiding places, and I take off with percussion on the same rhythmic pulse that they have established. That's one of my favorite scenes. It's difficult. There are scenes in *Member of the Wedding*—Jody's lament, when Ethel Waters speaks about her dead lover—and a scene from *The Misfits* with Eli Wallach, Marilyn Monroe, and Clark Gable, where they're rounding up the horses—I did that in the form of a ballet. I think most of my favorites are in the smaller, intimate films, because I can identify with people as opposed to these large spectacles.

IB: Let's talk in general about film music. What do you think film music is supposed to do? Don't you think it has more tendency to suggest, because of the visual imagery and context, rather than to describe anything?

AN: No question about it. I think it depends on the film, again; if it's an epic kind of a film, then the music is more objective than an intimate film, where you can extend a character by writing a certain piece that penetrates the soul of the individual. And I think you can create much more tension than there is visually very often, which helps the audience, in a sense.

IB: I'm glad you mentioned that word "tension," because contemporary music—its harmonic language—is ideally suited to increase this tension, more so than the harmonic language of, say, the nineteenth century. You like doing music for films, don't you?

AN: Well, I was going to stop in 1960. After *Spartacus* I thought I'd run the gamut.

IB: But there is a certain excitement, a certain theater and drama?

AN: There is, and I feel that whatever gifts I possess have to do with the function of theater. And adding that other dimension to the film or to a play or to a dance that isn't there visually, in a sense, just enhances the drama of a film, establishes the character or goes beneath the character, and that's not easy to do. The audience may not grasp it, but you, as the creator or as the composer, you know yourself what you're saying. The audience may not realize it.

IB: Setting aside the thematic Alex North and the rhythmic Alex North, it's the lyrical Alex North that I really like the most.

AN: Well, thank you.

IB: I feel that lyricism—the ability to sing—is what music is all about. Not that that's important in every film.

AN: No, but that's my point of departure in most cases, which is an old-fashioned thing stemming from the tune or melody.

INTERVIEW with LALO SCHIFRIN

Irwin Bazelon: I'd like to ask you a little about your background and what kind of musical education you have. Did you always want to write film music, or did you have other musical ambitions?

Lalo Schifrin: My father was concertmaster for the Buenos Aires Philharmonic thirty years ago. He's retired now. I grew up in a classical music family. Everybody in the family played string quartets on weekends as relaxation. For me, classical music was not only serious music but conservative serious. For my father to accept Debussy or even Wagner was too much. He didn't like them.

IB: But you were surrounded by music as a child; your father was involved?

LS: Oh, yes. Later, when I was going to college, I never planned to be a musician professionally. I was studying law, and I discovered American jazz, which was in Argentina very esoteric music. I'm talking about *real* jazz, not dance music. And I became very involved—that was my private rebellion against what was going on at home. So through jazz, believe it or not, I discovered modern music. I felt a kind of schizophrenia, a moving in two directions. It was easy to be a Dr. Jekyll and Mr. Hyde; I could do classical music, and I could do jazz with ease. When I went to France, I took lessons with René Leibowitz. At the same time I was playing at night at the Club St. Germaine, and this was a tremendous influence in my development. I played for the first time with American musicians like Chet Baker, and it was very important in my development. Then I went back to Argentina, and I put together a big band—modern jazz band—which was very successful. I couldn't believe it. Maybe because they never saw a band with four trombones, five saxes, and four trumpets playing together. And the vitality—we were making no concessions whatsoever to commerciality. And also, I became involved in writing music for ballets, choirs, symphonies, chamber music, all kinds of things. But there was another side of my artistic personality, which was my love for film. Before I went to France, I was going to film classes. I was studying all the masters of cinema. I think if

I had not become a musician, I would have become a film-maker or had some involvement with films.

IB: When did you come to the United States?

LS: I came in 1958. Dizzy Gillespie brought me here. He was touring South America and heard my band and asked me to join him. I had done some films in Argentina already, so when I came here, I played with him for three years, and then I came to Hollywood. M.G.M. Records sent me out here to the movies, and I started to live here.

IB: What was your first film?

LS: It was called *Joy House* and starred Jane Fonda. M.G.M. sent me to France. Then after that I started doing television and other movies.

IB: I asked about your background first, because, although I know the kind of musician you are, I only knew about your jazz interests. I did not know about your basic traditional training. Defining a composer as a person who knows how to put a piece together and understanding the nature of films and the kinds of music written for pictures, do you think it is always necessary to be a composer in this context in order to score motion pictures?

LS: No, you don't have to be a composer. For example, one of the most effective scores, *The Third Man*, has a theme that is crude and banal, but it worked in the film, and you can't honestly say he [Karas] was a composer. I can cite other examples, I'm sure. Also, sometimes it pays not to be a composer—one can be a "juxta-poser."

IB: How much leeway are you given when you write your music to use any sounds you want? How much pressure is exerted on you to play it safe or not to use too much dissonance? Are you given a lot of freedom to write your music?

LS: Absolutely. I feel that the ability of a good film composer in cases where he has to use dissonance—he does it in such a way that no one will notice the dissonance.

IB: It's easier in films, because you have the visual imagery and the dramatic context. You put these same sounds together isolated from the screen action, and people hear it differently.

LS: Yes. For instance, I did a score, *The Hellstrom Chronicle*—of course, the producers of the film were very musically oriented in their way to what's going on in today's avant-garde music. I used aleatory, electronic, and serial techniques. I don't know what the reaction of the audience was. It was probably very annoying for some of them who listened to the score alone. I had a very good subject, which was insects.

IB: How do you work? I know you're a pianist, but do you work everything out at the piano?

LS: No. I have no rule. Sometimes I do use the piano, especially when the score requires something based on melodic lines. But when it is composition or juxtaposition, then I don't.

IB: Do you ever write music between assignments other than film scores?

LS: Oh yes. As a matter of fact, right now I'm commissioned by Claremont College to do a piece.

IB: What percentage of producers and directors that you've worked for know anything about music or even how to communicate with you on a basic, elementary dramatic level? How would you grade their overall, relative musicality?

LS: There are some producers and directors who are very aware of what's going on—extremely aware. You'd be surprised. You know they do go to concerts. I went with a friend of mine with whom I've worked on many films (a Boulez concert, I believe). There are others who are aware in other areas, like what's going on in jazz. Others are not musical, and it is difficult to find the ability to communicate with them musicwise—how to find the common language. Some may not know too much about music, but they know about film, and they know about the feeling they want—enough to communicate.

IB: How do you feel about the current title-song mania and the influx into the film scene of record companies paying music-production costs, owning the music, and creating hit records and instant composers?

LS: Well, I feel that this has been happening all the time. You have to remember that films are not only an art; they are an industry, because they are very expensive. If you write, for instance, a piece of music, the only expense you have is your pencil, your score paper, and perhaps rehearsal time for your musicians. That is peanuts compared with film costs. Same thing with a painter. He might have the expense of canvas and paint and brushes, but even if he does not sell the painting, it's not so much as a film. Film is an industry, and they have to sell it; they have to recoup the money any way they can. And if a song can help or music can help, I don't blame them. If I were a producer, maybe I would be aiming for the same thing. Also, it helps the publicity of the picture. You have thousands of disk jockeys all over the country playing the title song of a movie. They're doing instant advertising that the producers couldn't possibly pay for—the equivalent in newspapers.

IB: In other words, the people who are out here doing film music cover a broad spectrum—all types with all sorts of backgrounds.

LS: I think that's healthy. It's a very stimulating competition with stimulating contact. I think that this division of the composer who's in the ivory tower, the academic world, and then the other one—and I can say this because I've been involved on both sides of the fence. Quincy Jones says there are two kinds of composers: those who come from the street and those who come from the school. And I think for films if, in some way, you have the possibility of knowing both sides of the fence, it helps. Coming from the street means having played gigs all over and, you know, being in contact with the masses. And then coming from the school, knowing the music theories— the merging of both—I think film is one of the few media where this can be successful—and television.

IB: In this connection, why do you think there are so few contemporary concert composers in the mainstream of feature films? Is there a prejudice against them?

LS: You cannot expect that they're [the producers and directors] going to call you, unless it happens to be a miracle or a very big coincidence—like your symphony is going to be performed, and a producer goes to a performance and he thinks, "Oh, I'm doing a picture, and this music would be perfect." They are not going to call you; you have to come here and be part of a community and start to work. Also, it's how much feeling for the dramatic the composer has. Some are very good composers, but maybe they have contempt for the dramatic. Many films have to throw out scores done by good musicians. Some films are successful with a song like *Shaft*, but you should see how many are thrown out. And then, they call professional composers to do it all over again. And the same thing happens from the other side of the fence. I won't name names, but I know composers of prestige from New York—they have no idea—they would write high, loud sounds under dialogue, you know, things like that. They have to throw the score out.

IB: It's interesting when you talk about dramatic-visual talent. Don't you agree that this is not something you can learn in music school? It is instinctive. You can have all the training and education, but you must have an intuitive dramatic sense—it can't really be taught.

LS:

Well, what you can do is this: first of all, I've been teaching at UCLA. I was teaching composition for movies and television, and my students were graduate students of composition or advanced students of composition. In the first class, instead of talking or giving a lecture, I asked them, as qualified composers, to write for me an orchestrated sound of the color orange. And it started to develop this synthetic feeling of the senses. Then that led me to develop a theory, which is: music for films—we are making an extension, like the Prokofiev-Eisenstein "audio-visual" concept used in *Alexander Nevsky* and *Ivan the Terrible*. I want to go further than that concept. Let's take the counterpoint of the Middle Ages and make an extension to film. You have the cantus firmus, which is the dramatic content in a film; we cannot get away from the cantus firmus. Then we have the tenor, which would be the visual; and then we have the bass, which would be the music. And sometimes the bass stops and comes back again and stops. Now we have an extension to this. I have a feeling that some of my students who failed in their exercises were coming up with very strange ideas. I would say, "You are a good musician, but to be a musician is not what I'm going to teach you. What you need is to stimulate your audio-visual counterpoint and dramatic sense. But more than that, you have to see plays, go to movies—all kinds of movies—and try to see what the composer is doing. Good, bad, it doesn't matter. Try to analyze what they are doing, what actors are doing. Maybe even join an actors' studio for a while to understand what acting is all about. Because this is what you are working for—the dramatic element." And as you have said, it's important for us to teach them, but maybe just introducing them to the elements of drama is worthwhile. Get acquainted with Kabuki theater, for example. You know, many of the things I do are an extension of Kabuki music, which is so effective—the use of silence and the dramatic use of sounds and music are so effective in Kabuki theater. And, it's a different tradition—totally different from Western culture.

IB: Do you think there's still too much illustrative music in films today?

LS: I try to avoid it. On the other side, I'm not saying that I try to avoid it so carefully to the point that I won't do it. Because sometimes, if it is in good taste and there is a correlation or a cut where I can use a musical accent, I'll do it.

IB: Do you think there's too much music in films today or that films are overscored?

LS: There again, there are no rules.

IB: What other film composers do you admire? Any particular score or segment of a film that impressed you?

LS: Oh, there are many. Most of the people you have interviewed for your book. By my criteria, you have good taste, because I would name the same composers.

IB: What do you consider your best score or your best-scored scene? Do you have any particular favorites of all the films you have done?

LS: I've done so many, and most of them worked, too. I mean, some of them—if I could do them over again, I would do them differently.

IB: How often have you had a score thrown out? Has that ever happened?

LS: No. I never get to that point, but I was going to start a film, and when I felt that the difference of concept was such that I knew it would be trouble—unless I would sacrifice my artistic integrity—I walked out before it started.

IB: There's a lot of interest among young film students and among laymen about the division of labor in the motion-picture score. We know, for example—those of us who have real musical training—that if we use an orchestrator, we hand him a fully sketched-out score, and his work is basically glorified copying. Do you use an orchestrator at all?

LS: Sometimes when I am hurried and pressured. I write a condensed version—everything is indicated. I don't leave any freedom whatsoever to my orchestrator.

IB: Do you believe that bad music or controversial-sounding music can actually kill a film or cause the composer to be blamed for the film's failure?

LS: Well, let me tell you this: if the film is bad, the music is not going to help it. I once saw a film that was not too good, and I was sorry, because the director was a friend of mine. The composer was so bad that he took from the film the little possibility that the film had to survive. I believe the music was really bad, and I'm not saying this from a musical point of view. I'm saying it from a dramatic one. It was the wrong choice of material—the wrong attitude.

IB: How do you work with dialogue? Do you have any special way of handling this problem?

LS: In the beginning, I started doing single lines or counterpoints, sometimes with two woodwinds—something very simple underscoring the scene. Then I found you can do anything, as long as it's not obtrusive. The texture can be quite thick and still transparent. It depends on the scene and on the mood whether you use music at all.

IB: Was it your idea in *Bullitt* during the car-chase sequence to start off with driving jazz and then, when the lead car shifts into high gear and the action speeds up, to substitute sound effects—tires screeching, applied brakes, all kinds of realistic effects?

LS: Yes.

IB: Because, in a sense, out of the music comes the sound effects, actually a quasi-music track. It just pulls the audience right into the scene. It's very dramatic.

LS: It was my idea and the director's idea. This is a case of perception. Many people come to me and say, "Oh, the music for the chase was so exciting." And, of course, they don't realize that the music stopped before the real chase.

IB: I get the feeling from interviewing you that you really care about films, that you like doing film scores very much.

LS: Yes, I like films very much. The main attitude a composer should have when he's working for films is that he's part of a team in which the director is the brain, the cameraman is the eye, the composer is the ear, and the editor is the genetic code. It's a real human Gestalt, and unless the Gestalt is all geared to the same goal, the film is not going to work. I'm very happy to work in this medium, which I consider a new medium.

INTERVIEW with BERNARD HERRMANN

Pat Gray: Do you think one has to be a composer to write film music?

Bernard Herrmann: Well, it helps! Most of the people who write film music in the present and some in the past have not been composers. They've been people who've written a tune or something, and other people have arranged and developed it. The use of ghostwriters has been very rampant throughout the history of film music. It started that way, and it is going back to it now. But I would say you do have to be a composer to write good music for films.

PG: Do you believe that film music must mirror the popular culture of the time or what is currently the popular style of dance music?

BH: Well, I don't know why it has to mirror that. If the picture mirrors it, the music can, but each film is a separate problem of its own, and who says film has to mirror our civilization even? All it reflects is the imagination and fantasy of a gifted director or group of people.

PG: How do you see the role of the film composer? Has it changed much in the years you have been connected with the cinema?

BH: Well, I don't think there is a difference between being a film composer and any other kind of composer. Cinema is a great opportunity to write a remarkable kind of music in the sense that it is music of theater, and at the same time, it is music that becomes part of a whole new artistic phenomenon which is known as cinema, which is a combination of all the arts—and music is cinema.

PG: Then you don't think you can have a successful film without music?

BH: They've tried. I can think of several films without music. *The Grapes of Wrath, A Tree Grows in Brooklyn,* and *Les Diaboliques,* a French suspense film. This last film had a bit of music dragged in at the beginning later on by the distributors. I would say that every director has a dream—that is, to make a film without music. But it is not possible. Their egos are so great they would think it is not necessary to have music. I can give an example. A film called *Mademoiselle* with Jeanne Moreau made by Tony Richardson. It was a catastrophe. This film, firstly, had no music and, secondly, had no motivation psychologically. Music could have given a picture of her neurotic state of mind and her internal emotional behavior—Madame Moreau's face is not enough. It is not possible to create a film without music, but you can create a film without *good* music. But you must have some kind of music. You see, cinema is an illusion, and it is the combination of the camera, photography, music, and, of course, the word that creates the illusion of what is known as cinema. It is something that the audience partakes of and makes, and the audience need not know about music or photography—only that they are affected by it.

PG: Why do you think so few contemporary concert or serious composers are invited to score mainstream feature films? Is there a problem of director-composer communication?

BH: One can answer this in two ways. One is that composers have a snobbish attitude towards cinema. It's beneath them, really, to write for the cinema, or they don't give it their best; and then, of course, we have the other side. Most directors of contemporary cinema today are men of such little taste they would not know what composer to ask. Though the statement is not altogether true, there are many distinguished composers today writing for film. Darius Milhaud, William Walton, Rodney Bennett, Malcolm Arnold, Aaron Copland. I would not say they're not asked, but the vain hopes of the director with poor taste is that the music will make money for the film with a theme song or a title tune.

PG: Is the film scene, in your opinion, open to new talent from all parts of the music world, or does it only seem so on the surface? What chance does an avant-garde composer have?

BH: As good a chance as anybody else if it is the right film. I can think of one film with a magnificent avant-garde score—the Japanese picture, *Woman of the Dunes*—which was completely electronic and fitted beautifully. When I worked on *The Birds* with Hitchcock, we had an electronic score. I worked with an American composer by the name of Remy Gassman, who really created the effects, and we went to Berlin to do that, because at that time there was no electronic studio available in America. Before that—it's now nearly twenty years ago—I did *The Day the Earth Stood Still*, which also had an electronic score. Even as far back as that. The cinema has no bar or prejudice, it only has the opportunity. How people get it, of course—there are many factors.

PG: What percentage of directors and producers you have worked with knew anything at all about music, even how to communicate on a simple level with composers?

BH: I would say that with the exception of Orson Welles, none of them knew anything.

PG: When you wrote the music for *Citizen Kane*, did you discuss the music with Orson Welles?

BH: I wrote the music during the making of the film and discussed it with him. Orson is the only one who has any musical, cultural background. All the other directors I worked with haven't had the temerity to tell me anything about music. Hitchcock left it completely to me.

PG: What do you think makes good film music?

BH: Each film has a different face, and there are different problems. There are no rules. It is not possible to have any set of aesthetic ideas to cover the whole enormous field.

PG: How do you feel about the title-song mania and the current intrusion into the film scene of record companies trying to create hit records and instant composers?

BH: They're not getting hit records, and they're not getting instant composers. They just get a lot more garbage. And it is not worth discussing in a serious discussion about film music. After all, if we're going to discuss the novel, we don't talk about comic books, do we?

PG: What is your best score or scene from a film? Or rather, which do you feel happiest with?

BH: I'm sorry—I'm happy with them all. I don't have my favorites. I feel very sorry for anyone who has to live a life worrying that he's got one pet piece of music or one favorite. Certainly, he would have a very small, minuscule talent. I've always done my best, and I'm happy about that.

PG: Among other composers, whom do you admire, or rather, what film score impresses you most?

BH: I still think the greatest film score ever written was the score for *Ivan the Terrible* by Prokofiev, and before that—much earlier—the score for *Karamazov* by Karl Rathaus is one of the great scores in film. We have had a few people that created cinema music that was the same as the music of the art world. I don't, for instance, feel that Copland's music for *The Red Pony* is any the less than the music of his symphonies.

PG: Your music has been described by critics as having a kind of continuous flow. It can be heard as a sort of web of suspenseful sound. Do you agree with this analysis of your music?

BH: I think it's sheer garbage. I don't know who said it. Because they print it—it makes it sacred?

PG: How do you write your music for films? Do you use the piano?

BH: I don't write on a piano. I write my music down on paper in full score, and when we get to a recording studio, they play it.

INTERVIEW with DAVID RAKSIN

Irwin Bazelon: Today we have many people taking credit for having written music for films who cannot in any sense of the word put a real piece together, and yet, somehow, good or bad, right or wrong, the music works more or less effectively. Do you think one has to be a composer in the traditional sense to write film music?

David Raksin: Well, I think that perhaps the best way to answer that would be that one does not have to be alive to live either. In other words, one can be hooked up to all kinds of machinery after the brain has stopped working, and a semblance of life can be maintained. Whether or not it should be is another question. You know, there are guys who have gifts who cannot write music down. There are a number of very famous examples in the world of popular music, and they actually have melodic, lyric gifts. So since they've never learned to write, they've always had a transcriber. Then there are people who are a step above that who have more sophisticated notions of what and how to do things. I worked with one of those—Charlie Chaplin, with whom I worked on my first film.

IB: He was very musical, wasn't he?

DR: Charlie was extremely musical. He not only had thematic ideas, but notions about what to do with them and with instruments—high or low, tense or relaxed, nutty, and that sort of thing. I'm not sure that my definition of a composer would coincide with yours. I do not need to know that Aaron Copland is able to put together a concert piece to know that he is a composer, because I can hear it in his film music. It is not whether or not a man can put together a concert piece that determines whether he is a composer but whether or not he can write *music*.

IB: But do you feel that there are people out here getting credit who really can't write music?

DR: Yes, but that's a different thing. These are people who actually can't write music; they can't write a score. They may come up with their little tune and somebody else elaborates on it.

IB: A lot of these kids who play chords on their guitar and strum their way through something.

DR: Yes, that goes on. There's always been a certain amount of that. Nowadays it goes on more than ever, because a real education in anything is considered antiartistic. But, you see, I have actually in the past admired film composers whose qualifications would not include being able to write anything of any great consequence. But they had dramatic gifts, and consequently, what they did was quite wonderful in certain films. To write music is great. Sure, you can be a film composer without being able to write a long, extended piece; but on the other hand, the real trick is to do the dramatic work for the picture (which is primary—I mean, that's really the first order of business) and, at the same time, try to write some *music* in the picture. You know, there are some guys who can do that, and those are the composers I admire most.

IB: How do you see the role of the film composer? Your career in film music goes back a long way. When were some of your first films?

DR: The first film I worked on was as an arranger and orchestrator. That was *Modern Times*. After that I began orchestrating scores, and pretty soon I was doing scores of my own—by 1936.

IB: Do you think that in all the years you've been active, the role of the composer, his position in the hierarchy out here, and how he functions in this culture has changed much?

DR: Well, it has changed. In the old days, there was a certain kind of respect, but it was a different kind of respect. Composers, except for a very few, were not very high in the pecking order—even composers who had done rather splendid jobs. If you did something that had great public acceptance and became very famous, people might say, "That guy's made it." And then all of a sudden you're a big man and they defer to you, because you've had public acceptance and great success. Al Newman used to call people who judge according to those standards "pulse-of-the-public boys." On the other hand, even at that time, the producer's word was law. I used to differ with them quite frequently, and it didn't help a hell of a lot. I mean, I didn't figure I was in there to echo producers' opinions but to give my own as a musician. Today, you've got people who haven't got the vaguest idea how a score is made but whose eminence in the world of popular music is so great that the producer doesn't dare challenge them.

IB: What percentage of producers and directors that you have worked for know anything about music or even how to communicate on a simple dramatic level with a composer?

DR: A very, very small number. I would say maybe four or five percent. I don't really know how to judge it.

IB: I want to find out a little bit about your working habits. Do you use a piano much when you compose?

DR: Yes, I use it quite a lot, but I use my head more than you would imagine. What I really do is—I like to think when I'm away from the piano. I like to think when my mind is diverted. If I've got a score running around in my head, trying to work its way out, I do a lot of work while riding in the car, or I do a lot of walking around, or just thinking or sitting somewhere, testing elements of the score against the requirements of the film and against one another. In one way or another, the music works itself out. What I then do is verify a lot of stuff at the piano. There are also times when I concoct things at the piano, you know, that my head won't hold.

IB: The song "Laura" is more than just a great song; as one of the serious composers said to me one time in New York, there's a kind of immortality in that song that he wishes he could claim, even though he's written quite a few symphonies. And I've always felt—you may not feel this way—that *Force of Evil* and *Laura* have the quality of early Alban Berg. Do you feel it, or is it just something that hit me?

DR: Well, the thing is this: I've been influenced by a lot of composers. I think that the two composers who influenced me more than anyone else in the world were Alban Berg and Igor Stravinsky. I studied for about a year and a half with Schoenberg, that marvelous old gent, but he never taught me anything about the system of composing with twelve tones, because he figured, and rightly so, that I ought to learn a little about music first. But I love the music of Berg, and I'm sorry that music didn't go that way—that it took the other road, that it went the way of Webern—because I think the latter kind of music is too open to comprehension and imitation by people who are not really musical. In other words, you can figure it out. Berg you can't figure out.

IB: Just to stay with "Laura" for a couple of seconds, do you remember how you actually wrote "Laura?"

DR: Oh sure, I can remember. I was assigned to the picture by accident; they wanted Al Newman to do it. Al heard that it wasn't all that good a picture, and he was working on another picture, so he wasn't about to extend himself. So they thought, "We'll get Benny Herrmann; he's very good with melodramas." Benny heard that Al didn't like the picture, so he decided he didn't want to do it either. They thought of the picture as a detective-story melodrama. I was doing detective stories and horror stuff at the studio, so they assigned me to it. I saw the picture as a love story. Otto Preminger, who was the director, had a given tune in mind that he was going to use; I thought it was quite wrong, and I tried to convince him of that, but he thought I was a nut. But Al Newman persuaded him to give me a chance at it. So Preminger said to me, "My dear boy, this is Friday afternoon. You come in Monday with a tune, or we're going to use the other song." So I worked like a crazy man on that tune—and I can write tunes, as you probably know, a mile a minute, but there was not one among them that was worth anything. On Saturday morning I received a letter from someone whom I cared about a great deal, and I read the letter with kind of misgivings without understanding what was in it, and I put it away, because I didn't want to be upset by that letter. I knew I had my hands full, and I was about to blow a great opportunity; and the next evening, when I'd just about given up, thinking, "My God, I can't go in with any of these pieces. If they accept one of them, I'll be ashamed, because it's not me." Well, in those days

239

when I had a block, I had a thing I used to do, and sometimes I still do it. I'd put a poem on the piano or sometimes a picture to divert my mind, and I'd improvise. In this case, I just happened to reach into my pocket, and I came across this letter. I put it on the piano, separated the two pages, and began to read it; and all of a sudden I realized that this lady I was in love with was telling me, "Get lost." And it hit me like—you know—a B-58 in full flight. And at that moment, as I was improvising, out came this tune. That's exactly how it happened.

IB: How do you feel about this title-song mania and the record companies getting into the film scene, paying for the music production costs, and trying to create hit records? Do you think it's just another phase?

DR: Well, it's another phase, but it's lasted quite a while, and it's going to last a lot longer. Now it may seem very incongruous to hear from a guy who's written his share of film-title songs that he does not like the current thing, especially since it might sound like sour grapes. But there have been plenty of times in the past when I have refused to use songs I have composed in the underscoring when I thought they were wrong for the occasion. Another picture, which was the second one I did for Preminger, the next one after *Laura*, was *Fallen Angel*. I refused to use my song in the main title because, I said, "It will ruin your picture. Your picture should not begin that way." And Preminger had learned to have confidence in me by then, so he agreed and didn't use it. Now today, we have a kind of a terrible hangover of the anxiety syndrome in which people who are making pictures find themselves contending with other films and other forms of entertainment for interest, for publicity, for all that sort of thing, and they must find some way of gaining attention for their pictures. Well, they have always known, since radio is very important (in Los Angeles, for example, there are about seventy radio stations), that if their theme gets to be a big thing on radio, the picture will get mentioned every time the song does. Consequently, they try to promote songs and gimmicks, and you have A-and-R men (artists-and-repertoire men) sitting in the booth and telling the composer what's going to work and what isn't. The problem with that is that I can't really see what it has to do with the picture. In other words, it's the same procedure that operates in trying to retail popcorn, and once you start responding to that, you cease responding to the law that is important to films—in other words, what's the music doing for the film? Is it just getting the publicity at the expense of what it should be doing: helping to guide the emotional reaction of the audience? Some pictures I can't conceive of with a score other than a pop score or a rock score. On the other hand, this business of having rock and pop in everything is just absolutely absurd, because that suggests that there are no areas of human experience which can't be depicted by the ever-present fender bass and electric guitar.

IB: Sometimes I get the feeling these guys get together and sort of wing the whole thing.

DR: Well, that frequently happens. I don't know that it really matters, in a way. It throws a few good composers out of work, but the point is that that goes across the whole field of art. You go into a gallery now, and you see things on the wall that are taking the place of pictorial art or graphic art. You see things standing in the middle of the hall that are taking the place of plastic art, of real sculpture. And the fact is that nobody seems to be able to say, "The king has no clothes." It's a pity, and I know that the attitude could be considered reactionary, but there's so much garbage in the world today—this is kind of a hyped-up seller's market—and you've got stuff that is dreadful. I don't have to listen to it, and I don't want to listen to it. When somebody does something that's good, that's okay, but I can't see man at his most intimate— unless he is no older than, say, a teenybopper—depicted by the kind of thing that goes on for the most part.

IB: Do you think there's still too much illustrative music in films today?

DR: No, I think there's too little of it, and I'll tell you why. If there is not some perceptible connection between the film and the music, if it does not look and sound as though the composer saw the picture *before* writing the score, then there's a big mistake somewhere. Too often, music, in an effort to be cool, disregards what is on the screen. Now I don't mean that every time someone puts a light on in a room you hit a bong with a chord or something—that's ridiculous. There was a time when, I'm embarrassed to say, we did that to some extent.

Whether or not it was any more gauche than overlooking cues, I don't know. But there are many, many times when I see television films and theatrical films where the music goes on, and very significant things which absolutely have to be acknowledged by the composer just go by without any attention being paid to them at all. This is an aesthetic of its own, with which I do not agree very often. It's a foolish conceit that you gain sophistication by pretending to be unaware of action on the screen that should be helped by the music.

IB: Hanns Eisler used to say, "If you go against the picture, it still has to be objectively planned." You have to have a dramatic function for why you're going against the picture.

DR: Yes, except that Hanns, who was a very dear and wonderful man and a fine musician, developed an aesthetic which was arbitrary. He was an intelligent man, but he was absolutely a slave to a kind of doctrine about films, which I say not because of his political orientation but because it shows in his work. There's one of his pictures which I still use in class all the time, and I always have to defend the music: *The New Earth*. There are interesting things about that picture and, seen in the context of its time, it's an important film score; but both music students and film students jump all over it, because they think it's terribly gauche. It is a result of a doctrinaire approach in which musical processes are held to follow from nonmusical considerations and aesthetics. You see, you do the old trick of the bed of Procrustes. In other words, you say I've got the only idea worth having, and anything that does not conform to that idea is not logical. You have therefore made yourself the custodian of logic, and that's as stupid as electing yourself the custodian of art.

IB: What about music behind dialogue? It really is a difficult problem when you're dealing with the words. After all, people have to understand what they're talking about. Do you have any special mannerisms or any special way of approaching all that?

DR: Well, I am hardly the person to talk with any great authority on the subject, since you'll find a lot of people who think that I do altogether too much under dialogue.

It may very well be. You see, I have a theory that one way to do a film score (if one wishes to write any music in it) is to try to find different levels of expression—which I have expounded for years to my students as the "Gulliver proposition." The analogy is this: If you read *Gulliver's Travels* on the surface only, it is a charming story about a man who finds himself among pygmies, giants, horses, and all the rest. If you read it on a different level, it is a political fable with all kinds of undertones that are quite fascinating. And you don't have to know about the second level to enjoy it on the first. Now if I want, as I have on certain occasions, to write a piece which is a free fugato using episodes, I am not about to expect the citizens of Topeka to erupt in joy when they recognize the entrance of the subject in the bass, or maybe, let's say, an inversion or canon or something like that. My idea is that if they hear nothing but the melodic line, *that* has got to do the work. So therefore, the rest of it, while it is not for my own amusement solely, keeps me busy as a composer. I'm not interested in simplistic music, although I have very great admiration for certain of my friends who do that sort of thing. For instance, I could never stick with a single pattern the way Benny Herrmann does, and yet he does it marvelously, and I quote him constantly to my students. I say, "Look, here's a guy—look what he does: with such simple means, he gets such marvelous results." I think the rarest bird in the world of music today is an absolutely straight lyric expression, the absence of which from today's music I really do believe is as sick as the absence of the human visage from graphic art. My idea is not that lyricism is everything, because I can also deal with other things that do not require ordinary lyric expression, but I do think that sometimes there is a kind of amorphous music that heaves and pants and does all that sort of jazz without ever really making a statement. The one thing that some people really do not want is to be seen for what they really are, I'm afraid, and the one way to risk that is to write a tune. You know, there's that great remark of Oscar Wilde, "To be understood is to be found out."

IB: Do you think there's too much music in films today or that films are overscored?

DR: I think there's too *little* music in films. There are several young composers in town in whom I take a particular delight, and whose music I admire, because I really do not relish the role of sour ball. It would be ridiculous, with my years and experience in the business, for me suddenly to say, "I don't understand what all these young cats are doing—they're nowhere." So, when I run across one in whom I can have great confidence and love for his work, I really relish that. Well, I saw a TV film last week written by one of the very best of these guys. Now, I mean really a talented guy who's going to be absolutely a leading figure in pictures. And yet, there was so little music in it that you almost ask, "Well, why did they bother?" Well, the reason they bothered was that where there was music, it was very telling. But it was one of those films where, in order to avoid coming to grips with the substantive issues that involve music, you don't play music. Someone seems to be unaware that great achievements in film music are not made by the absence of music but by the presence of talent.

IB: I always get the feeling that the films that have the least amount of music should have more and the films that have the most should have less. But somehow, the balances are lost along the way.

DR: There was a day when they used to score films almost from beginning to end. And a lot of people made fun of it, but just think who was writing then: Eric Korngold, among others. There are very few films I see that have been scored by good men in which the music is not superior to the film. If everybody in the business had the competence of film composers, I guarantee that films would be a hell of a lot better than they are.

IB: How much control do you have over the dynamic level of your scores after they leave the recording stage?

DR: Very little, very little. After the recording stage, the idea is to hear the *word*, which is a very limited symbol.

IB: Of all the scores that you've done, what do you think is your best score or best-scored scene?

DR: I have a number of favorite scores. One of them is *Laura;* another is *Forever Amber*, which wasn't much of a picture, but, you know, the score is really something. Then there's *Force of Evil*, which is a favorite one—even though the picture's been cut and very badly edited twice, the music still survives; and then the original version of *Carrie*, before that was all sliced up, had some of my best music in it. *The Bad and the Beautiful* is another film score I like. The original version of *Separate Tables*. Two more I should mention, because I think they're unique: one of them was a film that was not much of a film, but it was one of those things where the composer has a great opportunity. It's called *The Redeemer*, and my friend Hugo Friedhofer, who's one of the most knowledgeable people in the world on the subject, said he thought it was one of the finest scores for a religious film ever composed. It was done, you know, without heavenly voices and angels and all that jazz. It was done in the mid-sixties, and I don't think it's ever been shown in the United States, although it's been shown a lot abroad by religious organizations. And I would also say that the score of *What's the Matter with Helen?*, which is a terrible title but rather an interesting film, is one of my best. That was done in 1971.

IB: What film composers do you admire, or what segments of scores have impressed you?

DR: Of the composers still functioning, the ones I admire most are: Hugo Friedhofer, who, if I had to pick the three best composers who ever wrote for films, would certainly be one of them; another is Bernard Herrmann; another is Leonard Rosenman; another is Alex North, who has almost no peer in the profession; and Laurence Rosenthal; another one is Jerry Goldsmith, who's a very good composer; Billy Goldenberg is another fine composer—one of the younger chaps and very talented. I'm probably leaving out a few, but those are the ones who come first to mind.

IB: How often are your scores thrown out? What is your reaction?

DR: The original score of *Separate Tables* was thrown out—or had one big sequence thrown out. I replaced it. I don't think I've ever been totally replaced by another composer, but I've had good chunks thrown out. And, I think, arrogant though it may be, that it was in many, many ways due to the fact that the people who made the picture didn't realize what they had.

IB: Do you believe that bad music or controversial sounds can kill a film, or cause the composer to be blamed for the film's failure?

DR: I really doubt it. Music in a film can do harm. It can overload a situation. Vulgar composers do vulgar things. (Sometimes a composer who's not fundamentally vulgar will do vulgar things.) It is partly the style in which scores are done, and it's a great fashion to look back at the scores of the forties and fifties and say, "How corny!" But just think how the people will think of the scores of today twenty years from now. It will be absurd! The whole idea that everything in the world of imagination and feeling and response and emotion can be depicted by a relentless beat is just too funny for words. Music can't save pictures, but it can help.

IB: Do these producers really think that Dr. Raksin or Dr. Goldsmith can come in and save a film?

DR: Some people say things like that. I don't think they say it all that much any more, because it also represents an admission of default on their part—you know, that they didn't really make it on their own. But there are many times when film music makes the difference between whether or not a scene is understood or misunderstood, and there's no doubt in the world about that. All you have to do to get the point of film music across to the skeptical is to make them sit through the picture *without the music*. And, you know, next to the water torture, I would say that's the most far-out of man's inhumanity to man. Yet today there is among certain people a great vogue of not having music in films, as though that made events on the screen more "real." I'm sure you know this dopey old story, which dates from years ago when I was working at Fox. I was walking through the commissary one day, and a couple of girls I knew hailed me, and one of them said, "Listen, you know, Vi's boss says there isn't going to be any music in the picture that he's doing." I knew I was being put on, and I said, "Well, why in this case does the great man say this?" "Well," she said, "because the director says 'after all, this is a picture about a lifeboat out in the ocean, and where would the music come from?'" So I said, "Go back and ask him where the camera comes from, and I'll tell him where the music comes from." People don't understand that music is a convention of pictures.

IB: There's also the idea that people who make films always seem to think that they know their business and they know yours, too!

DR: Al Newman used to have a remark—he used to call these guys "plus-music boys." And they don't know our business, they absolutely do not, and the sad thing is that often they don't know their own. What else is to account for the kind of pictures that are made? Dreadful. Dreadful. So many of them.

IB: I sometimes tell my students to watch the old films on TV. They'll understand that it should be a tremendous encouragement to realize how many incompetents make films that are still playing the circuits years and years later.

DR: There again, I feel, as a film composer who's worked for a number of decades, that to this day I am hard put to think of a film score of mine that was not at the very least as good as the picture it was in and, more often than not, far superior to it.

INTERVIEW with BERNARDO SEGÁLL

Irwin
Bazelon: In the context of defining a composer as a person who knows how to put a piece together and understanding the structure of films and the nature of the music written for them, do you think one has to be a composer to write film music?

Bernardo
Segáll: I don't think it's always necessary. It doesn't hurt, though. It's almost like asking a great draftsman whether his knowledge could make a collage. However, a great painter could put together a much better collage. In a sense, I think that the talent for putting together a picture is very much like a collage. In fact, some of the best scores are collages, because they are a mixture of silence, sounds, voice, sound effects, and music. We are quite insignificant to that whole domain. We're adding some form of lyricism or rhythm to all of that other sound.

IB: You're the first person who's mentioned this in just this way, and I think it's quite right.

BS: The entire film realm is really an art of collage, and it's a great stunt to use all these elements and mix them, edit them, and come up with a picture.

IB: Did you always want to write film music or did you have other musical ambitions or did you stumble into the medium?

BS: I think I stumbled into the medium. I did compose as a child. By the time I was twelve, I had five compositions published. And when I came to America to continue my career and studies as a pianist, I was fifteen. I was born in Brazil. And Siloti, whom I studied with, was like a god to me; everything he said was sacrosanct. He said to me, "You know Rachmaninoff suffered from the dichotomy of whether he was a great composer or a great pianist? I don't want you to suffer like that; I want you to devote yourself entirely to playing the piano." And I took that as the gospel. But then, many years later, I met a very charming, talented dancer, and I started writing for ballets. That's when you met me. But I've always had a love of theater. The making of theater, which is a great part of composing psychologically.

IB: So your first scores were for ballet and then for theater?

BS: Ballet and theater. As you know, I did *Camino Real* by Tennessee Williams and *The Cavedwellers.* Then I did documentary films.

IB: Meantime, you had a complete concert-piano career going?

BS: Exactly. This was a diversion. And strangely enough, the thing that really motivated and interested me was going back to the collage thing, the mathematical possibilities of putting together notes for dramatic purposes—that was a diversion. And then I was offered some films, and I enjoyed doing them.

IB: Since you've had this dual career and you've come into contact with so many contemporary composers, why do you think so few contemporary composers in America are invited to score mainstream feature films?

BS: I think there's a tremendous intellectual gap between producers, directors, and serious composers. Generally, a composer is disciplined, has a sense of his own aesthetics, has a sense of the meaning of structure; whereas you'll find that even a director who'll talk about realism or neorealism or have theories about expressionistic films is really not on firm intellectual ground.

IB: What percentage of producers and directors that you have worked for know anything about music or even how to communicate on a simple dramatic level with a composer? How would you grade their overall musicality?

BS: I've only met about two men who've had any sense of communication; the rest has been guesswork. One tries by seeing the film and by the form that has been used to make sure that when they say romantic, did they mean romanticism or did they mean realism? In essence, I think that today most films are done in a documentary style—realism—so when they think of music, they really are thinking of realistic sounds we hear in nightclubs, etc. And that's why a lot of this nonmusic is coming into films.

IB: How much leeway are you given to write your music, especially as regards the use of controversial sounds?

BS: In my experience, TV leaves you much more alone, because of the time factor; they have to trust you, and you can do more experimental things. More avant-garde composers get a chance with TV than with the high-pressured theatricals, where all that money is involved—where they feel they have to have that pop sound, or have French or Italian composers who stick in the melody and a little rhythm.

IB: I know you also teach piano classes at USC, but what's it like being a composer in this medium? Do you get caught up in a circle of competitiveness, or are you able to avoid this?

BS: Well, as you know, it's a competitive business; however, I have really not gotten into the throes, because I teach at the university, so when I get work, it's kind of amusing, it's a relaxation, and it's a world that offers dadaism—it's so mad and all of them are so insecure that when you come with a bit of security from another field, like teaching or concertizing, it's kind of fun. You have your own professional sense, your own security.

IB: Tell me something about your working habits. Being a pianist, I assume you use the piano. When you get an assignment, do you sit at the piano and try to improvise a little bit to get a feeling, or do you lay it all out on a page timewise?

BS: Well, of course I do it at the piano, as I am a pianist. I need the piano for the colors and the textures that I imagine that eventually I could get. Because, in essence, the composing for a film largely consists of texture and time. Occasionally, you're called upon to provide a certain lyricism. Actually, I think that music can best serve films with its lyric quality. And really, I think that people like Bacharach and Mancini, who provide a simple *melody*, are most successful, because they are providing a lyric element.

IB: Do you think music can actually describe anything, or do you think it needs the visual imagery in the dramatic context to suggest certain things, even emotions and feelings?

BS: I think that the fact we have inherited the whole romantic period, which is all description from Liszt on—Liszt, Wagner—that period has inculcated, has made clichés of, what that music represents so that when we use that formula, we actually are using descriptive clichés.

IB: Do you think there's too much music in films today, that films are overscored? Or do you think there's too little?

BS: Well, I think today there's a great suspicion. People try to avoid music for purely financial reasons, so they tend to want less and less music.

IB: What do you think is your best score or your best-scored scene from a film? Do you have any particular favorites?

BS: Yes, *The Luck of Ginger Coffey*.

IB: What particular scene did you like?

BS: The opening is when you're asked to really compose. You're given at least two or three minutes to develop something. Generally, our title music is the music we like best.

IB: It's also the first sound, and, because it comes first, it has an impact over and above anything else, and in many ways you can catch the audience right then and there. Set the scene and tell me what you did in *Ginger Coffey*.

BS: Well, it's a scene in Montreal, Canada—snow on the ground, approximately 5:30 A.M., the sun is just about to come up, so you have this wonderful, kind of Corot haziness. And the camera is traveling down empty streets, and eventually into the window of the protagonist. The picture has a sadness.

IB: Yes, it was a picture about a loser.

BS: A loser picture. At the same time, it had a kind of nostalgia, so I used a kind of baroque theme. In films,

251

when they do chases, as you know, they always want a kind of ostinato that keeps it moving—they're always afraid there isn't enough movement visually.

IB: That's contradictory, because an ostinato chains you down rather than propels you forward.

BS: Exactly. They're afraid of the changes, they're afraid of the contrasts. I used baroque, because baroque uses a pattern of a sixteenth note that keeps it moving. And also, I wrote a contrasting idea that was very French.

IB: It started out with a solo flute?

BS: Solo flute, that's right. Then the accordion came in as a French sound.

IB: How come a brilliant pianist like yourself is so fond of the accordion? In fact, your use of the bass accordion, which is an unusual instrument to begin with, is really quite interesting, because it's part of your thinking—it's part of the Segáll sound.

BS: Well, actually, when I was doing documentaries, the budgets were low, and the accordion was a very practical instrument. You could mix it with three celli.

IB: You taught me that trick—to make it sound like ten celli. But you don't use it in the singsong, French way; you use it as a solo line. It also conveys a solo tone color. What other film composers do you admire?

BS: I admire Jerry Goldsmith above all of them. I think he has a true dramatic sense, which I think is very important, even in an abstract, symphonic style. He can also create a very simple mood, which I admire.

IB: Have you ever used anybody to help you orchestrate your scores, and if so, how much did he actually contribute?

BS: I did once, because I thought that I didn't have enough jazz background, and I used him for a contemporary, a legitimate jazz sound.

IB: Do you believe that bad music or controversial sounds can kill a film?

BS: First of all, the responsibility lies not with the composer but with the director. Generally, if he [the composer] is killing the film, it's because he wants to help the film; generally, where scenes don't work is where musicians are asked to function; because the scenes themselves don't work, they blame it on the music.

IB: What about music behind dialogue? How do you handle this problem?

BS: Generally, I don't like to score behind dialogue, but sometimes those scenes don't work—say, two people are quarreling—and if you can juxtapose, work the other way—say, they were once in love—with one single line, the quarreling might work better dramatically.

IB: Do you think that the best film music is understated rather than overdramatized?

BS: Understated, yes.

IB: You use the small ensemble. Other composers work that way, too. I always get the feeling that everything is understated, and, as a result, the dramatic action on the screen is allowed to come through without being commented on all over the place.

BS: Exactly.

INTERVIEW with LAURENCE ROSENTHAL

**Irwin
Bazelon:** In the context of defining a composer as a person who knows how to put a piece together and understanding the structure of films and the nature of the music written for them, do you think one has to be a composer to write film music?

**Laurence
Rosenthal:** It seems to me that this question arises principally because a lot of films have been scored by people who might not strictly qualify as composers. Now, this would include different types of musicians—and I use the word in its broadest sense. Let's leave aside, for the moment, men who are unquestionably composers. When Prokofiev writes a film score, it's a film score by a composer. But beyond that, everything depends on the nature of the film. For example, there are certain films expressly designed for a musical background or foreground, as the case may be, primarily composed of songs. These songs are arranged, elaborated upon, fragmented, reprised, sometimes ad nauseam, but nevertheless, they have a perfect validity in relation to the kind of picture they accompany. In this case, certain songwriters really qualify as composers. It would be a pretty stuffy type who would call Jerome Kern merely a songwriter. He was a superb craftsman who worked within the idiom of the song form.

IB: There seem to be a lot of young people who have given themselves the title of composer at an early age, whose principal qualification is that they have learned to manipulate sounds and put them together, as well as being able to write a good tune. I don't think this ability qualifies them to be composers, and yet some of the things that they have done for films certainly work dramatically in the picture.

LR: I guess a good example is a film like *The Graduate*. Now I certainly wouldn't call Simon and Garfunkel film composers. What they did was to write and perform a series of songs—I guess some were precisely designed for the film and others not—which were played behind the action of the picture. It seemed to work very well, but that does not indicate in my book that Paul Simon is a film composer. He's an excellent songwriter. And Mike

Nichols is a most imaginative director who saw how it all could relate.

IB: And I can give you another film, such as *The French Connection*, where there are some strange sounds functioning, but I'm not sure that these people could qualify as composers in the context of putting a piece together.

LR: It's really very hard to answer the question completely. However, I would say that from my point of view these examples of scores composed of songs or, perhaps, of random sounds or by way of somebody fooling around with a synthesizer and fiddling until he gets something which sort of works would certainly tend to be the exception rather than the rule. In principle, I'd say you have to be a composer to write music, and in the same way you have to be a composer to write music for films.

IB: Henry Mancini and others have gone on record as saying that film music mirrors the pop culture of its time. Do you believe this?

LR: I would say that's a rather limited view of the whole subject of film music. Certain films scored by certain composers do in fact mirror the pop culture of the time, but clearly, not all films mirror the pop culture of the time.

IB: How much leeway are you given to write your music, especially as regards the use of any controversial sounds that you may or may not want to put into your scores?

LR: I've been pretty lucky; I've had a great deal of freedom—based on the fact, I think, that I've worked with a few directors whose sensitivity to music was quite remarkable. They would often say nothing to me about what they had in mind, but if they did, they always managed to speak in terms that would not hamstring me in any way. One of the best examples of that is a director with whom I've worked a great deal, Peter Glenville, who has a most perceptive approach to music, especially in the relation of music to image. He'd always discuss the score in broad aesthetic terms. He would never say, "This kind of music; that style; this sort of instrumentation."

IB: Why do you think so few contemporary composers are invited to score mainstream feature films?

LR: Well, I suppose that the producers of these films are nervous about the excessively (from their point of view) esoteric idiom, especially of avant-garde music or of anything that would sound strange or unconventionally related to the idiom of the film. They've got their mind on the box office; they can't help it. Many of them still go along with the absurd and archaic idea that the best film scores are the ones you never notice. Others think in terms that are equally repulsive to me—they are victims of this mania about big themes and about the idea that a musical score is principally a potential commercial adjunct to the film's money-making campaign. But on the other hand, there are many (to use that unfortunate term) serious composers to whom the particular discipline occasioned by composing for films is anathema.

IB: Let me ask you a few things about your working habits. You're a pianist, aren't you? Do you use a piano when you compose?

LR: Almost all the time.

IB: Do you use a Movieola at home?

LR: I've only on rare occasions had the opportunity to do that. I remember when I was a kid I read that Aaron Copland always insisted on having the film in his studio on the Movieola so he could run the picture constantly while working on the music. This is an ideal method. I remember doing *The Miracle Worker* that way. It's amazing how much nuance and how much atmosphere you can forget, no matter how detailed the cue sheet is. There are all kinds of visual elements that appear on the screen, like how much sky is showing. It may sound absurd, but that factor could conceivably influence the quality of sound you're trying to create. But unfortunately, it is usually considered impractical, time-consuming, and expensive. As far as I know, nobody does it that way in California. I suppose if one absolutely insisted, the powers would accede to it. Personally, I love working that way. I love having the Movieola at the piano and literally playing things against the film; trying them out.

IB: Do you ever write music between assignments other than film scores?

LR: Yes. But I must say that for the last few years there's been precious little time for it, because the assignments have just been coming back to back.

IB: You had a piece played by Leonard Bernstein and the New York Philharmonic, and you've had other concert works performed.

LR: Yes, but I'll tell you something: people ask me, "Do you ever have time to write your own music?" And I always find that a strange question, because it doesn't seem to me that I ever write anything but my own music.

IB: I believe what you believe, that a person has a style, and no matter if he gets paid for it or not, this is the way he works. Although, granted, anybody who does film scores has to have a tremendous amount of versatility to mold his style into certain dramatic shapes as regards functional purposes.

LR: Well, it's perfectly true that sometimes the subject matter of a film will lead you into a direction or an idiom that you might not otherwise have pursued, but that could be true of any stimulus. You could read a novel that you found quite by accident on an airplane and suddenly decide to write an opera on that subject, even though it's something that might never have occurred to you the day before. I suppose, to be perfectly honest, that there are moments in any film and sometimes, perhaps, in an entire film, in which you are going against your natural grain. But, in principle, my whole musical nature has always been tremendously attracted to theatrical forms. I find that my best inspiration comes from images, from dramatic situations, from ideas, from words, from atmospheres; to me, it's much more unnatural to sit down and start writing a string quartet or an abstract piece for orchestra than it is to write something for the ballet, to write something for the voice, for a poem that I happen to like, or for the musical stage.

IB: What percentage of directors and producers that you have worked for know anything about music or even how to communicate on a simple dramatic level with a composer? How would you grade their overall musicality?

LR: Well, on a scale from zero to ten, I'd certainly rank Peter Glenville a ten. There are others whom I would rank at the opposite end of the scale. It's very hard to make a generalization. There are some directors who have a wonderful grasp of the possible function of music in films and others who not only totally lack this sensitivity but are really not even very interested. I mean, they almost say, "Just write something that's nice and doesn't get in my way."

IB: Don't you think that these are the guys who tend to hire the same people over and over again, because they almost know beforehand what they're going to get, so they don't have too much of a problem?

LR: I'm not sure whether I can say yes or no to that, but I think that what you suggest may also hold true of a director who does have a good sense of music, once he finds a composer with whom he feels a real rapport, because he doesn't have to start covering all kinds of basic ground at the beginning of every film. They know basically what they're talking about, and sometimes a word or a phrase or even a gesture or glance would be sufficient.

IB: Do you believe that music in itself can actually describe anything, or do you think it has a tendency to suggest through the visual imagery and dramatic content what is going on?

LR: Well, certainly, there's no question about it that however philosophically you can prove that music is incapable of describing or expressing anything, when you listen to the opening music of Die Walküre, if you don't know there's a storm going on, you're out of your mind. At least, you feel the powerful agitation of a storm. I also think that music can be very much of a chameleon, that in one visual-dramatic context the same music could produce a completely different effect from what it might produce in another. And I have always been interested in the idea that music is so frequently used to underscore dramatic action, when actually that is often a waste of its possibilities. Because an important function of music in films is to add a new dimension, a new dramatic and psychological dimension to the drama. Merely to duplicate what the film is already perfectly successfully doing is, of course, just a redundancy.

IB: Do you believe there's still too much Mickeymousing going on?

LR: Probably. But I wouldn't for a moment deny that there are times when that's the only thing to do. And that endlessly going against the action can finally become as much of a mannerism as monkeylike Mickeymousing.

IB: Do you believe that certain instruments like strings, for example, have a way of depersonalizing themselves, or do you believe in solo instruments or single lines behind dialogue? In *The Miracle Worker* the importance of trying to make this little girl speak was so strong, and, remembering your music, you didn't try to buck that, you got out and allowed that to come through.

LR: Well, I'll tell you, very often if you have a scene that is playing beautifully, played by really good actors, music only gets in the way. However, there are times when music is trying to open another dimension, trying to say something that is not visible or audible from the screen, and then all kinds of things are possible. Strings have probably been overused, largely because of their transparency—the voice can cut through.

IB: In addition to that, you can listen to strings for hours. You can't really listen to percussion and brass for too long.

LR: It would be dangerous. But I'm always rather fastidious about orchestral timbre. If there's a possibility of getting a little woodwind into a pause in the dialogue instead of right on the word, I use that possibility, because it really pays off.

IB: I'd like to get back to *The Miracle Worker* because it's a film I have great esteem for. In it, I recall, your lyric voice comes through; it's almost a contrast to the fact that you're dealing with a story where the protagonist cannot speak or hear. It's not that I thought that your music was a substitute for her dialogue. But there is a singing quality that really enhances the spectator's involvement in the film itself. What did you do when you were dealing with the tremendous dramatic power of Anne Bancroft and Patty Duke?

LR: Well, it's a little bit hard to talk about it in a specific and objective way, partly because it's been quite a long time; and secondly, because—as I mentioned before—I worked in direct contact with the film for many weeks. It made a very deep impression on me. I confess that I was so profoundly moved by certain sequences that sometimes I had to go out and take a walk after looking at them before I could even put pencil to paper. It got to me that much. Sometimes I wonder if the lyric passages you speak of were almost expressions of my personal reaction to the film. I was both composer and spectator. It's a strange thing to say, but sometimes I wonder if that wasn't the case.

IB: There's a scoring sequence when Patty Duke, groping her way in the yard through a maze of clothes hanging from the line, got tangled up in the washing. It conveyed beautifully the strange kind of thing that was going on in her mind, trying to find her way through that maze—a maze not only exterior but interior.

LR: Yes, it even gives me goose bumps to hear you talk about it. I remember she was wandering through the washing, which was blowing in the wind, got tangled up, and fell to the ground. Her mother rushed out of the house, extricated her from the sheets, and just held her.

IB: The thing that always comes to my mind is the tremendous warmth of the music.

LR: The music that accompanied that sequence seems to have emerged as a blending of lyricism and pain, an enormous pathos and a feeling of compassion for a child who's living in a world of darkness and silence; and indeed, also for her mother, who probably suffered more.

IB: Maybe you've just answered this, but what's your best score, the best-scored scene from a film? Do you think it's the one we're talking about?

LR: Well, it's certainly one of the best. There are several scenes in a modest sort of Western that I thought were of quite good quality.

IB: Do you mean *A Gunfight?* I did an analysis of it in my book.

LR: Well there were a number of sequences in it that I like. We spoke earlier about a certain contrast that was brought about by the use of themes of a familiar, Western stamp against a much more modern texture, a sort of grainy haze.

IB: I called it a "stringent harmonic texture," because I remember it was based on major-second and minor-second intervals.

LR: One of my favorite moments is the scene that takes place immediately after the moment of the gunfight itself. Two men have agreed to engage in mortal combat for money, a notion that thrills and titillates the crowd, which encourages them and eggs them on. But when the climax finally comes, the spectators are absolutely stunned. The reality of one man now lying there dead as an entertainment for the crowd is almost more than they can bear. That moment in the music was one of the more interesting ones to me, because it contains the theme, which is rather simple and stark, played on two trumpets. One of them is electrified and the other one just normally muted against a background of densely clustered strings and electronically echoed woodwinds and vibraphones, and eventually the electronic reverberation of chimes and churchbells, which were part of the scene. To me, that seemed to be one of my better achievements.

IB: Do you think there's too much music in films today and that films are overscored?

LR: Yes, I think so. My principle in writing film music, and this is one that I can really say I apply to every film and even every little TV thing that I approach, is that there should be as little music as possible. In fact, there should be no music at all unless the picture can't do without it. Then, when it's there, it really counts.

IB: Bergman and Eric Rohmer would love you.

LR: They sometimes go to extremes of restraint! Bergman is so sparing in his use of music.

IB: He thinks that films are a composition in themselves and that by using music, you're piling music on music, in a sense.

LR: That's a legitimate attitude, and I would say that from the viewpoint of his aesthetic it's certainly true.

IB: What other film composers do you admire? What particular score or segment from a score of one of your compatriots do you like?

LR: There are lots of them. I have certain all-time favorites. I love the score of *Alexander Nevsky*. I think Prokofiev did something really extraordinary there. I always liked Walton's Shakespearean scores for Olivier's films very much, especially *Henry V*. It's music of an essentially conventional nature, perhaps even old-fashioned, but it's dead right for the film. It fuses with it so perfectly. And all of Copland's work in films is superb.

IB: What about contemporaries?

LR: Well, I'll tell you one score I adore—for a film I never saw. I was living next door to Jerry Goldsmith while he was writing it. The film was *The Mephisto Waltz*, in which part of his job was to incorporate certain aspects of Liszt's *Mephisto Waltz*, and to me, the sheer invention and imagination in his use of the orchestra, especially some of his writing for strings, percussion, and electronics was absolutely staggering.

IB: Really kind of a satanic twist he gave to that music.

LR: It was quite wonderful and quite an unconventional approach. I can say that, because it's much different from the way I would have probably treated that subject myself, and I think I like his way better.

IB: How much control do you have over the dynamic level of your scores after they leave the recording stage?

LR: Very little. The dubbing studio is composers' purgatory. As you may know and have undoubtedly heard from others, the recording stage is the composer's golden moment. After that everything is downhill.

IB: How often have you had a score thrown out, and what was your reaction to it?

LR: The gods have been kind to me. I don't know how I would react. It's never happened to me. I've just been lucky, I suppose.

IB: Do you believe that bad music can kill a film? I've always said that a film can be choked a little by bad music but not actually strangled to death.

LR: I'm not sure it could be strangled by it, but I would like to say something about that, and I won't mention the film, because it would be indiscreet. There was one film, which was fabulously successful—it was an enormous money-maker—it was one of the great films of the last ten years—great, I mean, from the point of view of its huge distribution and overwhelming public appeal. It had a score with a theme that was a monumental commercial hit. It seemed to me that the theme, indeed the score in general, was so badly related to the picture that, for me, it destroyed the film. It didn't destroy it for the general public, and it certainly didn't destroy it for the studio, which, I'm told, was understandably proud of the fact that the sound-track album had sold two-and-a-half million copies or something like that. But to me, this film's entire character was spoiled by the saccharine and silly sentimentality of the music, which was in no way related to the seriousness of the subject. It may not have been the greatest film of all time, but it was a hell of a lot better than it seemed, being continually inundated by this insistently cloying theme, which was in no way indigenous to the film, and which virtually transformed it into a super-soap opera. The composer, by the way, is by no means untalented, and I'm told that the theme was created as a result of relentless pressure from the director, whose musical taste it finally reflects—a taste that has been, from one point of view, vindicated handsomely at the box office.

INTERVIEW with JOHNNY MANDEL

Irwin Bazelon: Where are you from, and what is your musical background?

Johnny Mandel: I was born in New York, and raised half in New York and half in Los Angeles. I always had music around the family, around the house—my uncle is a composer. My mother was an opera singer but wasn't allowed to go into it professionally, and we always had jazz people around the house, because my uncle was tight with the whole Chicago bunch—like Eddie Condon.

IB: Where did you study music?

JM: The first teacher I ever had was when I was thirteen, and, believe it or not, it was Van Alexander. It was probably the best thing that ever happened to me, because Van taught me how to write before I knew any better. I hadn't studied any theory or anything; I had just started to play the trumpet. Van started me writing charts for dance bands right off. And even though I didn't know anything about music or musical theory, he started me off transposing scores. I did that all through high school; I went to New York Military Academy on a band scholarship, where all I did was play marches all day, and I was able to do a lot of writing there. We had a pretty big marching band. After that I went to Julliard and Manhattan School of Music. Fine schools. I'd been on the road about three years before that. I was playing professionally from the time I was sixteen.

IB: What kinds of bands were you with?

JM: Live bands. Three Buddy Rich bands. A really good Count Basie band for a year. I was in bands from '42 on, partly because of the scarcity of musicians. Everybody was drafted. This isn't modesty—I wouldn't have had a prayer of getting a job the way I played if everybody wasn't overseas. I got better later, but I got a nice early start because of it.

IB: Did you ever have any idea of doing motion-picture music or did you have other ambitions? Did you stumble into film music?

JM: Stumbled into film music. I'd done everything else first. Written for acts, singers, bands.

IB: Out of all of this you have found a style and developed it as a composer. I find this fascinating, considering that at fifteen or sixteen you were playing pop music in dance bands.

JM: Don't take this as an offense, but I think that a jazz background is the best possible background anybody could have in this film age, because you start from a very flexible base. It can lead you into symphony music, it can lead you into contemporary pop music—you can go in a lot of directions. A perfect example is a symphony player. What's worse than a symphony trumpet player? They're good with standard repertoire, but when you come right down to it, it's much easier to take a good, well-schooled, jazz first-trumpet player. His inherent flexibility will allow him to digest traditional repertoire with little difficulty.

IB: Those are the guys I look for. They can all read, and they have that wonderful flexibility that, as you say, symphonic players don't have.

JM: I don't write jazz scores per se. I mean I have, but I never think of it as that; it's whatever is called for. I learned theory and composition after having been on the road for three years, so I had a vantage point—it meant more to me.

IB: Do you use a piano at all when you compose? Do you use it fairly extensively?

JM: Yes, more than I really should. I use it as a crutch sometimes, but I can write without it. I have many times.

IB: Do you have your own Movieola to keep in constant touch with the film?

JM: I like it sometimes; sometimes I do. But more often than that, I spend so much time spotting a film to begin with—maybe twice as much as most of the guys do. And I make a sound recording of the film, and I get so I know just where every cut is—exactly what cuts are where—and when I play back the dialogue track, I really know what's going on in the film by that time. With a Movieola, I usually end up having to splice, etc. I like working with a Movieola in a cutting room, but I find it rather time-consuming if I have it at home, because I start using it as a delaying tactic. I just keep watching the film.

IB: Do you ever write music between film assignments other than film scores?

JM: No. Let me say this: what I really like to do more than anything else is write songs. I never wanted to write symphonies, I never cared about writing chamber music —I'd much rather listen to it, and I have written some. But I'm not a frustrated symphonic composer who's "whoring it off" for films.

IB: What percentage of producers and directors that you have worked for know anything about music or even how to communicate on a simple dramatic level with a composer? How would you grade their overall, relative musicality?

JM: You know, it's almost an impossible question to give a general answer to. Everybody's different. I've worked with a lot of good directors who are very conscious about their inability to communicate musically, and I tell them not to worry about that at all, because I don't want to know how much they know about music. What I want to know is how they feel. I have to look at a picture the way a director looks at it, and we're working with dramatic values; the music is only a tool for this. He can give me an example of what he wants—that's fine—but he doesn't have to talk my language. It's much better if he can tell me how he feels about it; i.e., if he wants a feeling of tension. We can work much better that way. Sometimes, when they start getting musical and feel that they have to, it can confuse the issue. Music's so damned abstract as something to talk about that you're better off talking about emotions or feelings or temperatures or colors when you're working on something like this. The notes are just the tools.

IB: Do you think there is still too much illustrative music in films today?

JM: I hate that, really. There's more of it in television, because you're working with an audience that's liable to be in the kitchen or screaming at the kids or whatever. You don't have the captive audience of feature films, so you can be about as subtle as a bricklayer on TV.

IB: How do you feel about the title-song mania? And the current influx into the film scene of record companies paying music-production costs and creating hit records and instant composers, many of whom don't seem to be really qualified to be composers? I sometimes wonder what they actually contributed to some of these scores.

JM: Very often just a melody line, with somebody in the back doing all the work.

IB: Yes, and they get the credit. Is there more of this going on now or less?

JM: Yes, there's more of it going on now.

IB: Does it bug you at all?

JM: Sure, it does. For one reason, I'm a songwriter, and it bugs me on that count alone.

IB: Well, you obviously do the rest of the scoring too.

JM: Right. Well, record people are oriented toward chart action, they want to get a name, but, you know, the damn thing is that the odds against their being able to bring it off, to get a *Shaft* or to get a *Superfly*, are ridiculously high. No sane businessman would gamble on those odds, yet they always think they can pull it off. Once a year now you'll get a *Superfly* or a *Shaft*, and that's happening partly because of the black-oriented-picture phase that's going on right now, which, as soon as the novelty wears off, will be like any other picture phase. For the first time, you can see a black man on the screen who isn't sweeping floors or anything, which is beautiful; but because of it, you've got a built-in audience for films. So all of a sudden we've got a black detective. Well, great. But in five years that won't be such a new thing any more.

IB: What gave you the idea of opening the main titles of *Point Blank* with that alto flute? I think it was an imaginative stroke behind those stills. In a film that has so much violence, the music is beautifully nonviolent.

JM: Well, you know something? The violence in that film was, strangely enough, peripheral. Lee Marvin showed tremendous scope; he's one of those guys who makes something very difficult look easy. There were moments of great tenderness in that picture on his part. John Boorman, the director of that picture, is, I think, one of the finest I've ever worked with, and he did things in this picture—the entire beginning of the film was in blues, grays, and greens; he kept all the primary colors out of it. Then he started adding some white; then, around the time Angie Dickinson came into the picture and that whole business up in the apartment—red, oranges—he worked very consciously with color and used color emotionally. When you do a picture, you've got to get inside of it. And, to answer your question—the alto flute playing that line at that moment felt extremely gray and disembodied.

IB: The alto flute's tone color gave the feeling of loneliness. It was a single line, and then the trumpet came in and began to weave a counterpoint. The whole score was understated.

JM: Well for one thing, I was on the picture from the beginning. And I was on Alcatraz while the filming was taking place. And the feeling, the vibes, that place gave off contributed a lot to the way I actually scored those scenes. It's the eeriest feeling in the world, especially when you get into the places like down in the basement. There were a lot of intangible things that went on. They had a piano down in the basement that was rotting away, and when you played it half the keys didn't work—it had been sitting there since they closed the prison. God knows who played on that piano—Capone and whoever else—but it had gotten out of tune in such a way from all that dampness and temperature changes. I really wanted to use that piano; it was impossible, of course.

IB: Another scene that impressed me took place in the discotheque. The people are hollering into the mikes, and in the background is all the violence, and then somebody sees the bodies and screams, and nothing happens! The audience thinks it's part of the discotheque show.

IB: What do you think is your best score or your best-scored scene from a film? Do you happen to be very partial to *Point Blank?*

JM: Yes, I really like that film. The scene I think is the best scored—actually there are a couple of them I like. There is one where his wife has taken sleeping pills, done herself in. He's walking around this empty apartment, then suddenly—you get this time lapse going—he smashes a glass, he drops bottles into the bathtub—you see these horrors going on—then you hear his wife's voice humming this tune against it; the tune was on the track, and I wrote the stuff to that. That was one scene. The other one I liked in particular was when he finally makes it with Angie Dickinson after she hits him on the head with a pool cue, and you get this series of flipovers where it's him, then it's his ex-wife, then his lover—that was a tough scene to write, it really was, because I overlaid it with organ and the only way I could figure out how to do it was to make a thirty-six-foot loop—you know, you never have anything longer than an eight- or nine-foot loop—and we'd keep going over and over the score. To feed the loop through, I had to have about four sound men just holding the stuff— it went through three rooms, and they were just passing it back and forth! And they thought we were crazy, but it was the only way we could do it. That one worked very well, I thought.

IB: What other film composers do you admire? What scores or segments from scores have impressed you?

JM: Oh, I have lots of favorites. I think most film composers who have been at it for a long time are good. But they've got to be, because if you're at it for that long, you get a lot of the rough edges rubbed off by some of the people you work with, because they're tough. Jerry Goldsmith immediately comes to my mind as being very good. And please don't forget Alex North, Hugo Friedhofer, or John Williams. Laurence Rosenthal—his score for *The Miracle Worker* was one of the most brilliant pieces of work I've ever heard. And I'm leaving out quite a few.

IB: Do you have much control over the dynamic level of your scores after they leave the recording stage?

JM: Not really. You go in the dubbing room and you fight. Once in a while you fight with them to keep it down—they play it too loud—but that's a minority of times.

IB: Now, of course, the music for *Point Blank* is entirely different from what you did for *The Sandpiper*. I read what you wrote on the program notes on the back of the album, when you were talking about wanting to create a kind of a haunting, lonely mood, reflective of the Big Sur location, which is obviously a very favorite spot of yours.

JM: Anybody who has seen the Big Sur coastline will realize it dwarfs any drama you've set against it, particularly the way they shot it in that picture. What it was, was a remake of *Rain,* although nobody would ever admit it—exactly the same story. Plus the way it was directed; it was kind of a monotone; there were no highs or lows emotionally. So what I did was something you should never really do. I scored the scenery and just totally left out the whole damn thing and tried to carry it by itself. You should have seen that picture silent.

IB: You did *Harper, Pretty Poison,* and *The Russians are Coming.* Any other films that you've worked on?

JM: *M*A*S*H* I had a lot of fun with. I had to take the weight off the hospital scenes—that picture I was able to make a bigger contribution to than most pictures, because that whole business of the loudspeaker came from me. I remember years ago, about the time of the Korean War, I heard the first Japanese attempts to play American jazz, and it was some of the funniest stuff I've ever heard. (Of course, they've gotten very good now.) When we did the picture, it flashed back to me that this might be just the thing to take the weight off a lot of the operating scenes.

So how do you qualify it? You've got to have a source. So why not have it coming from Radio Tokyo? So I suggested to the director that he shoot some exteriors and interiors, day and night, of loudspeakers. And Bob Altman, who is a genius, I think as far as film-making is concerned, starts getting ideas and starts writing up camp announcements and reads up on publicity sheets on old World War II films. And from that, the whole character of the speaker evolved. And I did another film with Altman, which was one of the most interesting ones I've worked on, called *That Cold Day in the Park*—a film he did with Sandy Dennis. Just totally opposite. About a crazy lady, but you don't know until the end that she's really whacked out. I scored that picture with disk music boxes; I used them and worked around that kind of material, trying to get a very Victorian feeling in the picture.

IB: Have you ever had any of your scores thrown out?

JM: No, I've never had a score thrown out, but I expect it any day. I've had one decapitated—*A New Leaf.* They kept some of the score and replaced the rest with sound effects, and they didn't get any new music for it. No, I've never lost one, but everybody does; so I figure I'm bound to sooner or later.

IB: Producers believe they know their job and yours too.

JM: Everybody knows their job and the music. It's an old cliché, but it's true. Since everybody's so in the dark about the music, including most directors—even some of the best ones are dummies when it comes to music. When a film bombs at a preview, it's very easy to say, "It's the music." It's so easy, because who's going to disagree with you?

IB: This culture has an awful lot of composers and people who think they're composers. Is it hard to maintain friendships with composers whom you know and like but whom you're constantly competing against? It must make for some tensions.

JM: No, not really. You know, composers as a group are more congenial, I find. You know, the guys really like one another—with very few exceptions. There's nothing most of us like better than to go to a bar and get good and smashed and just rap. Composers run hot and cold—some people have good years and some people have bad ones. The competitive thing isn't there that exists among many actors, for example, or certain drummers or certain trumpet players, probably because you're forced to bend more. If you won't bend, you won't stay in films very long. And that doesn't mean compromise. It means getting used to working with a greater variety of personalities. No two directors are alike—if you're working for the director. Sometimes you're working for the producer. Sometimes the producer and the director don't see eye to eye, and you get caught in the middle, which is the first thing you ought to avoid, but you can't always successfully do it.

IB: What are some of your personal reactions to living out here and working in the film industry? Do you like films?

JM: Oh, I love films, I hate working on bad films, and I love working on good ones—it's that simple.

INTERVIEW with PAUL GLASS

Irwin Bazelon: In the context of defining a composer as a person who knows how to put a piece together and understanding the structure of films and the nature of the music written for them, do you think it's absolutely essential that one be a composer to write film music?

Paul Glass: It used to be. In the present state of the film business it seems that the trend is that he doesn't have to be a composer. It's unfortunate, but it seems to be the trend. However, there is still that little fringe in the business that requires the composer. Now the percentage of films being made seems to be less and less from year to year. But there's still a need for the composer to express his personality. For the real craftsman—there is still a need for that.

IB: You are one of the few contemporary American concert composers who regularly scores mainstream feature films. Is there such a thing as commercial-mindedness that influences film people to avoid so-called serious composers?

PG: Yes, basically because the film business began in the silent days with the pit band. And even the musicians were sometimes referred to, you know, in not really a serious manner. As a matter of fact, the contract orchestra in the old days always had five saxes. It grew up out of the pop music. I just found a list—my father was a silent-film star—and it said, "Tear this off and give to the conductor in the pit." And it had a list of these dreadful, stupid, awful pieces of music. And that's part of the reason in this country.

IB: Do you think the film scene is opening up to new talent from all parts of the music world? For example, what chance does an avant-garde composer have? Do pop songwriters and pop-music talent have an edge in getting a film assignment out here?

PG: Yes. And this is a trend we're all hoping will change. We hope that, with the opening of new possibilities with the cassettes, we're going to have a lot more varied kinds of music for more discriminating tastes.

IB: How long have you been out here? What is your background?

PG: I was born in Los Angeles in 1934. I studied music composition at U.S.C. Later, I worked one year with Roger Sessions at Princeton and then three years with Witold Lutoslawski on a grant from the Polish government and a grant from the American government in Warsaw. So from about 1957 to 1969 I went back and forth basically between more or less living in Europe and a few assignments in films. I did my first picture, *The Abductor*—a Fox film—in 1957.

IB: Did you always want to write film music? I know you have other musical ambitions, but did you stumble into film music?

PG: In high school I was asked to write my ambition, and there it was: I wanted to write music for films. I've always felt that a musician who is not functioning—I don't believe in sitting in the university getting your pieces played by amateurs when that big, beautiful orchestra's out there. And I also believe that the film is the workshop of having to write it today, hearing it tomorrow, and trying all those things out before you put them in your symphony.

IB: That's right—a laboratory. I did the same thing in documentaries for over twenty years in New York. Every piece that I have written I had the opportunity to try out first. It's a marvelous place for experimentation. How do you work? Do you use a piano much?

PG: I'm not a pianist. I can get by on the piano as much as I want. If I'm doing a score that involves spatial notation techniques, I probably will not use the piano at all.

IB: Do you ever write music between assignments other than film scores?

PG: Always. Constantly. I have to, because some of the best ideas I get, I get too quickly, and I don't get a chance to work them out; usually my so-called symphonic music is the working out of some idea that came up when it fused with what I had to do today and didn't have time to finish tomorrow.

IB: What percentage of producers and directors that you have worked for know anything about music or even how to communicate on a simple level with a composer?

PG: People that I have worked with—I'll cite one example, Luther Davis. Here's a man who wants to know as much as he can about any kind of music, and when he asked me to do a picture on the basis of some tapes I had played for him—I remember I went over to his place on a Sunday, and he said, "Bring all the contemporary records that you have; I want to be acquainted with it." And in the U.S. of A., unfortunately, the music is not at everybody's disposal. It's hard to get to, especially outside of New York City, and you really don't get a chance to hear what's going on. These guys, some of them, want to know, but they just haven't had the opportunity.

IB: Well, that question I asked you is really almost answered by what we've already been discussing. The kind of music that you write—the people who hire you better damn well know how to communicate with you, or they wouldn't have gotten to you in the first place. Do you think music can actually describe anything, or do you think it tends to suggest through visual imagery and dramatic context?

PG: I think it's this way—that you take a scene that you decided to score, and you find out what the form of the scene is visually. And then you find in your own compositional craft what kind of musical things it suggests. It might be an A-B-A scene, it might be a rondo-type theme, or whatever, and you can actually work out your material. And this is the best and the quickest way to do it, according to the musical forms you work with on your own. Yes, you can describe an action—rather, suggest an action—and you might in certain cases. I'm the type of person who doesn't like to look at a film too many times. Because if you know the film and memorize it from a point of view of the sequence of action, then you tend to double it rather than add to it.

IB: Do you think there is still too much modern Mickey-mousing music in films today?

PG: I have a funny feeling about Mickeymousing. I think that if you are a serious composer and you use the Mickeymouse synchronization technique with subtle musical elements, it's good. But if you use the Mickeymouse technique with dumb musical elements, it's terrible. And I think it happens much, much too often.

IB: Do you think there's too much music in films today—that films are overscored—or do you think there's too little music in films today?

PG: It's very funny. Back again, we're stuck with the rule of the tradition, which always turns out to be a third of the picture.

IB: What other film composers do you admire? What scores or scored segments have impressed you?

PG: Aaron Copland. Some of the segments in *Our Town* are just magnificent. Bernard Herrmann's score for *The Devil and Daniel Webster*. I think some of the things that Hugo Friedhofer has done: some of the things from *The Young Lions*, for example. Some of the things from *One-Eyed Jacks* with Marlon Brando. I think David Raksin is definitely one of the top people. Some of the cues from *Laura* are absolutely amazing.

IB: How much control do you have over the dynamic level of your scores after they leave the recording stage?

PG: Practically none.

IB: What do you think is your best score or your best-scored scene from a film?

PG: *Interregnum* was an interesting assignment, because I had somehow been involved with that whole German Expressionism scene—I was one of the first kids in my school to go twelve-tone. So consequently, when you're talking about German Expressionistic painting of the twenties, you're talking about twelve-tone music, you're talking about George Grosz, Kokoschka, and that whole gang who were Schoenberg's and Alban Berg's friends. So the idea was—it wasn't really the style I was writing in, but it was a style I had written in to try and recreate the Expressionism of the twenties, and I thought it was the best way to go, since we were talking about the concentration camps and persecution. Schoenberg was one of the ones who got the worst end of it as far as the persecution; he had to leave home. So I tried to go as best I could with some of the latest things Schoenberg did; not the things he was doing in the twenties but more or less what he was doing later on when he came to the United States but still seemed to fit. So it was an assignment of not writing Schoenberg's music, because I wouldn't have taken such an assignment, but somehow to express the Germany between the wars. And I think I did it very well, and it was an interesting assignment, because there were all kinds of possibilities to do things that I wasn't doing anymore, because my style had grown to a different thing.

IB: Considering the fact that your musical style is not the typical style of Hollywood music, how much leeway are you given to write your own music, especially as regards the use of controversial sounds?

PG: I never realized that what's going to be the biggest help for young people who are going to go into composition is the fact that these poor people who have a musical background are looking for freaky sounds through rock means, through electronic music, through thunder basses, through pedals on guitars. And when somebody does come along from the so-called European freaky school—the European freaky school is a skilled way to do what they're looking for. So I think that these people are not hurting us—they're helping us, because they're making all kinds of strange sounds that years before you couldn't do. The whole concept of the symphonic orchestra and so on—it's very rare that one gets to do that any more.

IB: In your opinion, how much effect does music actually have on a spectator's responses? Do you think it's conceivable that almost any kind of music could work behind a film, because the people might be engaged in watching the imagery and not pay a hell of a lot of attention?

PG: I think that if they do hear the music, it's wrong. I think that music should accompany the action. I also believe that the cue, taken away and played on a tape recorder, should also make sense as a piece of music. There must be form and structure in the piece of music. It is a piece on its own, and it is also a piece that fits the picture.

IB: While the functional demands of the film come first, I've always felt that if the piece is constructed right with real objective planning, it will stand on its own.

PG: And also, there's a whole other point: you can write a piece of music fortissimo under a dialogue scene if you stay out of the way of the dialogue by having a different tessitura—I just did that recently on a cue. I had high, screaming quarter tones when a man was talking in a baritone voice. It can go as high as I want—it still won't get in the way.

IB: Have you ever had any scores thrown out?

PG: Yes. I just did.

IB: How did you feel about it?

PG: Well, it was a very funny thing that happened. It was for the TV series "Columbo." The producer was unaware of what happened. He called me six months later and said, "I'm sorry, and I'm going to make this up to you." He called me on his own volition and said that there was a misunderstanding of what was needed in the score. He said, "Because of that, I really feel that I hurt you at Universal, and I'm going to make it up to you." It was totally thrown out. And I think it's one of my best scores.

IB: Considering what's happening on the scene today, do you believe that film music mirrors the pop culture of its time or what's currently the pop style of dance music?

PG: Well, it depends on the subject matter. If it's about some freaky kids out on a commune or anything like that, you got to have it, 'cause it's their music. It's not our music. However, the only thing about the pop culture is this: if you have a film with people who are constantly screwing up and doing dumb things, getting in stupid trouble, having no sense, then that's the kind of music you're going to want to have. But if you have a genuine hero (say, Fredric March) and you emulate him, you've got to have great symphonic music to go with a character like that. Here comes a man who has moral strength—then that's the kind of music you're going to have to have. But if you've got some idiot in a pair of Levi's picking his nose, you're going to want, as Quincy Jones puts it, "hoopity ding ding," which is that bass kind of ba boom.

IB: I thought that Stan Kubrick's idea of using *The Blue Danube* in *2001* was very pointed, because it functions as a kind of Muzak to get you up to the space station where Howard Johnson and Conrad Hilton have taken over. Did you see *2001*?

PG: No, I didn't. I know the score and I disagree. Bergman does it, too. If a producer wants a piece that sounds like Bach, he gets a guy who can write a piece that can sound like Bach. Because if it *is* Bach, I don't care about the picture; I'll go with that familiar piece. I did a movie for TV last year called *Sand Castles*. The score had to be Schumannesque, but not Schumann. I wrote in the style of Schumann, because that's a trip for me. That's an academic, fun thing. But I don't ever believe in using familiar pieces as a picture score, because as far as I'm concerned, it's like someone just turned on the radio or a concert or something else. If I see an orchestra playing, let 'em play Beethoven.

IB: You realize in America when you use the word "composer," ninety-nine out of a hundred people think that you write pop songs?

PG: But then again, I'm kind of funny, because I have a great deal of respect, especially—two of my favorite composers outside of the world of serious music are George Gershwin and Jerome Kern. Because that kind of melodic invention is rare.

INTERVIEW with JOHN BARRY

Pat Gray: Do you believe that film music must mirror the pop culture of the time or what is the current popular style of dance music?

John Barry: No, of course not; it depends on the subject you are dealing with. In the last fifteen years there has been an incredible external influence on film music through the various forms of popular music, electronic music, etc. The audience for films today is a ninety-percent young audience, and therefore pop music has had an effect on it—some bad and some good influences.

PG: Is the film scene, in your opinion, open to new talent, or is it completely closed; and what chance does an avant-garde composer have?

JB: It is always open. It is a question of the opportunities, the specific subject of the film that would carry an avant-garde score, if you like, by some young composer who wished to do it that way. I don't think it is closed. I think it is a completely flexible situation.

PG: Is it difficult to get into the business of writing music for films?

JB: It is difficult in that it is the circumstances of the actual fact of writing music for films, i.e., the timing. They've spent whatever millions they have spent on a picture, and apart from the final dubbing, music is the last thing that happens. You are going into the studio maybe with a large orchestra, and they have delivery dates, so there is an element of risk for an inexperienced composer. They like to take people they can rely on to deliver. One usually gets started on very low-budget films—at least I did—until you can establish yourself and get some sort of a record for reliability in the business.

PG: What percentage of directors that you have worked with knew anything at all about music or how to communicate on a simple level with the composer? How would you grade their overall musicality?

JB: I think about twenty-five percent of the people I have worked with knew anything at all about music. They look very strongly to a composer to guide them. I think John Schlesinger is one who knows exactly what he wants, and, on another level, Bryan Forbes or Sam Spiegel have a way of expressing what they require. A lot of other people talk a lot of nonsense, and you have got to steer them away from it and put them on the right track. One of the main problems in writing music is finding out this musical personality or lack of it in the producer or director when you become involved. I like to talk to them first and find out what they know—if they know anything.

PG: Do they have an overall say on the music? Can they knock your music?

JB: They can. I have done scores for films that I thought were right and they thought were wrong. I have had this before. For example, *The Knack,* which I did for Richard Lester, which received quite a lot of acclaim for the music. Richard said, "Look, you've done everything I wouldn't have done, but it works." This was a case where we fought desperately over the film for the style, but he finally admitted it worked. But it was hell going through it.

PG: In the long run do they leave it to you?

JB: On this we had one extra session to straighten things out and move things a little his way or attempt to move things my way. Essentially it was ninety-five percent what I wanted to do.

PG: What do you think makes good and effective film music?

JB: I like to try and get, for want of a better word, an "interior" score as opposed to a physical, exterior score. That is, getting into the characters, the personalities and trying to be moved by what their response would be emotionally. I think a good score depends on how accurately you are able to do that.

PG: Do you often try to enter into the plot by trying to change the viewer's perception of image—musically, I mean?

JB: No. I think you can add another dimension; I don't think you should try to change anything. If the characters are well drawn in the script and again in the performance and the direction is a certain way, then you are working within the limitations of that prior work, and I don't think you should try to change it. I don't think you can; but you can imply and bring another dimension to that character.

PG: Do you think there is too much Mickeymousing in films?

JB: It depends on the character of the film. You know, I did the James Bond series—the whole style of the series is Mickeymouse music. It had to be. Subtlety is not a virtue in a film of that kind of design. But usually I try to keep well away from that kind of scoring. But it's not a golden rule that you have to. Every film has a life of its own, and you have to go with that.

PG: How do you feel about the current title-song mania, the hit-record business in film scores? Does it tend to create instant composers?

JB: I think it depends. With the Bond movies it has always been the style to have a title song, but I integrated it with the dramatic material. The song has been a complete part of the theme, countermelody, and harmonies of an integrated score, and I think that works. I think in a lot of movies where you are asked to do a title song and there's really no room for it whatsoever, then that is disastrous.

PG: What's it like being a composer in the film medium? What is your personal reaction to this milieu?

JB: I was born in the theater business, so it's been a part of my life. My father had theaters and cinemas. I don't socialize very much with people in the business. I find it very funny a lot of the time. I think you have to retain a sense of humor and a sense of your place within it. But, I think, like anything, when you are working with intelligent people, it's a very stimulating business. When you are working with idiots, you just want to finish the job and get out.

PG: What film composers do you admire?

JB: Of the European composers I like Nino Rota and most of the work he has done with the Fellini pictures. They were a marvelous marriage of Fellini's mind and approach, and I think they are some of the most interesting scores. In America, I like Alex North very much, and I think the score he did for *A Streetcar Named Desire* was exceptional.

PG: I see you use a Movieola.

JB: Yes, and a piano and tapes. I record what I write in a rough way, just getting the feel on tape, and play it back into the Movieola. Not always. Sometimes I don't feel I have to go to that trouble. Other times I just record it from the piano. Sometimes, if one is a little uncertain or trying things over the top, the Movieola is a good indication. Often, with a bad scene, I find it helps when you're a bit fuzzy because the scene is fuzzy. You can go back over it and try different things, attitudes, and usually just seeing those images and hearing one or two approaches to it clarifies certain things for you. Viewing it in a theater, there are subtleties of change which you miss if you don't have a Movieola. Your memory cannot retain all the nuances. You do, of course, get your timing sheets right down to the last third of a second, but you can miss the nuances, and when you begin to write, you shift emphasis. I wouldn't be without a Movieola.

PG: Do you write music between assignments, or do you work only in films?

JB: I have a recording contract whereby I do two albums a year. I am involved this year in doing a musical play, *Billy Liar*. It is something I've set up; it's my idea, and I've got the elements together. It's a departure.

PG: How do you think music detracts or enhances the spectator's involvement in a film? Is music necessary?

JB: It depends on all sorts of things. I think it is correct to use music in the correct position in the structure of the film, and this can be incredibly helpful. You can also get one or two bad scenes over the hump. I don't think it can make a bad scene work for you, but it can act as a binding force in many areas, and I think music should— this old wives' tale that if you hear the music, it's bad—work. There are whole areas of *Midnight Cowboy,* for instance, where the director decided to go with the music, and it's a part of the framework of the whole picture. The same with Tony Harvey in *The Lion in Winter.* There were moments of, if you like, repose, when a sequence shot that way with music gave you a complete, added dramatic dimension that otherwise would not have been there.

PG: Equally, you might have films without music; isn't that the dream of every director?

JB: Well, an instance when Tony Harvey made a one-hour film of the play *Dutchman,* and he wanted to do without any music whatsoever—just the sound of underground trains. He did this, and then he called me up and said, "Look, we've no money left, the sound effects are not working, what can we do? Would you like to take a look at the film?" So I took a look and we used three small pieces of music; one at the beginning, one at an interlude moment, and one at the end. The music lifted it—it was almost a musical sound effect. Dramatically, one could get more stridency and horror through the music, which was the effect we were looking for.

PG: What do you regard as your best score? Have you a favorite?

JB: No, I think anything that works is always interesting. I don't care what level it's at. Of the Bond films, I think the *Goldfinger* score was the best, because it worked. I like *The Lion in Winter,* where I was able to write a large dimension musically, saying that the Church of Rome at that time was a powerful fact in the life of the King of England. This is something that was only referred to at the end of the script when the King had to go to Rome, but the music implied all the time the weight of the Catholic influence on the King, and I think that worked. I think *The Knack* worked. I think *Born Free* worked. That was almost a parody of a sentimental, Walt Disney score. It's knowing what you are doing with it and having an idea and an approach to a score and bringing it off.

PG: Do you use an orchestrator?

JB: No, I orchestrate my own music. I think that's all the fun of it. Orchestration is texture, and I think one of the most important things in a picture is the texture of the music. There are some scenes that you score where there is virtually nothing but textures—with lack of rhythm, lack of melodic values; just sound, purely sound. This is just as refined a thinking process—what that sound should be—as writing a melody or an active, rhythmic piece, but sometimes, under the great pressures forced on composers, they have to use orchestrators. The composer can write into the score the way he wants it orchestrated, but it is the subtlety the composer gets when he orchestrates his own music that is valuable. After all, composition is orchestration. It's like Stravinsky writing something and getting someone else to orchestrate it. It is the whole fabric of the composer's craft.

PG: Did you always want to write for films, or did you just stumble into it?

JB: No, I always wanted to do it. How it came about is just a question of chance or accident. I don't think you'll find one composer who says, "Right, that's what I wanted to do, and I did it." It is always by accident or luck that one gets into it in very diverse ways. I always wanted to have something to do with film or theater music. I was brought up with theater and cinema.

PG: Do you believe producers are trying to indoctrinate the idea that bad music can kill a film?

JB: I don't think music can ruin a bad film. If you have the wrong composer on the wrong picture, he can add absolutely nothing. It is a question of sympathy with the subject. I will not do a picture unless I see it, because you have to feel that you are right for the picture and it is right for you. More and more now, one is brought in earlier. When I read the script, I say, "It's an interesting script, but I'll wait until you make the picture," because they can change the script completely before the end of the picture. Maybe halfway through a rough-cut stage you see that it is really coming into shape, and you want to be involved. Some producers don't like that, because they say, "Who the hell are you, passing an opinion on my work?" I have had films offered where the producer said you must commit yourself now at the start. I've had that on a Frank Sinatra picture, and I said, "No thank you." He even phoned me from Hollywood, and I said, "Let me see the picture, Frank, please!" And he wouldn't, and I said, "No chance!" I was told it would be a pleasure to work with Sinatra and that it would be good for my career, and I said, "Let me be the judge of that." I love the way he sings!

INTERVIEW with GAIL KUBIK

Irwin Bazelon: In the context of defining a composer as a person who knows how to put a piece together and understanding the structure of films and the nature of the music written for them, do you think one has to be a composer to write film music?

Gail Kubik: Well, of course, I think the answer is yes. As far as I'm concerned, you start out by being a composer, which is to say that you've been dropped on your head in such a way that you find that you can only express who you are, your vision of the world, your reaction to the world, most completely and authentically through the use of sound—through that kind of marvelous, special language which music is. That you engage from time to time in writing for films is, I think, just testimony to the fact that there are now in the twentieth century many, many audiences for a composer. There is, of course, the mass audience—that of the film, radio, television, recording worlds—all media that exist because of the microphone, that marvelous electronic gadget which has opened up the mass audience to the creative artist in music. But, as a man who writes music, I want to reach all the audiences I can. Naturally, I want to reach the audience made up of people like you who are professionals, who can enjoy that which is a puzzle piece, music which only the sophisticated musical mind can decipher and derive some kind of spiritual nourishment from. But I also want to reach the audience that listens to radio jingles. With simple songs, I want to reach the huge audience of children of all ages. I want to reach the school bands, and, to repeat, I certainly want to reach the mass audience of the millions who go to the films, watch television, listen to the radio. So, for me, my writing a film score is just another aspect of writing music, one by which I hope to reach lots of people.

IB: It seems to me that this field is, in addition to being open to legitimate composers, also open to people who really don't qualify as composers—and yet somehow manage to get the job done.

GK: Well, of course. But then, that's not too surprising. First of all, it must always be remembered that making films is a business, and it's just sheer delusion to think that when you're talking about film music, about the motion-picture field, you are talking about the idealistic art of concert music. A symphony, a poem, a piece of sculpture—those are artworks in which communication is a one-to-one affair. But you get into the mass-audience fields, and, by definition, the very words indicate that communication is no longer a one-to-one affair. For we're now talking about an art that has to be boiled down to some kind of common denominator, an art that tries to please huge numbers of people. And the minute you get into mass art, you also get into big money, you invite all of those unseen powers that are there to tell you, "Look, Bazelon, there are too many notes in that chord. Either make it simple or get out." There are always those pressures. In a word, it's a business. As you and I both know, your score is no more successful than the film is. I've written scores, scores that I thought were first-rate, but if the film didn't do well, the world just wouldn't give that music the time of day. No one ever says, "Great music, but a lousy film." As you know so well yourself, it's all a power play. Inevitably, the composer who is best at playing poker is going to get the job, and for the simple reason that the producer or the director—the power men (or for that matter, the wife of the man who's invested a hundred thousand dollars may not like the shirt you have on)—these people just don't care that much about music: the distinction between a serious composer of symphonies and the commercial composer of nearly all mass-audience music is just not real to them.

IB: That leads me to this next question that you've touched on. Why do you think there are so few contemporary concert composers in America who are ever invited to score a mainstream feature film? Now a lot of us have done documentaries, and the situation is not the same in Europe: in England, for example, Richard Rodney Bennett, William Walton, and Peter Maxwell Davies have scored films; in Germany, Henze has done some films; and it's not the same in France or in Russia. Do you think it's a problem of director-composer communications or ego involvement? Do you think there really is such a thing as being afraid to use so-called serious composers that influences film people to avoid them? Outside of the five or six scores that you've done and a few that Aaron Copland and Virgil Thomson have done and an isolated concert composer here and there, none of us have ever gotten into the mainstream of feature films. What do you think is behind all this?

GK: Well, when I was a youngster, I had this enormous idealism: I was so convinced that if I could get my sounds onto that tape or that celluloid track, that if I contributed from time to time a few hours of music to this mass-audience medium, the film—well, I thought that doing that was going to change the taste of millions and millions of people. Now if that idealism could function without hindrance, then I'm sure that you and I would be joined by dozens of our colleagues, dozens of the serious composers. But very quickly you learn, first of all, what I just now remarked, that not one film-maker in a dozen knows or cares about music. But there he is, he's the big mogul, he's got the power, and inevitably he feels he has his finger on the pulse of John Q. Public; and therefore, he feels quite qualified to get into the composer's act, to tell you your music is getting too complicated, that the public will never like it. So you ask me, why aren't more of our colleagues in the field? Many of them would like to have written the documentary scores that you have. But they're not willing —and who can blame them?—to put up with that almost inevitable interference from the power people. And so most serious composers just walk away from the mass-audience media. Now it's true, I have to spend nine months teaching to make what I would make out of one solid film score, but at least people don't interfere with my artistic prerogatives. I can write that symphony—nobody gets into the act, nobody tells me to change a note—and so again, the reason why we are not surrounded by more of our colleagues is that unless you've got the willingness to scream louder, like a youngster than the director or the producer—in a word, to put on the genius act and finally just say, "I'm sorry, I'm not altering one note. Now I'm running this part of the show." Unless you're willing to scream louder than the producer and go through that kind of emotional torment—and you know it's very upsetting—I can understand why many of our friends reluctantly keep their distance from the Hollywood film factories. Also, there's another aspect. While I enjoy doing an occasional film score, certainly no composer worth his salt is going to want to write more than a modest amount of music which is only heard behind dialogue. I'm too much of an egotist not to want people to sit themselves down and listen to my music, and I don't want to have competition from the visuals on the screen or the dialogue of the writer and certainly not from the sound-effects man, who can change that magnificent little C-major chord into something that's now surrounded by screaming brakes and closing doors. I want that C-major chord to be heard for its own delicious sound.

IB: It's interesting that you say that, because many of these producers and directors go on record as saying they're afraid of the controversial sounds or the complexities they might get from the concert composer, and yet we know that by the time a film score has been recorded, a form of neutralization takes place in which the matter of how modern it is or how conservative it is is basically academic. In the years that you've done film music on and off, what percentage of the producers and directors that you've worked for knew anything about music or even how to communicate with you on a simple dramatic level?

GK: I would say that I was certainly luckier than the boys in Hollywood. If you're talking about the documentary field in New York, the main reason why a lot of us get a toehold in doing films is that it's in the nature of the documentary that the director or the producer making a film takes a position, a point of view. They know that a documentary, almost by definition, is a film that is out to change the world. It's out to show a facet of the world, a particular facet of the world, and thereby convert the audience to that point of view. As a result, the men who make those films—they're not put off by the idea that your music is a unique kind of sound, my music is a unique kind of sound. They want that, because they're committed to the idea of trying to do something that isn't designed to please every Tom, Dick, and Harry—that isn't a search for the lowest common denominator. Well, on that basis I've been very lucky: the documentaries that I've done (all of them) had directors that, as a matter of fact, sought me out because I had a style, because I had a point of view. But you get into Hollywood, and there film-making is a business. Well, I must confess, if I were a film director or producer out there, I suspect I'd probably feel the way they do. Because, you know, everybody wants to build his monument. The man who has sought out those million dollars to make a film—naturally, he goes home to his wife and says, "*My film. I'm making my film.*" He's not going to let me, from his point of view, ruin that film or endanger that film in any way. At that point, I'm at the mercy of his cultural background. You know, I did two documentaries for William Wyler—*The Memphis Belle* and *Thunderbolt*. A few years later Willy brought me over from Paris to do *The Desperate Hours*. Now the great thing about Willy was that he knew that there was a difference between the typical Hollywood sound and the music of Marc Blitzstein and Gail Kubik and Aaron Copland. Willy knew that there was a difference between so-called serious, creative music and the industry-produced music of Hollywood. Well, that's rare. But William Wyler wasn't always able to or didn't choose to stand up and support us the way we felt he should. Aaron had a bad time with him on *The Heiress*; I certainly had a bad time with him on *The Desperate Hours*. Nevertheless, I can't be totally condemnatory of Wyler, because when the chips were down, he first had to give in to pressures that were out to remove me and my kind of sound from big films. On *The Desperate Hours* it was just fantastic. At the preview of *The Desperate Hours*, a lot of people commented on the music, and already that's exceptional; because, as you know, music doesn't often get very much notice, very much attention. In the face of that industry confirmation that the score was dramatically sound, Mr. Don Hartman, who was head of Paramount at that time, walks up the aisle, sees Wyler, and says, "Willy, great film, great acting, but Willy—that *music!*" And he did a parody of a sequence that I had written, a pointillistic sequence. He said, "We've never had music like 'poo poop pee poop pee poop.'" And he parodied this kind of pogo-stick sequence that I'd done. The principle behind my use of a pointillistic sound—and in the film, it worked marvelously well—was to write a series of sounds which were completely unpredictable: you didn't know when the next sound was coming or where it was coming from. It was a score which was literally more or less what Hartman had described: "ba bom ba boom ba ba ba," and the idea was to build and support the unpredictability inherent in the scene. And so, as they say in Hollywood, a lot of my score was left on the cutting-room floor. Why? Not because it wasn't dramatically sound. The earlier, preview-audience reaction had demonstrated that it came off very well. But the opinion of one powerful man who could only measure sounds against his private taste left Gail Kubik mangled on the cutting-room floor.

IB: They screened *The Desperate Hours* recently in New York on television, and I believe the only thing I recognized—and I know your music—was the main title.

GK: There was a bit more than that, but not much more.

IB: Tell me something about your working habits when you compose for a film. First of all, do you sit at the piano and improvise to get ideas? There are a lot of composers out here who are really pianists, and they have a tendency to sit down and improvise a scene or try to find a style and somehow think it through at the piano. You were a violinist, so you wouldn't normally be attached to the piano in that way.

GK: Well, I'm not much at the piano, but yes, I've used the piano on occasion. The working method, I should think, that would bind us all together, that would be common to all composers of whatever musical persuasion, would be that you have to get to know the film completely. You have to look at it a great many times.

IB: Would you use a Movieola right near you if you could?

GK: I have on occasion. I did a film for Metro—for English Metro, that is—and they flew in a Movieola from Rome. I was living in Paris at the time, and it was marvelous to have the film right under my thumb. But you asked about the piano; once you get to know the film—well, if the piano helps, why not? But I've written a film score on a subway, and certainly my use of the piano is not an absolute necessity.

IB: How do you see the role of the film composer? I know there's been a turnover of composers, but do you think the role of the film composer has changed, and do you think he's given greater opportunities today? Has film music evolved in the way you thought it might?

GK: Well, I think there are a number of men around who are very bright, who seem to me to have a unique talent for film tracks. A man like Elmer Bernstein seems to have very bright ideas. Certainly, Henry Mancini, ten years ago, opened up areas of sound that were new. I think that there are fewer men in the serious field working in films today than there were twenty years ago, not merely because producers want a composer who can perhaps be counted on to supply a hit tune, but also because the optic, the point of view, of the serious composer has also changed very drastically in the last twenty years. Twenty years ago, twenty-five years ago, thirty years ago, the mass audience exerted an extraordinary fascination for many serious composers. You had the case of Virgil Thomson, of Aaron Copland, of Marc Blitzstein, of Henry Brant, of myself—men who had found, who were beginning to find a style. But no matter at what stage of development we were, we had this awareness of the mass audience. The depression made us aware of this audience that numbered in the tens of millions. The depression brought the professional artist into contact with masses of people. There was concern on our part that hadn't existed before. And Aaron Copland, I think, coined the term—at least it was a term that turned up in the mid-1930s—"stylistic simplification." We had this feeling that we had a responsibility to take our complicated sounds and find a simplified language that would reach the mass audience. Acting under that philosophy, several of us made an effort to translate that philosophy into a working job of getting commissions to do film and radio scores. But now contemporary music has fluttered off all over the place. The years since the war have seen such a disillusionment in the arts: you've seen a bunch of youngsters come along doing an art that is plainly in revolt against the past; composers who say, "I just don't want to have anything to do with the world that was created up through the Second World War." And among the casualties in that new attitude, that attitude of revolt, has been a concern for the mass audience. The men in the serious business of treating music as a philosophy, as a statement of man's relationship to society, no longer think very much about the mass audience. Therefore, they don't make an effort to supply music for that field. On the other hand, you've seen this marvelous generation of youngsters come along. They've developed rock, they've developed a kind of mass-audience sound, they've said, "To hell with 'moon, June, spoon' "—all the musical styles that dominated American popular music, world popular music, up through the Second World War. They've been in revolt. We've had the Beatles come along, Dylan, all these people who have revolutionized the pop field. And since, in the eyes of the movie producers and directors, this new pop music has to their ears (by contrast with the earlier, musical-comedy sound) the sound of something new and modern, they say, "Well, gee, that's modern music." The movie producer cheerfully forgets—even if he knew, which he probably didn't—that by comparison with Henry Brant or with

Stockhausen, pop music is pretty simple, pretty boring. In a word, the movie-music scene has changed enormously. The Roy Webbs, the Max Steiners, the Alfred Newmans, even the Dave Raksins—their days are gone forever. Those men have had to face the competition of the youngsters who have a rock-pop background, an electronic sound. And although that music in comparison with Max Steiner sounds new and different, it is still pop music, a very simple sound as compared with the way your music has gone, the way my music has gone, the way serious composers have gone.

IB: Do you think there's too much music in films today, that films are overscored?

GK: Well, I wouldn't want to generalize. I think, really, you're also asking the question, "Is the ability to keep music out of a film part of the talent of being a fine film composer?" And I would say yes, it is.

IB: In other words, where *not* to add music is almost as important as where to have music.

GK: Exactly. I've always admired Benny Herrmann for the score that he did for *All That Money Can Buy* for exactly that reason: he knew where *not* to use music. The judicious use of music, the reservation of music, the reserving of music for those places where it can really change the quality of that film: that is an essential part of the dramatic talent of any composer who writes for films.

IB: As you are well aware, through the years the composer has never owned the rights to his music, and the composers are now in revolt and trying to organize and get these rights. Already C.B.S. has granted them their rights for television. You were involved, were you not, in a very interesting story in England about a film you did that by your inadvertently not signing a contract dramatically brought up the question of the composer's rights in his film music?

GK: Well, that failure to sign a contract wasn't inadvertent! We, MGM and I, were involved in a power play. I was pretty much aware of the significance of my not having signed my contract before recording. Let me just preface this by saying I've been fighting this business of rights for years, and in only one instance have I given to a film company the complete rights to the score. Even that story (*The Desperate Hours*) finally ended happily enough. The case to which you make reference was a film that I did in England for Metro called *I Thank a Fool*. A film with Susan Hayward and Peter Finch. Initially, I said to Metro, "Look, I'll give you all the rights that you can use in the film but no rights that aren't usable in the film; I'm retaining those rights." They didn't quite believe that I was serious. They let me—and I kept saying, "You know, we haven't signed a contract, we haven't worked out the rights problem." They let me, foolishly, finish the score and record it. (I had a seventy-piece orchestra, the London Philharmonic!)

IB: Did they pay you?

GK: Oh, they had to pay me. There wasn't any question that I had done the work, delivered the score. They paid me. But I still hadn't signed a contract about the rights. Now the end result of this (oh, and I had a fantastic contract. It provided, among other things, that if I wanted to take the time and rewrite the score into a concert piece, Metro was committed to keep the orchestra so that I could record this work in that fashion—which I did, incidentally. Beautiful recording.)—still no contract on the rights. Okay, we now finish the film, we dub it, the film is flown to Hollywood for the approval of the front office. The head of the studio turns to his lawyer and says, "Has Kubik signed his contract?" "No. He refuses to sign unless he retains all the nonfilm rights." The lawyer says, "Take the music out of the film." And they did. Now what developed was, as the lawyer explained, "If we let this man get away with this, we will open the door to half a million dollars that Metro is currently getting from ASCAP through its ownership of film-music rights." I wouldn't budge on the issue, and they wouldn't budge. They took the score out. Fortunately, I had these provisions for making a concert piece. But that was the end result—they took the score out. It was a mediocre film, so in a way I was lucky not to have my name connected with it. But still—MGM must have poured down the drain fifty or sixty thousand dollars.

IB: I know it opened in New York and closed the next day, so I never got to see it, but they were willing to throw out all that money rather than establish a precedent! What do you consider your best score or best-scored scene from any of the films that you've done? Do you have any favorites?

GK: Well, I think the best overall score, the film where the use of music is most perfectly coordinated and synchronized with the film, is the little cartoon *Gerald McBoing-Boing*. I needn't expand on the reason why the score was written first; that film took on a really musical architecture. You know that story. As for sequences from another film, sequences where the boundaries of film music were really pushed forward, I would nominate a score of mine for a little film, *C Man*, that I think was completely innovative. Some of the sequences in *The Desperate Hours* were, I feel, quite original. Many of those innovations, as remarked earlier, never saw the light of day. Incidentally, I'd like for the record to say, as a matter of honesty, that Paramount ultimately published a large-scale concert piece that's called *A Scenario for Orchestra*, which was fashioned from that *Desperate Hours* score that got so badly treated in the film. The studio, a year after the film was released, stepped forward and said, "We want to publish your concert score." And it must have cost them ten to fifteen thousand dollars. I've never known why. Maybe they were, in a way, saying, "We're sorry, Kubik, you got badly treated a year ago." I've never forgotten Paramount's gesture, and I have always been quite grateful that from *The Desperate Hours* score there emerged my *Scenario for Orchestra*. I did the premiere of the *Scenario* at a contemporary-music festival in Pulerimo some years ago. And at that performance no one interfered!

IB: Many people who do not know the inner workings of motion-picture music always assume that everybody that writes a score has somebody who orchestrates it. Now you and I know that there is really no such thing as orchestration, that the orchestration and the birth of a composition, to real composers, is a simultaneous thing. We don't write something in sketches and then suddenly decide we're going to give a tune to this instrument here and that instrument there. But have you ever had anyone help you orchestrate anything that you've done for a film? And if they have, do they ever actually contribute anything to your score?

GK: Well, in the true sense, no. I would accept your statement of the relationship of orchestration to the creative sketch. Of course you hear the orchestra in your head; a sketch is nothing but a shorthand by which you get that orchestral sound quickly down on paper. But I have been aided in two or three situations where the pressures of time—the film for Metro in London that I just now mentioned, *I Thank a Fool,* was a case in point—required me to have the assistance of an orchestrator. I had an English musician, Gerard Schurmann, to help me on that orchestration, but Gerry didn't really orchestrate that score at all. My sketches are very complete. What he did was simply to transcribe those sketches into a notation for the orchestra.

IB: Do you believe that producers have tried to inculcate the film public through the years with the idea that bad or even controversial music can cause people to leave the theater? Have you ever known a film that was actually strangled to death because of the music?

GK: Well, not really, no. No. Oh, they're always looking for a fall guy. But that, I might say, can sometimes work in reverse. That when a film does badly, they have second thoughts that maybe they *should* have let the music be more controversial, be more outstanding. That happened in the case of *Desperate Hours.* After the film was out a year and wasn't making any money, the people at Paramount, some of them, concluded that maybe they had been wrong to tamper with my score. Of course, a score can help, just as it can certainly fail to help. But a bad film is bad for reasons much more fundamental than the score that goes with it.

IB: I'm of the opinion, sometimes, that by the time everyone's had their hands in a score and it's been tuned down and neutralized, almost anything could work behind the film.

GK: Well, good music in films can make an extraordinary contribution to films, but it so rarely does, simply because so few of the people who make films and have the power have the cultural background and the willingness to believe that music could do all that. It's not often that composers get a chance to prove that that could indeed happen.

TO BE ALIVE. Composer: Gene Forrell. See page 38.

TO BE ALIVE. Composer: Gene Forrell. See page 38.

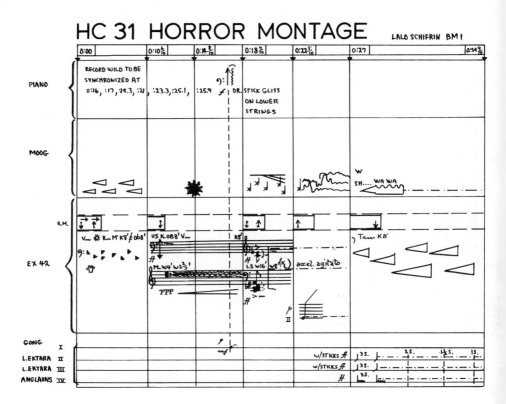

Permission granted by Lalo Schifrin.

PLANET OF THE APES ("Post scarecrow sequence"). Composer: Jerry Goldsmith. See page 86.

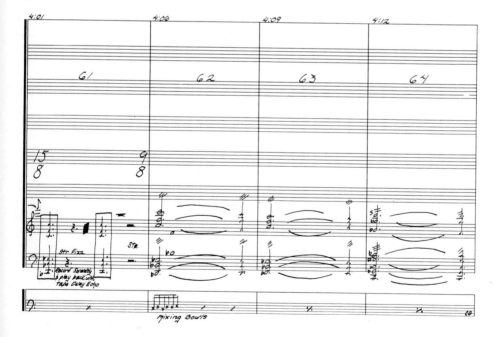

IMAGES ("In search of unicorns"). Composer: John Williams. See page 94.

World Wide Music, Nems Enterprises Ltd.

IMAGES ("Killing Marcel"). Composer: John Williams. See page 94.

IMAGES ("Kathryn's drive"). Composer: John Williams. See page 95.

World Wide Music, Nems Enterprises Ltd.

307

VIVA ZAPATA ("Peasant's telegraph sequence"). Composer: Alex North. See page 95.

7

VIVA ZAPATA ("Peasant's telegraph sequence"). Composer: Alex North. See page 95.

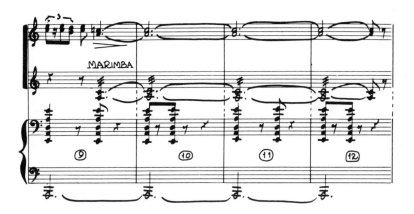

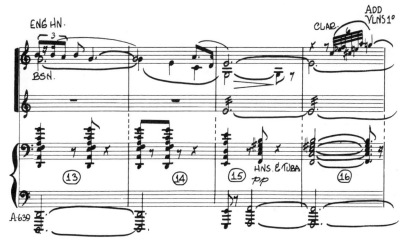

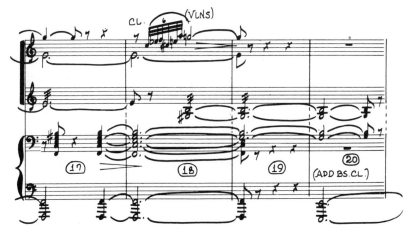

VIVA ZAPATA ("Peasant's telegraph sequence"). Composer: Alex North. See page 95.

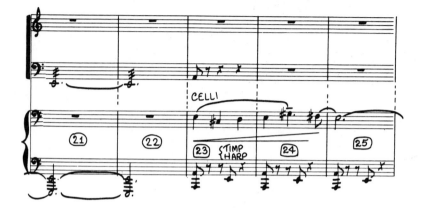

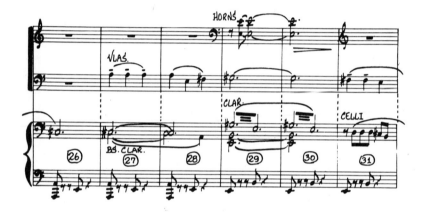

VIVA ZAPATA ("Peasant's telegraph sequence"). Composer: Alex North. See page 95.

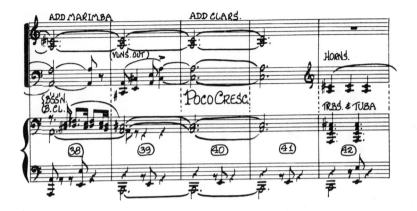

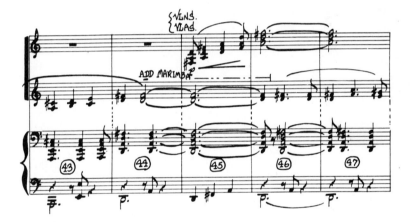

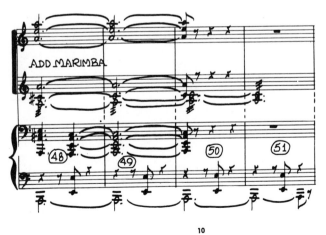

10

WHAT'S THE MATTER WITH HELEN? ("Main title"). Composer: David Raksin. See page 100.

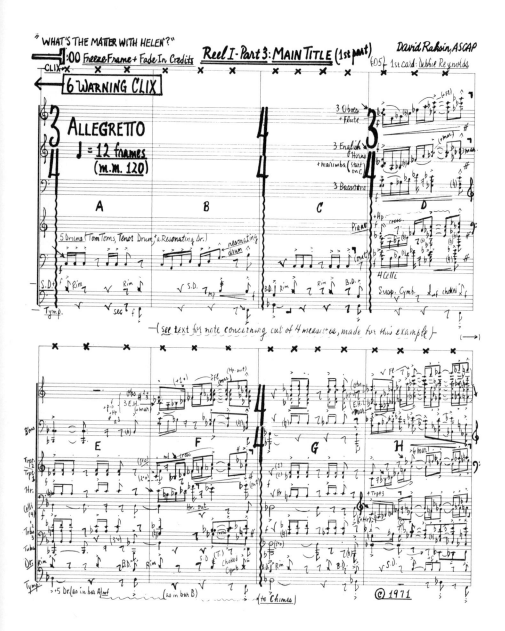

WHAT'S THE MATTER WITH HELEN? ("Main title"). Composer: David Raksin. See page 100.

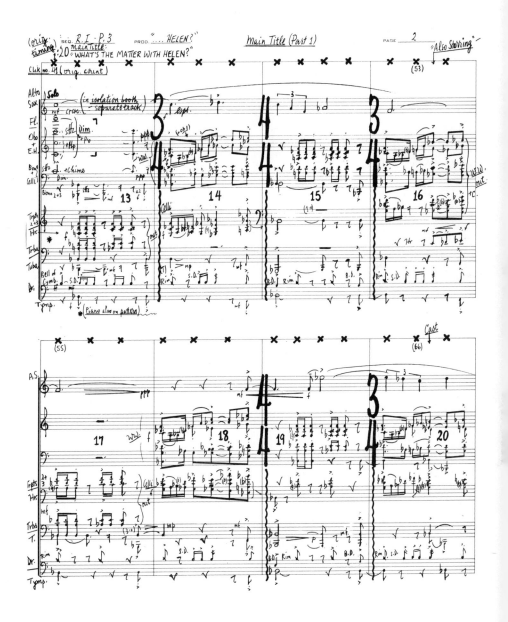

WHAT'S THE MATTER WITH HELEN? ("Main title"). Composer: David Raskin. See page 100.

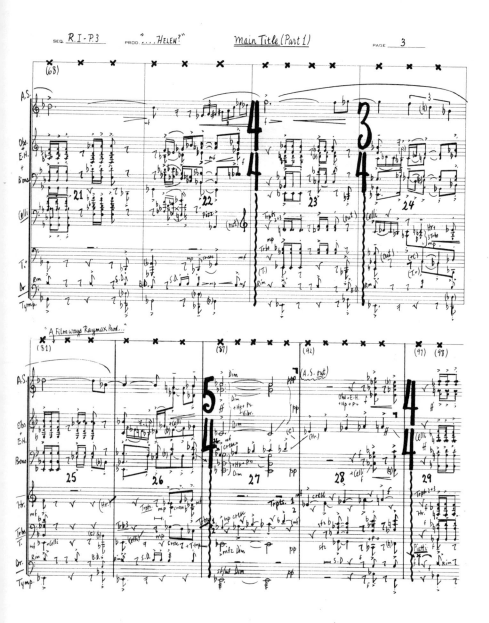

THE MIRACLE WORKER ("Helen tangled in the clothesline"). Composer: Laurence Rosenthal.
See page 102.

TO KILL A MOCKINGBIRD ("Opening sequence"). Composer: Elmer Bernstein. See page 103.

SECONDS (Opening titles). Composer: Jerry Goldsmith. See page 104.

-2-

SECONDS (Transformation scene). Composer: Jerry Goldsmith. See page 104.

SECONDS (Transformation scene). Composer: Jerry Goldsmith. See page 104.

-2-

SECONDS (Transformation scene). Composer: Jerry Goldsmith. See page 104.

SECONDS (Transformation scene). Composer: Jerry Goldsmith. See page 104.

SECONDS (End title). Composer: Jerry Goldsmith. See page 105.

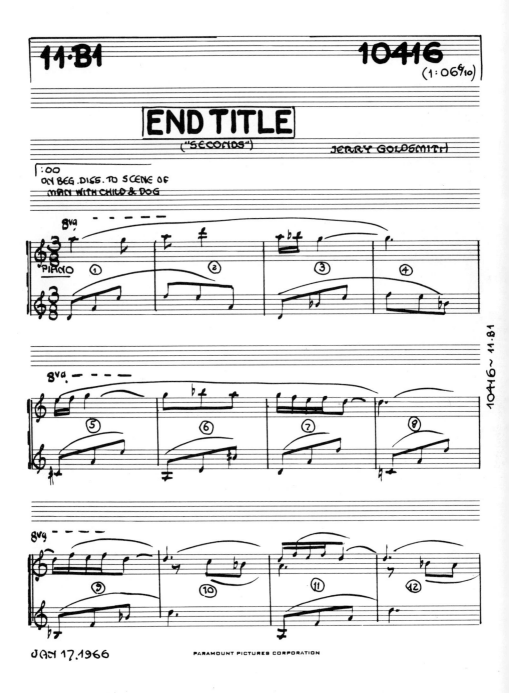

THE LUCK OF GINGER COFFEY ("Clock theme"). Composer: Bernardo Segáll. See page 106.

THE LUCK OF GINGER COFFEY ("Clock theme"). Composer: Bernardo Segall. See page 106.

POINT BLANK ("End title"). Composer: Johnny Mandel. See page 108.

END TITLE. From the Metro-Goldwyn-Mayer Inc. Motion Picture "POINT BLANK." MUSIC
BY: JOHNNY MANDEL. COPYRIGHT ©1967 METRO-GOLDWYN-MAYER INC., N.Y., N.Y.
Rights throughout the world controlled by MILLER MUSIC CORPORATION, N.Y., N.Y.
USED BY PERMISSION.

POINT BLANK ("End title"). Composer: Johnny Mandel. See page 108.

POINT BLANK ("End title"). Composer: Johnny Mandel. See page 108.

2001: A SPACE ODYSSEY ("The foraging"). Composer: Alex North. See page 111.

-14-

THE SAVAGE EYE ("Strip tease"). Composer: Leonard Rosenman. See page 122.

THE SAVAGE EYE ("Strip tease"). Composer: Leonard Rosenman. See page 122.

INTERREGNUM ("Ball hausmusik"). Composer: Paul Glass. See page 122.

INTERREGNUM ("Ball hausmusik"). Composer: Paul Glass. See page 122.

Boy Fights Alligator

(Fugue)

from "Louisiana Story"

Virgil Thomson

47066c

GERALD McBOING BOING (Opening music from the published score). Composer: Gail Kubik.
See page 129.

5

Gerald McBoing Boing

Dr. SEUSS
with additional lyrics by Gail Kubik

GAIL KUBIK
(1950)

GERALD McBOING BOING (Opening music from the published score). Composer: Gail Kubik. See page 129.

GERALD McBOING BOING (Opening music, sequence #1 from the film). Composer: Gail Kubik. See page 129.

THE SAVAGE EYE ("Judith Alone"). Composer: Leonard Rosenman. See page 142.

CLEOPATRA ("Assassination"). Composer: Alex North. See page 143.

CLEOPATRA ("Assassination"). Composer: Alex North. See page 143.

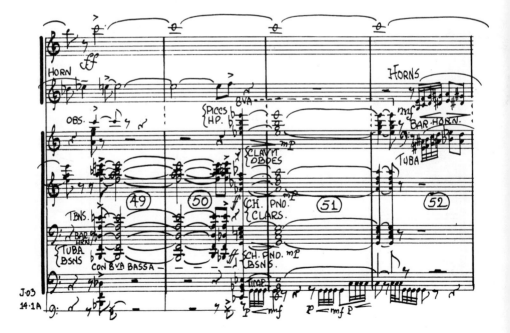

CLEOPATRA ("Assassination"). Composer: Alex North. See page 143.

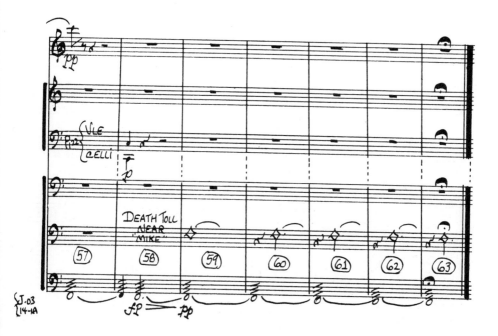

MEN IN WAR ("Walking through the forest"). Composer: Elmer Bernstein. See page 144.

SCENARIO FOR ORCHESTRA (Night scene, "The Desperate Hours"). Composer: Gail Kubik.
See page 145.

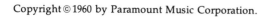

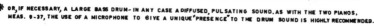

Copyright © 1960 by Paramount Music Corporation.

SCENARIO FOR ORCHESTRA (Night scene, "The Desperate Hours"). Composer: Gail Kubik.
See page 145.

Index

351